LOUISIANA LAW OF OBLIGATIONS IN GENERAL A PRÉCIS

LOUISIANA LAW OF OBLIGATIONS IN GENERAL

A PRÉCIS
Fourth Edition

ALAIN A. LEVASSEUR
Professor of Law, Emeritus
Louisiana State Unversity, Paul M. Hebert Law Center

2015
With the Assistance of: Kimberly Ulasiewicz

NOTE TO USERS
To ensure that you are using the latest materials available in this area, please be sure to periodically check the LexisNexis Law School web site for downloadable updates and supplements at www.lexisnexis.com/lawschool.

Editorial Offices
630 Central Ave., New Providence, NJ 07974 (908) 464-6800
201 Mission St., San Francisco, CA 94105-1831 (415) 908-3200
www.lexisnexis.com

MATTHEW◆BENDER

Louisiana Code Series

CIVIL CODE SERIES

LOUISIANA POCKET CIVIL CODE
2016

LOUISIANA CIVIL CODE PRÉCIS SERIES

LOUISIANA LAW OF OBLIGATIONS IN GENERAL
ALAIN LEVASSEUR
3RD ED. 2016

LOUISIANA LAW OF CONVENTIONAL OBLIGATIONS
ALAIN LEVASSEUR
2ND ED. 2016

LOUISIANA LAW OF SALE AND LEASE
ALAIN LEVASSEUR & DAVID GRUNING
3RD ED. 2016

LOUISIANA LAW OF TORTS
FRANK MARAIST
2010

LOUISIANA LAW OF SECURITY DEVICES
MICHAEL H. RUBIN
2ND ED. 2016

LOUISIANA LAW OF PROPERTY
JOHN RANDALL TRAHAN
2012

LOUISIANA LAW OF PERSONS
Forthcoming

LOUISIANA LAW OF SUCCESSIONS
Forthcoming

About the Author

Professor Alain Levasseur is a graduate of the Universities of Paris (France) and Tulane. He was an associate with the Paris firm of Mudge, Rose, Guthrie & Alexander for a while but left the firm to become a technical assistant at the World Bank in Washington, D.C. Professor Levasseur taught at Tulane Law School from 1970–1977 when he joined the LSU Law Faculty. He is a member of the International Academy of Comparative Law, the Société de Législation Comparée, and the Louisiana State Law Institute; he serves on the editorial or advisory boards of the American Journal of Comparative Law, the Revue Internationale de Droit Comparé, the Revue Trimestrielle de Droit Civil, the Revue Générale de Droit, the Foro de Derecho Mercantil, and e-Competitions. He is a member of the Scientific Committee of the Fondation pour le Droit Continental; he is president of the Louisiana Chapter of the Association Henri Capitant and of the International Association of Legal Methodology. He has published extensively in the fields of Comparative Law, Civil Law (Civil Law System/Tradition, Obligations, Contracts, Sale/Lease . . .), EU/EC Law, US Law (in French with Dalloz) . . . He has been a regular visiting Professor at the Universities of Aix-Paul Cézanne and Lyon III.

Table of Contents

Table of Contents

Table of Contents

Table of Contents

Table of Contents

Table of Contents

Table of Contents

Chapter 1

OBLIGATIONS IN GENERAL LSA-C.C. ARTS. 1756 TO 1762

The demands placed on man are many. Some are of a moral or religious nature, others could be described as social, political or intellectual. These demands may often take on the general or "generic" label of "obligations." We can read in Webster's II New College Dictionary that an "obligation" is "the act of binding oneself by a social, moral, or legal tie." With respect to an "obligation" as being a "legal tie," much has been written in legal literature on the variety of meanings of the word *obligation*. In its broadest sense and most popular acceptance, the word obligation refers to all sorts of duties that the law or good morals, for example, would impose on a person.

There is, indeed, at the very heart of the notion of obligation the compelling belief of a duty. It is common to speak of an obligation to be polite, to respect one's parents, to be charitable, to help one another, etc. It was in this general sense that former **LSA-C.C. Art. 1756** described an obligation as being "in its general and most extensive sense, synonymous with duty."[1]

The breadth of this notion subjected it to easy criticism, as all "duties" do not have the same compelling force. It is a fact that many of the duties encompassed in this general and most sensitive definition could receive only a moral or a religious or, still, a social sanction. Some duties lacked, and still lack, the sanction of the proper state institutions which can transform "duties" into legally binding obligations between an *obligee or creditor*, in the sense of a person who holds a right to demand a performance from another person who will then be referred to as an *obligor* or *debtor*. As the Latin meaning of the word "obligatio" explains, this word is made up of the prefix "ob" (to or towards) and the verb "ligare" (to bind). In a certain sense the verb "ligare" can be found in the English word "ligament" that joins or binds or acts as a "bond" between two or more bones or cartilages.

In its narrow and technical legal sense derived from its Roman law origin,[2] the notion of obligation can be defined as a bond of law, "vinculum juris," meant to impose a performance on a person, the *obligor*, for the benefit of another, the *obligee*.

One can find in Justinian's Institutes the following definition of the concept of obligation:

---

[1] Article 1756 of the Louisiana Civil Code of 1870.

[2] Harpers' Latin Dictionary, Oxford Latin Dictionary. The very etymology of the word "obligation" explains its nature. It comes from the Latin verbs "obligare" which means to bind together, to tie up, to make legally liable and 2) "ligare" which also means to bind, to tie.

1

"Obligatio est iuris vinculum, quo necessitate adstringimur alicuius solvendae rei, secundum nostrae civitatis iura."

"An obligation is a legal bond whereby we are constrained by the need to perform something according to the laws of our state"[3]

It is this meaning which is reflected in **LSA-C.C. Art. 1756**: "An obligation is defined as a legal relationship, whereby a person, called the obligor, is bound to render a performance in favor of another, called the obligee. Performance may consist of giving, doing, or not doing something." In the *Dictionary of the Civil Code*, under "obligation" we find the following description: "In a technical meaning, the passive side of a personal right (or right to a claim, performance); bond of law (vinculum juris) whereby one or more persons, the obligor or obligors, is/are required to carry out a performance (doing or not doing something) for the benefit of one or more persons, the creditor(s) as a result of either a contract . . . ".[4]

The use of the adjective *legal*, in the sense of juris, in combination with the word relationship or vinculum, conveys the idea that the relationship must be lawful, recognized by law and enforceable under the law. Such an obligation that can be enforced, will bear the name of "civil obligation," as its specific performance can be requested from a court, unlike a "natural obligation," which **"is not enforceable by judicial action" LSA-C.C. Art. 1761**.

It is obvious, then, that there may exist an innumerable number of such legal relationships or bonds bringing the sanction of the law to man's varied needs of others. Despite both the extreme variety in the kinds of bonds that can be created between men and the intensity of these individual legal relationships, it is possible to bring all these bonds or relationships under a "system," a "classification" of obligations that will help in outlining and defining the specific effects of each class or category of such obligations.

Behind this necessary and deeply weighted concern in attempting to classify the different categories or kinds of obligations, there is more than a mere dogmatic or didactic motivation. Indeed, the law of obligations has always been considered and identified with the *civil law* par excellence and as the ideal field of creativity of the civilian scientific reasoning process and logical method of reasoning. The present Louisiana law of "Obligations in General" dates back only to 1984. It is still, even some thirty years later, in the process of developing and shaping its own identity within the broader framework of the civil law tradition. It is, therefore, open to guidance and suggestions from the many existing civil law systems, the French civil law system in particular, but also other legal systems whenever a "transplant" would fit within the mold of the Louisiana civil law system.

The Louisiana Civil Code articles we will be studying here, offer us the dual opportunity of dealing, on the one hand, with a large number of fundamental substantive concepts of the law of obligations common to all civil law systems, and

---

[3] The Institutes of Justinian, Book III Title XII. De Obligationibus. Text,Translation and Commentary by J.A.C. Thomas. North Holland Publishing Company, 1975.

[4] *Dictionary of the Civil Code*, Cornu, Association Henri Capitant, Levasseur and Laporte-Legeais, LexisNexis 2014, p. 403.

of speculating through reasoning, on the other hand, on these still barely adult code articles. We will indulge, indeed, in some legal reasoning and juridical analysis to take the code articles of the Louisiana Civil Code through and beyond their apparent and literal content by calling upon civilian techniques of legal methodology.[5]

"Obligations" can be classified according to their different sources or according to their objects or, even, their effects.

ARTICLE 1

CLASSIFICATION OF OBLIGATIONS
ACCORDING TO THEIR SOURCES

In the narrower sense of the word *source*, the source of an obligation is the particular juridical act or fact susceptible of creating a legal relationship between an obligor (or obligors) and an obligee (or obligees). There are, in this respect, two broad categories of sources of obligations. One can identify formal sources specifically listed and identified as such in the Civil Code. There is another category of sources which actually transcends the Code but that can be created and illustrated out of the last few but extremely meaningful "legal" words of **LSA-C.C. Art. 1757: "and other acts or facts."**[6]

§ 1.1.1.   SOURCES OF OBLIGATIONS ACCORDING TO THE CIVIL CODE.

The second Civil Code article on "Obligations in General," Article 1757 is the fountainhead of all sources of obligations. One need to be informed that this Article 1757, through its listing of the sources of obligations, refers to and describes what is known as a *"civil obligation"* by contrast with what is referred to a "natural obligation."[7] **LSA-C.C. Article 1757** states:

> **"Obligations arise from contracts and other declarations of will. They also arise directly from the law, regardless of a declaration of will, in instances such as wrongful acts, the management of the affairs of another, unjust enrichment and other acts or facts."**

On the basis of this Code article, one can list the five formal sources of obligations as being: 1) contracts or conventional obligations and other declarations of will; 2) the law in the sense of legislation and custom; 3) offenses; 4) quasi-offenses; 5) quasi-contracts or obligations arising without agreement.

A few words about each one of these sources of obligations will help draw a distinction between them and better understand their respective scope of application.

---

[5] See *Deciphering a Civil Code*, Alain Levasseur, Carolina Academic Press, 2015.

[6] See immediately below. Actually, the concepts of "juridical acts" and "juridical facts" are inclusive of all sources of obligations as explained below.

[7] On natural obligations, see below § 1.3.1.

A.   Contracts and Other Declarations of Will.

The will of a person is creative of obligations when it meets the requirements necessary to establish a legal relationship binding an obligor to an obligee. As **LSA-C.C. Art. 1757** states: "Obligations arise from contracts and other declarations of will." These requirements, essential to the validity of a contract or to the binding nature of other declarations of will as sources of obligations, are to be addressed in a subsequent paragraph dealing with juridical acts[8] and in greater details in another Précis on "conventional obligations."

B.   The Law.

As **LSA-C.C. Art. 1757** states: "[Obligations] also arise directly from the law." The law, in the sense of Articles 1, 2, 3 and 4 of the Civil Code,[9] may impose obligations regardless of any declaration of will or juridical act, or the occurrence of any juridical fact on the part of an obligor. Such are, for example, the obligations of tutorship by nature [**LSA-C.C. Art. 250**], inconvenience to neighbor [**LSA-C.C. Art. 668**], which are created by legislation on the basis of a particular juridical situation.

C.   Offenses [Delicts].

Louisiana Civil Code Article 2315[10] is the fountainhead of this other source of obligations. Offenses give rise to obligations as the consequence of the unlawful, voluntary and intentional acts of man. At civil law an offense (or delict) is a "juridical fact" by contrast with a "juridical act."

D.   Quasi-Offenses [Quasi-Delicts].

Louisiana Civil Code Articles 2315 and **2316**[11] contemplate the creation of obligations as a result of a quasi-offense or quasi-delict. The latter concept is defined as an unlawful and voluntary act of man that causes damage to another as a result of negligence, imprudence or want of skill. The missing element here, as contrasted with offenses, is the lack of an intent to cause a damage although the act itself was voluntary in its perpetration.

E.   Obligations Arising Without Agreement [Quasi-Contracts].

Some obligations arise without an agreement between persons when they result from the lawful and voluntary act of one person, from which an obligation may be created for the benefit of a third person or, sometimes, a reciprocal obligation between two or more persons. **LSA-C.C. Art. 1757** lists two quasi-contractual

---

[8] On juridical acts, see below § 1.1.2.

[9] LSA-C.C. Art. 1; Art. 2; Art. 3; Art. 4: see Appendix.

[10] LSA-C.C. Art. 2315 (in part only): see Appendix. See, Précis on Louisiana Law of Torts, Frank Maraist, LexisNexis 2010.

[11] LSA-C.C. Art. 2316: see Appendix.

obligations: the management of the affairs of another (negotiorum gestio)[12] and unjust enrichment. The latter is then rephrased under the more technical civil law title of "Enrichment Without Cause."[13] One will find under "Enrichment Without Cause," the statement of a general principle[14] and the legal regime of another quasi-contractual relationship known as the "Payment of a Thing Not Owed" (Condictio Indebiti).[15]

§ 1.1.2.   JURIDICAL ACTS AND JURIDICAL FACTS AS SOURCES OF OBLIGATIONS.

The last few words of **LSA-C.C. Art. 1757** and other acts or facts, as sources of obligations, hide some fundamental concepts of the civil law of obligations behind their ambiguity.

In the context of the code article itself, the words **"acts or facts"** are related by "and" to the concept of *unjust enrichment,* which immediately precedes them. This does not make much sense, as we will explain. Are the words meant to refer to two broad categories of sources of law into which the specific sources of law identified in Art. 1757 would fall?

In the civil law, a juridical act, *stricto sensu,* in the technical sense of the words, is any manifestation of the will of a person meant to have legal effects. The *Dictionary of the Civil Code* defines a juridical act as an, "[a]ct, expression, of the will meant (in the mind of the person or persons who expressed the will) to create legal effects."[16] By contrast, a juridical fact can be described as an event occurring outside the will of a person and which, by itself, brings about legal effects. In the *Dictionary of the Civil Code* we read that a "fait juridique," a "juridical act" is "[w]hatsoever fact (be it a question of intentional or unintentional act of man, a social event, a phenomenon of nature, a material fact) to which the law attaches a legal consequence (acquisition of a right, creation of an obligation, etc.), which has not necessarily been sought for the author of the fact."[17] This event or fact may lack the intentional element which makes man wish a particular set of legal effects: for example, the fact of driving at a high speed does not convey the intent to cause an accident. Most certainly, the payment of compensatory damages was not something intentionally willed by the driver. The event may also consist in a natural and purely material occurrence [*example: death*] which gives rise to legal effects [*succession, for example*].

A juridical act which is the expression of the will of one person with the intent to create a legal or civil obligation (or obligations) is called a "unilateral juridical act." It is an "[a]ct carried out by one person only or by several persons with the same

---

[12] LSA-C.C. Arts. 2292–2297: see Appendix.

[13] LSA-C.C. Arts. 2298 to 2305: see Appendix. Also known as "actio de in rem verso".

[14] LSA-C.C. Art.: 2298: see Appendix.

[15] LSA-C.C. Arts. 2299–2305: see Appendix.

[16] *Dictionary of the Civil Code,* — word: acte juridique, p. 18.

[17] *Dictionary of the Civil Code,* — word: fait juridique, p. 236.

interest in mind, for the purpose of creating legal effects."[18] An example of such a unilateral juridical act is an "olographic testament," which is "one entirely written, dated, and signed in the handwriting of the testator."[19] Another example is the "acknowledgment" of a child. Indeed, "the acknowledgment creates a presumption that the man who acknowledges the child is the father."[20]

On the other hand, when two persons are each one bound to the other by an expression of their will, the juridical act entered into is qualified as "bilateral," i.e. a "contract," because two wills have been exchanged to create one or more obligations. The best example of a bilateral juridical act is a contract which is described in **LSA-C.C. Art. 1906** as **"an agreement by two or more parties whereby obligations are created, modified, or extinguished."**

As is discussed and emphasized in the Précis on "Conventional Obligations," it is important to stress here that, if a contract is, *itself*, a bilateral juridical act, because *"it"* binds together two wills that have been exchanged, that adjective "bilateral" has to do with the *creation of a bond of law* by the wills of two parties and between these two parties only. However, this same adjective is not indicative of *the number of obligations* created. Indeed the mere fact that two parties have entered into a contract does not mean that each one is bound to the other to perform an obligation. The nature, name of the contract or, in other words, the legal label attached to a contract will be indicative of the number of obligations that have been created and whether they are due by both sides of these obligations. For example, in *the contract of donation* we have two parties involved; two wills have been exchanged between the donor and the donee. However, only one party, the donor, is bound to carry out an obligation, i.e. to "donate" or transfer something gratuitously to the other party, the "donee"; the latter merely accepts (or rejects) the donation. Since there is only one obligation created from the donor to the donee, the contract will be referred to as *"unilateral,"* in the sense that two parties created only one obligation going *"one way."* Conversely, in a contract of sale, the seller must deliver the thing to the buyer who, in turn, must pay the price to the seller; two "reciprocal" obligations have been created as a result of which the contract of sale will be classified as a "bilateral contract." In other words, "unilateral" and "bilateral" in the civil law have nothing to do with the legal meaning of "unilateral" and "bilateral" in the common law!

ARTICLE 2
CLASSIFICATION OF OBLIGATIONS
ACCORDING TO THEIR OBJECT OR PERFORMANCE

LSA-C.C. Article 1756 suggests, in its second sentence, a classification of obligations according to the nature of the performance to be rendered by one person in favor or another. As far as the nature of the performance is concerned, in other words, as regards the "object" of that performance it **"may consist in giving,**

---

[18] *Dictionary of the Civil Code,* — word: acte unilatéral, p. 18.

[19] LSA-C.C. Art. 1575 in part: see Appendix.

[20] LSA-C.C. Art. 196 in part: see Appendix.

doing or not doing something." So, the performance involves "something" that has to be given, done or not done.

To this classical or traditional distinction based on the object (or item) of the performance of an obligation it is appropriate to add another one suggested by doctrinal writers and applied by the jurisprudence. This latter distinction aims at contrasting *obligations of result* with *obligations of means* and borrows, therefore, its *raison d'être* from the object of the obligation, the "something" that has to be performed.

One may ask, again, why this concern for a classification of legal concepts? The theoretical answer is found in the essence of the civil law methodology, which is both inductive and deductive in its reasoning. We will give here two practical illustrations of the benefits of classifying legal concepts which simply means that one endeavors to fit a legal concept within an articulated legal regime or framework so as to subject that classified concept to a predetermined and coherent legal regime. For example, if one classifies an obligation as being one "to give" (as in a contract of sale, where the seller must transfer the ownership over a thing, i.e. give a real right over that thing to the buyer), automatically one will attach the right to demand specific performance which is of the nature of the obligation to give. On the other hand, it is extremely rare, if not impossible, to obtain specific performance of an obligation to do, i.e. to "force" someone to provide some service to another. No one can be compelled by force, manu militari, to perform services.

Another example of the practical consequences of such classifications concerns the *raison d'être* of the distinction between *obligations of result* and *obligations of means*.[21] In a malpractice suit, the plaintiff carries the burden of proof of the defendant's malpractice simply because the defendant owes only an obligation of means, i.e. to use the best means in the performance of his services towards the plaintiff.

On the other hand, if an obligation is to achieve a result (such as carry a passenger to his place of destination), if that result is not there, not achieved, the obligor will automatically be in breach of his obligation, and it will be his burden to prove that a fortuitous event, force majeure or some impossibility of performance, prevented him from reaching the result wanted. In other words, this classification of obligations between *"means and result"* has important procedural consequences should an obligee not obtained the performance due by the obligor. Is it not wise to have this distinction in mind when entering into a contract?[22]

---

[21] See below Obligations of Result and Obligations of Means § 1.2.2.

[22] See below under Alternative Obligations § 1.2 for another practical consequence of this distinction.

§ 1.2.1.   OBLIGATIONS TO GIVE, TO DO, AND NOT TO DO.

A.   Obligation to Give.

The verb *to give*, used in connection with the word obligation, must be understood in the technical sense of its Latin parallel *dare* (to transfer, to grant) and not in its more colloquial sense of *donare* or to give as a present, to transfer gratuitously. **LSA-C.C. Art. 2655** defines a giving in payment as follows: **"Giving in payment is a contract whereby an obligor gives a thing to the obligee, who accepts it in payment of a debt."** It is obvious, therefore, that the verb *to give*, as used in the Civil Code, should be understood as meaning *to transfer* to an obligee-creditor the ownership of a thing, such as a sum of money for example, or more broadly speaking, to grant to someone a *real right* in a thing. Such a transfer can take place either onerously [see, for example, **LSA-C.C. Arts. 2439 and 2456**][23] or gratuitously [see, for example, **LSA-C.C. Arts. 1468 and 535**].[24]

Whenever an obligation is meant to transfer a real right over a thing, it is an obligation to give. There are, actually, few obligations to give per se since, in a large number of instances, the transfer or giving of a real right takes place by mere exchange of consent.[25] The same juridical act that creates the obligation simultaneously amounts to its perfection, which is the vesting of the title transferred in the obligee. As **LSA-C.C. Art. 2456** illustrates perfectly, **"[o]wnership is transferred between the parties as soon as there is agreement on the thing and the price is fixed, even though the thing sold is not yet delivered nor the price paid."** Actually, the perfection of such an obligation to give, in the sense of the actual alienation of the real right, may be altered by the will of the parties or by law as would be the case of stipulating a term or a condition.[26] Depending on the circumstances, it may remain for the obligor *to do* something, *i.e.*, to deliver the thing.

It is important, therefore, to make the distinction between the "perfection" of the obligation by mere exchange of consent and the "performance" of that obligation. An obligation *to give* may have to be preceded by an obligation *to do*. Such would be the case when an object is to be manufactured before its ownership can be transferred or when an object has to be identified and individualized out of a larger quantity, such as is the case of things that have to be weighted, counted or measured.[27] Since a real right cannot exist in the absence of a thing over which it will bear, the obligor would be under an obligation to give as soon as the object is manufactured, individualized or, somehow, comes into being. Furthermore, in those instances where the parties to a contract agree to delay the transfer of ownership from one of them to the other until some time period or some event agreed upon, it can be said that, in addition to an obligation to do, the obligor would be under the obligation to give the obligee-creditor the real right of ownership at the time or

---

[23]   LSA-C.C. Art. 2439; Art. 2456: see Appendix.

[24]   LSA-C.C. Art. 1468; Art. 535: see Appendix.

[25]   See, for example, Art. 2456: see Appendix.

[26]   See below Term § 2.2-A and Condition § 2.2-B.

[27]   See the Précis on Louisiana Law of Sale and Lease, Levasseur and Gruning, LexisNexis 2015.

upon occurrence of the event agreed upon.[28]

The principal obligation to give a real right over a thing carries with it two accessory obligations, which are: 1) the obligation to deliver the thing and 2) the obligation to preserve and care for the thing until it is delivered. The obligor must "attend" to the good care of the thing, as is expected from a prudent administrator (particularly an administrator of a thing that may belong to another as the result of a mere exchange of consent which, by itself, may transfer ownership.)

The obligation to deliver the thing is well illustrated in, first, **LSA-C.C. Art. 1986**[29] in a broad manner and, second, in **Arts. 2477**[30] *et seq.* in a specific manner.

The obligation to preserve the thing and care for it until it is delivered is illustrated in **LSA-C.C. Arts. 2489 and 2930.**[31]

B. Obligation to Do.

An obligation to do requires that the debtor-obligor perform some positive act, such as supporting and educating children, physically delivering a thing, providing medical care, building a swimming pool, etc. **LSA-C.C. Arts. 227, 2746, 2756**[32] are codal illustrations of such obligations to do.

The personal and actual involvement or participation of the obligor in the performance of an obligation to do may be either essential (in the technical sense of *the essence of the obligation*) or indifferent to the creditor-obligee.

Practical experience suggests that some obligations to do are of such a nature that their performance would require the personal and exclusive involvement of the obligor. Such would be the case, for example, of a painter who would have agreed to paint the obligee's children's portraits, or the case of a known actor selected to fill a particular part in a play. In such instances where the skill, talent, and expertise of the obligor is most important to the obligee, one can speak of a *strictly personal obligation* as to the obligor. In other kinds of obligations to do, the obligee might very well be satisfied with the performance of the obligation by a third party where the obligor himself would fail, or be unable, to render the performance required of him. It is very common for the owner of a car repair shop, the actual obligor, to have the repairs performed by his employees, who are third parties to the legal relationship existing between the owner of the car, or obligee, and their employer-owner of the shop, the true obligor of the obligation to do.

Once again, there are an important legal and practical justifications behind the distinction made here. Indeed, for example, whenever an obligation is to do and because of the particular factual circumstances it must be labeled as *strictly personal* on the part of the obligor, it results from a combined reading of **LSA-C.C.**

---

[28] See below Modalities such as Term § 2.2-A or Condition § 2.2-B.

[29] LSA-C.C. Art. 1986: see Appendix.

[30] LSA-C.C. Art. 2477; Art. 2481: see Appendix.

[31] LSA-C.C. Art. 2489; Art. 2930: see Appendix.

[32] LSA-C.C. Art. 227; Art. 2746; Art. 2756: see Appendix.

Arts. 1766 and **1855**[33] that the breach of such an obligation will, most likely, not be susceptible of specific performance.[34] The courts are, rightfully so, most reluctant to infringe forcefully (*manu militari*) upon the obligor's personal freedom. It ensues that the obligee, as he should have anticipated, will not receive the actual performance of the obligation he had bargained for. Instead, such a breach of a *strictly personal obligation* will give rise to the payment of damages which "should" be considered as the "compensation" for the breach of the principal object and performance of that obligation.[35]

Whenever an obligation is not so personal to the obligor as not being susceptible of an equivalent performance by a third party, for example mowing a lawn, repairing a vehicle, carrying a passenger, the obligee should still have the right to demand the specific performance of that obligation and the court could, in its discretion, grant it.[36] However, in most instances, a court would allow the obligee to have a third party perform the obligation at the original obligor's expense.[37] In such an instance the obligee would receive the actual performance of the obligation he had bargained for but through the intermediary of a third party. Should the obligee be unable to obtain performance either from his obligor or from "another" at the expense of the original obligor, the obligee would "recover" damages for the obligor's failure to perform or his defective performance or his delayed performance.[38]

C.   Obligation Not to Do.

An obligation not to do requires that the obligor refrain or abstain from doing something which, under normal circumstances, he would have the right to do. An illustration of such an obligation is provided by **LSA-C.C. Art. 2931**, which forbids the depositary from making use of the thing deposited unless authorized by the depositor. Another statutory illustration can be found in **LSA-C.C. Art. 663**, which provides that a "landowner may not build projections beyond the boundary of his estate."

The breach of an obligation not to do may entitle the creditor to demand specific performance where, for example, it would be feasible to obtain an injunction under Articles 3601 *et seq.* of the Code of Civil Procedure.[39] However, in most instances, obligations not to do, like obligations to do, are not susceptible of specific performance. The courts do call on the following Latin maxim so as not to compel specific performance: "*Nemo proecise cogi potest ad factum.*"[40] In the alternative,

---

[33] LSA-C.C. Art. 1766; Art. 1855: see Appendix.

[34] LSA-C.C. Art. 1758; Art. 1986: see Appendix.

[35] LSA-C.C. Art. 1994: see Appendix.

[36] See Art. 1986 infra note 40.

[37] LSA-C.C. Art. 1758 A(2): see Appendix.

[38] LSA-C.C. Art. 1758 A(3): see Appendix.

[39] LSA-C.C.P. Art. 3601: see Appendix.

[40] *No one can be compelled to do something.* As LSA-C.C.1986 states in part: "**Upon a failure to perform an obligation . . . such as an obligation to do, the granting of specific performance is at the discretion of the court.**"

the creditor-obligee could demand damages **under LSA-C.C. Art. 1986.**[41]

As will be further explained in a subsequent section on specific performance, it can be argued that the essence of and reason for **Articles 1986** and **1987**[42] of the Civil Code and 2504[43] of the Code of Civil Procedure would support a reasoning *a pari ratione* sufficiently convincing to provide a court with the legal grounds to authorize an obligee to have his obligor, or a third party, *undo* what the obligor has done in violation of his obligation not to do. However, the actual circumstances, particularly the economic and financial discrepancies between "undoing" something that has been built by an obligor in violation of his obligation not to build, and "compensating" the obligee under the form of monetary damages, will enable the courts to use "their discretion," which means, in most instances, allocating damages to the obligee.

§ 1.2.2.   OBLIGATIONS OF RESULT AND OBLIGATIONS OF MEANS OR DILIGENCE.

This classification of obligations is a creation of doctrinal writers and was first suggested in 1925 by René Demogue.[44] It was further refined by Henri Mazeaud and Andre Tunc.[45]

A.   Obligation of Result.

There exists an obligation of result whenever the performance or object of the obligation is so precisely determined as to amount to a definite result to be achieved. An obligation to give a specific thing and an obligation not to do something would be obligations of result.

Whether an obligation to do is one of result or one of means[46] might be a matter of interpretation and policy. What would you say of the obligation of an airline to transport its passengers "safely" from the place of origin to the place of destination? Is a passenger merely contracting for the airline to do its best to transport her safely to some place of destination, or does the passenger want to reach her place of destination first and foremost with the implicit obligation on the part of the airline to take her safely there? What is the obligation of a professional photographer at a wedding mass or reception: one of means or one of result?

One can see in **LSA-C.C. Art. 2754**[47] an obligation of result imposed on a carrier since he is held liable for a breach of his obligation as soon as the object of his commitment, i.e. the safe keeping and preservation of the thing entrusted to him,

---

[41] See supra note 40.

[42] LSA-C.C. Art. 1987: see Appendix.

[43] LSA-C.C.P. Art. 2504: see Appendix.

[44] René Demogue, *Traité des Obligations*, En général. T5 § 1237 p. 538, 1925.

[45] Henri Mazeaud "Essai de classification des obligations" 35 R.T.D.C. (1936); André Tunc "La distinction des obligations de résultat et des obligations de diligence." J.C.P. 1945, 1, 449.

[46] On Obligations of Means, see next section.

[47] LSA-C.C. Art. 2754: see Appendix.

has not been achieved. It will be the carrier's burden of proof, as a likely defendant in a lawsuit, to show that the "loss of the thing or the damage to it had been occasioned by accidental and uncontrollable events." The same can be said of the obligation of the manager of another's affairs who must have been successful in his management before he can be granted an action for reimbursement of his expenses against the owner (**LSA-C.C. Art. 2297**).[48]

B.   Obligation of Means or Diligence.

There is an obligation of means or diligence when an obligor is expected to use the best possible means available to him, or to act with the utmost care and diligence in the performance of his obligation but without that obligor being in a position to guarantee a definite result. For example, a medical doctor is expected to do his best to cure his patient without assuring the latter that he will definitely be cured. Yet, the same medical doctor could transform his obligations of means into one of result should he, by contract, bind himself to cure his patient. The same is true of a lawyer who is expected to use proper care to safeguard the interests of his client by preparing adequately and giving appropriate and competent attention to his legal work. [See the Code of Professional Responsibility of the A.B.A., canon 6 EC.6.4.]. The Civil Code offers many examples of obligations of means, from among which we can cite **LSA-C.C. Arts. 2683, 2894, 2930**.[49]

C.   Importance of the Distinction.

The relevancy of the distinction based, once again, on a classification between obligations of means and obligations of result is built around the assignment of the burden of proof.

If an obligation can be classified as one of result it will carry with it the presumption that the obligor is at fault whenever the result he was bound to secure has not been achieved at all or not been achieved within a certain period of time. The burden of proof of the failure to perform is thus shifted from the plaintiff to the defendant who, to exculpate himself, will have to prove that a fortuitous, accidental or uncontrollable event prevented him from rendering his performance as expected.

In contrast, if an obligation is classified as one of means, the obligee-plaintiff will have to carry the burden of proof. He will have to show that the obligor-defendant did not act with all the care and diligence required of a *bonus paterfamilias*, a faithful or prudent administrator.[50] A malpractice lawsuit aims at establishing that a doctor has failed to perform his obligation of means.

One must acknowledge that the distinction between an obligation of result and one of means is not always easy to make. The *result* of the performance of an obligation may be susceptible of different degrees of assessment as can be the diligence shown by an obligor.

---

[48]   LSA-C.C. Art. 2297: see Appendix.

[49]   LSA-C.C. Art. 2683; Art. 2894; Art. 2930: see Appendix.

[50]   See LSA-C.C.Art. 2895: " . . . **use it as a prudent administrator.**"

As Colin and Capitant[51] pointed out, the painter of a house binds himself to a certain result, to wit, paint the house. Yet, this result may be more or less accomplished in a workmanlike manner. If the obligee, the owner of the house, is dissatisfied with the result presented to him, he may have the burden of proving why the undertaker did not execute the work in the manner that would have led to a satisfactory result.[52] In this respect, one may want to rely by analogy on **LSA-C.C. Article 2460**[53] to make the performance of the obligation owed by the obligor conditional upon the approval of the thing by the obligee.[54]

ARTICLE 3
CLASSIFICATION OF OBLIGATIONS
ACCORDING TO THEIR EFFECTS

The fundamental legal nature of an obligation determines the greater or lesser extent of its effects. In this respect it is traditional to distinguish *natural obligations*, which carry few legal effects, from *civil obligations*, which carry full legal effects. Such *civil obligations* can further be divided according to the extent of the right of enforcement available to the obligee; a distinction is thus made between *personal, heritable and real obligations*. This latter distinction will be presented in the next chapter entitled, "Kinds of Obligations."[55]

Article 1757-1 of the Civil Code of 1870 had been the subject matter of a lot of controversy and much confusion.[56] It was therefore wise not to incorporate it in the 1984 revision of the law of obligations. A comment to the post 1984 Civil Code Article 1760 summarizes as follows the conclusions of the committee on the revision of the law of obligations: "*If imperfect obligations have no legal effect then there is no need for the Civil Code to grant recognition.*"[57] As a result, there remain in existence in the post 1984 articles on the law of obligations only two kinds of obligations: the natural and the civil obligations.

§ 1.3.1. NATURAL OBLIGATION.

Although much has been written about the concept of natural obligations, it still remains somewhat ambiguous. There is one certainty however and it is that a natural obligation, although it expresses the existence of a right in a person and, conversely, creates what appears to be an obligation on the part of another, it cannot be a ground for an action to have that right enforced. The creditor-obligee of a

---

[51] Ambroise Colin et Henri Capitant, *Cours élémentaire de droit civil français*, 10th ed. vol. 2, 1948 p. 87 no. 123.

[52] LSA-C.C. Art. 2769: see Appendix.

[53] LSA-C.C. Art. 2460: see Appendix.

[54] See also the Civil Code Articles on Cause: Arts. 1966–1970.

[55] See infra Chapter 2.

[56] Article 1757-1 of the Louisiana Civil Code of 1870 read as follows: "If the duty created by the obligation operates only on the moral sense, without being enforced by any positive law, it is called an imperfect obligation, and creates no right of action, nor has it any legal operation. The duty of exercising gratitude, charity and the other merely moral duties, is an example of this kind of obligation."

[57] Comment (d), article 1760, Chapter 2. Natural Obligations.

natural obligation has no right of action against the *natural obligor*.[58]

A laudable effort of clarification and precision in legal terminology has been accomplished in the post 1984 drafting of **LSA-C.C. Arts. 1760, 1761,** and **1762.**

A. Article 1760 defines a natural obligation as one arising **"from circumstances in which the law implies a particular moral duty to render a performance."** As regards Article 1762,[59] by stating expressly that it merely lists examples of natural obligations, it puts an end to a controversy, which had been engendered by the ambiguous language of former **LSA-C.C. Art. 1758.**[60] It is clear now that **LSA-C.C. Art. 1762** is only *illustrative* of the different kinds of natural obligations that may exist. The reader or interpreter is therefore invited to add <u>new</u> and <u>additional</u> natural obligations to those listed in Art. 1762 and to do so by calling upon methods of reasoning, whenever, from the existing circumstances, the law implies a particular moral duty to render a performance (**LSA-C.C. Art. 1760**). The Louisiana Courts are then in a position to "fill gaps in the law" in finding and erecting " a particular moral duty" as the "reason" for creating as many natural obligations as they may believe are grounded in the general principles of law or equity and justice.[61]

Still, Article 1760 raises at least one problem of interpretation. The word *law*, in our opinion, ought to be taken in a very broad sense, which would combine the essence of Articles 1, 2, 3, and 4 of the Civil Code.[62] It is, indeed, most likely that when a statute, identified as the solemn expression of the legislative will, would create a natural obligation, it would do so expressly as is the case of **LSA-C.C. Art. 1762.** The use of the present tense *are* in this latter article, followed by clear legal illustrations of natural obligations arising from institutions of the Civil Code, makes these illustrations *explicit* or express natural obligations. It follows that **LSA-C.C. Art. 1760** gives our courts a rather wide discretion in their ability to create additional natural obligations whenever they would be in a position to conclude that the circumstances are such that the *law*, that is to say *natural law, reason and equity* (in addition to legislation), implies a particular moral duty to render a

---

[58] Already in Roman law "the chief effect of natural obligations was that, although he could not be sued for payment, a natural debtor who did pay would not be able subsequently to recover the sum condictio indebiti. . . . " J.A.C. Thomas, Textbook of Roman law, North Holland 1976 p. 220.

[59] LSA-C.C. Art. 1762: "Examples of circumstances giving rise to a natural-obligation are: (1)When a civil obligation has been extinguished by a prescription or discharged in bankruptcy. (2) When an obligation has been incurred by a person who, although endowed with discernment, lacks legal capacity. (3) When the universal successors are not bound by a civil obligation to execute the donations and other dispositions made by a deceased person that are null for want of form."

[60] Former LSA-C.C. Art. 1758, up to the revision of 1984, read as follows: "Natural obligations are of four kinds: (1) Such obligations as the law has rendered invalid for the want of certain forms or for some reason of general policy, but which are not in themselves immoral or unjust. (2) Such as are made by persons having the discretion necessary to enable them to contract, but who are yet rendered incapable of doing so by some provision of law. (3) When -the action is barred by prescription, a natural obligation still subsists, although the civil obligation is extinguished. (4) There is also a natural obligation on those who inherit an estate, either under a will or by legal inheritance, to execute the donations or other dispositions which the former owner had made, but which are defective for want of form only."

[61] LSA-C.C. Art. 4: see Appendix.

[62] LSA-C.C. Art. 1; Art. 2; Art. 3: see Appendix.

performance. The use of the adjective *moral* to describe the inherent value of a natural obligation is broad enough to bring under the label of natural obligations any duty *binding . . . in conscience and according to natural justice.*[63] On that basis we could easily find a natural obligation in an *implied* moral duty bearing on a brother to provide alimony to his sister or brother who might be in need. Shouldn't there be a natural obligation imposed on a person to take care of the funeral expenses of a close relative even though the former may not be an heir of the latter? One could make the argument that under the 1984 law of obligations, the concept of "natural obligation" is, today, an "objective" concept resulting from the "*law*" whenever it implies the existence of a particular moral duty. It was more a "subjective concept" in former Art. 1757-2 that stated that a party was bound "in conscience." However, Art. 1757-2 added "and according to natural justice," which was an objective standard or concept.

B. A natural obligation, because it is defined in part as an obligation, necessarily creates a right in someone who, logically, should be considered as an obligee. That right, however, is deprived of any means of action for the enforcement of the obligation which is its counterpart. In this respect, the natural obligation is to be distinguished from the civil obligation.

This and other effects of natural obligations are laid out in **LSA-C.C. Art. 1761**:

> **"A natural obligation is not enforceable by judicial action. Nevertheless, whatever has been freely performed in compliance with a natural obligation may not be reclaimed.**
>
> **A contract made for the performance of a natural obligation is onerous."**

The first sentence of the first paragraph of this Article restates the identifying feature of the natural obligation as not susceptible of enforcement by judicial action. This feature is so traditional and so well accepted that it deserves no further comment here.

The second sentence of the same first paragraph of Article 1761 calls for two comments: how is the word *freely* to be understood, and why can't the performance of a natural obligation be reclaimed?

The word *freely* conveys the idea of a person acting of her own volition without any compulsion or outside interference. Hence, one would not be acting freely if one's performance was the result of fraud or violence-duress committed by another person. In such an instance, the obligor of a natural obligation who has performed because of fraud or duress should recover his performance. But would an obligor be *freely* performing a natural obligation if he acted as a result of his own error as to the existence of a merely natural obligation when he believed erroneously that he was bound by a civil obligation? Such an error would be presumed to be unilateral (in the true sense of the word, meaning that only the obligor would be acting under his own error) and could not be taken into account because it would become the

---

[63] Former LSA-C.C. Art 1757-2, up to the revision of 1984, read as follows: "A natural obligation is one which can not be enforced by action, but which is binding on the party who makes it, in conscience and according to natural justice."

cause of an injury, damage, loss to the interest of the innocent beneficiary-obligee of that natural obligation who would have received the performance believing it was due to him under the "circumstances." If two innocent parties suffer a prejudice (the obligor in not being able to recover his performance and the obligee in having to return the performance), it appears much more reasonable and fair to hold liable, for any loss that may occur, the party who did set things in motion, the acting party, less innocent in this respect than the passive party who received a benefit without actively seeking it. This is all the more true when the benefit was due even though only *in conscience and according to natural justice,* or as the result of "**circumstances in which the law implies a particular moral duty to render a performance.**"[64]

On the other hand, an "honest or genuine" error made by the "obligor" of a natural obligation should entitle him to claim the restitution of his performance as having been carried out in the absence of any moral duty under the "circumstances," and when the recipient of the performance would be most obviously enriched at the expense of the obligor should he be allowed to keep the object of the performance.

An official comment to **LSA-C.C. Art. 1761** supports this interpretation of the word *freely* where it reads, "*it does not mean that his performance [the obligor of the natural obligation] cannot have been induced by error . . . .*" Former **LSA-C.C. Article 2303** of the Code of 1870 was very clear where it stated: "*To acquire this right (to reclaim what has been paid), it is necessary that the thing paid be not due in any manner, either civilly or naturally. A natural obligation to pay will be sufficient to prevent the recovery.*"

The denial of the return of the performance carried out on account of error when rendered under a natural obligation can be justified on two grounds. First, as explained above, the personal interest of the innocent obligee-creditor ought to be protected whenever he is free of any wrongdoing. A second consideration is more of a legal nature and can be found in **LSA-C.C. Arts. 2299** and **2300:**

> **Article 2299:**
>
> **"A person who has received a payment or a thing not owed to him is bound to restore it to the person from whom he received it."**
>
> **Article 2300:**
>
> **"A thing is not owed when it is paid or delivered for the discharge of an obligation that does not exist."**

The express law of the quasi-contract of *condictio indebiti* (payment of a thing not owed) further strengthens the above interpretation of the word *freely* in giving a purposeful meaning and reasonable justification to the statement that the performance of a natural obligation cannot be reclaimed.

Indeed, if an obligor of a natural obligation were to perform voluntarily and intentionally his moral duty, it would be tantamount to saying that this same obligor fulfilled a promise to perform as a result of a unilateral or a bilateral contract with his obligee. Under these circumstances, **Article 2300** would have no ground for

---

[64] LSA-C.C. Art. 1760.

application, as the obligation would have been turned into a civil obligation under the second paragraph of **Article 1761**.[65] Furthermore, and reasoning *a pari ratione*, why would an obligor of a natural obligation who, for example, had the power to plead prescription in his favor be denied that right if it were not for the fact that he was under the (erroneous) belief that he owed the performance?

The second paragraph of **Article 1761** describes another traditional effect of natural obligations: "**A contract made for the performance of a natural obligation is onerous.**"

According to this article an existing natural obligation stands as the *potential* onerous cause of a *future* promise to perform. The performance of a natural obligation is an onerous juridical act whereby the obligor intends to extinguish a previously existing debt, which, for reasons of law, could not be enforced against him. Thus the contract resulting either from the promise to perform a natural obligation or from the performance itself of that obligation is an onerous contract since its cause is onerous. The moral duty which prompts the obligor to perform is inspired by the desire to extinguish a debt (albeit a moral debt) and, thereby, this duty voids the natural obligation of any gratuitous motivation.

C. The fact that a natural obligation has a few legal effects raises some questions, which are suggested by contrasting the extensive legal regime of civil obligations with the skeleton legal regime of the natural obligation.

a: One may wonder, for instance, whether a natural obligation is heritable and, as such, whether it is part of one's patrimony?

If we assume a debt prescribed under **LSA-C.C. Art. 1762-(1)**, should the obligor's heirs feel bound by the same natural obligation that the law had imposed on the now deceased obligor himself? As long as a natural obligation has a monetary value and represents the extinction of a debt, there is little doubt that, as a general rule, it should be heritable, both actively and passively. As such it should fall into the patrimonies of both the obligee and the obligor. The heirs of an obligor of a natural obligation would find it in that obligor's patrimony and could possibly turn it into an onerous contract for the performance of the natural obligation.[66]

b: Two civil obligations can be extinguished as a result of compensation by operation of law if they meet the requirements of **LSA-C.C. Art. 1893**.[67] Can a civil obligation be compensated with a natural obligation? We do not believe that it can for the reason that a natural obligation is not demandable and it is not enforceable by judicial action. Furthermore, compensation by operation of law amounts to a compulsory payment since it takes place even unbeknownst to the parties. Yet, performance of a natural obligation can only be rendered *freely*; it cannot be imposed on the obligor. Thus we believe that compensation by operation of law or by judicial declaration between a natural obligation and a civil obligation cannot take place.

---

[65] See supra § 1.3.1. Natural Obligation.

[66] See next chapter on *Kinds of Obligations* for an analysis of the concepts of "patrimony" and "heritable obligations."

[67] Compensation: see infra *Extinction of Obligations* § 7.5.

The same reasoning would not be valid if the parties mutually *agreed* to compensation between a natural obligation, on the one hand, and a civil obligation, on the other hand. **LSA-C.C. Art. 1901**[68] raises no obstacle to the freedom of contract enjoyed by the parties in this matter and conventional compensation is but an illustration of such a freedom to contract. Such a conventional compensation could lead either to a reciprocal extinction of the two obligations involved, the civil and the natural, or to a partial remission of a debt, the higher of the two debts.[69]

This is not to say that the freedom of contract is absolute. It is, indeed, possible to imagine a conflict between, on the one hand, the moral duty of an obligor of a natural obligation determined to perform his obligation and, on the other hand, the rights that this obligor's creditors may have on his patrimony. Suppose that the obligor of a civil obligation which has prescribed wishes to perform although he could no longer be sued for performance: whose rights should prevail; those of the obligor of the remaining natural obligation or the rights of that obligor's creditors?

It goes without saying that preference should be given to the obligor's creditors who are in a *legal-civil relationship* with him (**LSA-C.C. Art. 1756**)[70] and are entitled to enforce their rights against their obligor. As regards the natural obligation itself it is now owed to a creditor who, on the one hand, "apparently" failed to act on time to claim that which was due to him (hence the presumption of the action) and a creditor who, on the other hand, was negligent in managing his affairs. On these two grounds, this creditor under a natural obligation should be the one to suffer the loss. It is in this sense that one ought to understand **LSA-C.C. Art. 3453**:

> **"Creditors and other persons having an interest in the acquisition of a thing or in the extinction of a claim or of a real right by prescription may plead prescription, even if the person in whose favor prescription has accrued renounces or fails to plead prescription."**

A reasoning *a pari ratione* or, even a *fortiori ratione*, could be made on the basis of paragraphs 2 and 3 of **LSA-C.C. Art. 1762**[71] to reach the same conclusion as above.

§ 1.3.2. CIVIL OBLIGATIONS.

Former Civil Code Article 1757-3 defined a civil (or perfect) obligation as "*a legal tie, which gives the party, with whom it is contracted, the right of enforcing its performance by law.*" The Dictionary of the Civil Code defines the civil obligation as an "[o]bligation, the specific performance of which may be requested from a court (unlike a natural obligation)."[72] The essential feature of the civil obligation, in contrast with the natural obligation is that the creditor-obligee had or has a right of action to compel the obligor to perform.

---

[68] LSA-C.C. Art. 1901: see Appendix.

[69] On Remission of Debt, see infra § 7.4.2.

[70] See supra p. 1.

[71] See supra p. 3.

[72] *Dictionary of the Civil Code* — word: obligation civile, p.101.

The new code articles on obligations do not include a definition, *per se*, of a civil obligation as did former Article 1757-3. However, the definition given of an obligation in **LSA-C.C. Art. 1756** can be construed to refer to a *civil* obligation, and we ought to preserve this adjective *civil*, which, although not used in the new 1984 law of obligations, remains useful to contrast it with a *natural* obligation which, itself, has survived as a concept in the post 1984 law of obligations.[73]

The selective terminology of **Article 1756**[74] in particular the words *bound to render a performance*, combined with the contents of **LSA-C.C. Art. 1758**[75] and the rights therein given to the parties can, therefore, only describe a legally binding obligation or a *civil* obligation, as it was previously specifically referred to in the Civil Code of 1870.

The essence of such a *civil* obligation is summarized in **LSA-C.C. Art. 1758**, which outlines, in broad terms, the basic rights and obligations of parties to a *civil* obligation, whatever its source under **LSA-C.C. Art. 1757**. The importance of this **Art. 1758** lies in the fact that it posits some general principles which have been extracted from specific rules[76] by the logical process of an inductive method of reasoning. In turn, these general principles can now become fertile in application as express or implicit sources of law to be used by the courts in un-provided for circumstances. It should be emphasized also that the effects of obligations listed in **LSA-C.C. Art. 1758** are *general* and must govern whenever they are not expressly rejected by specific rules in application of the maxim: *specialia generalibus derogant*, special rules or clauses derogate from general rules or clauses.

ARTICLE 4
GENERAL EFFECTS OF OBLIGATIONS

Two innovations have been brought about by the 1984 revision of the law of obligations: they are formulated in **LSA-C.C. Art. 1758** and **1759**.

§ 1.4.1.   GENERAL EFFECTS: LSA-C.C. ART. 1758.[77]

From a formal, didactic and civil law point of view this Article finds its proper place among the general principles of the law of obligations although its immediate legal impact may appear, to some, somewhat limited. The substance of this Article 1758 amounts to a broad listing and general formulation of the types of remedies that might be available to a creditor-obligee who seeks the performance of the obligation he is owed. The nature and extent of that performance will depend on the legal nature of the civil obligation in existence and of the rights and defenses which might be available to a debtor-obligor of that civil obligation. This is where the

---

[73] In a "comment b" to Article 1760 one is told that in this revision the word "obligation," without more, is always synonymous with "civil" obligation, that is, an obligation which is enforceable by legal action.

[74] See supra p. 1.

[75] LSA-C.C. Art. 1758: see Appendix.

[76] The "specific rules" or applications to particular legal concepts of the general principles stated in LSA-C.C. Article 1758 will be explained and illustrated in another Précis on Conventional Obligations.

[77] LSA-C.C. Art. 1758: see Appendix.

distinctions made above between different kinds of obligations will come into play.

This general and broad listing of remedies and rights, as well as defenses, is the outcome, albeit incomplete, of an inductive reasoning which led the drafters of this article to consider, as a first step, all the remedies available to creditors as granted by the different kinds of existing obligations. The second step in the reasoning process consisted in inducing some general considerations or principal effects which can be looked upon as common links between the different kinds of existing obligations.

The importance and benefit of such a general article is to provide gap-filling measures in the event that a particular type of obligation would either fail to specifically provide for certain effects or would not explicitly exclude some remedies. It stands as an umbrella article, which ought to be used always as the general introductory article to any analysis of the nature of the rights of an obligee who seeks the performance of the obligation owed to him.

On the other hand, the danger of such a broad listing might be to convey the impression that, if a remedy is not therein mentioned, albeit in general terms, it would then be excluded on the basis of the principle *inclusio unius, exclusio alterius*. This approach could not be more alien to an authentic civil law legal analysis. As an illustration, we could cite a general remedy that is mentioned in **LSA-C.C. Arts. 3141 and 3142**[78] and, yet, stands out as a general effect of a civil obligation. The right therein given to a creditor is the fountainhead of more specific remedies, which entitle the creditor to be paid or to receive damages out of the sale of his obligor's assets.

§ 1.4.2. GOOD FAITH: LSA-C.C. ART. 1759.

Article 1759 reads as follows:

> **"Good faith shall govern the conduct of the obligor and the obligee in whatever pertains to the obligation."**

The requirement of good faith on the part of parties to an obligation is not a new requirement, although it lost some of its importance over the centuries. The specific inclusion of this requirement in a code article has the merit of raising it to the status of a general principle which, as such, ought to guide the jurist in his analysis of the law of obligations. Coming from Roman law and developed by Canon law, this fundamental theory of *good faith* inspires and pervades the entire law of the Civil Code and the law of obligations in particular. Its underlying presence all through the Civil Code is the legal expression of moral, social, economic objectives that should never be forgotten. It will be particularly true as we look at the formation of a contract and the effects of conventional obligations.[79]

Here again an inductive reasoning led to the inclusion of this **Article 1759** in the Civil Code. From a series of existing code articles, a general principle was extracted and placed in such a manner as to govern all obligations.

---

[78] LSA-C.C. Arts 3133–3134: see Appendix.

[79] See below LSA-C.C. Arts 1948–2012.

Actually, this general principle or duty of good faith can be considered as including two sub-duties, which are incorporated in a great variety of code articles. One such sub-duty could be called the duty of loyalty and the other the duty of cooperation.

A. One can find illustrations of this duty or obligation of loyalty in **LSA-C.C. Art. 96,**[80] on the benefits of a putative marriage, or in **LSA-C.C. Art. 215,**[81] on filial honor and respect or in **LSA-C.C. Art. 576,**[82] on the standard of care owed by a usufructuary. We can also cite **LSA-C.C. Article 1954,** which deals with a relationship of confidence between parties to a contract, or **LSA-C.C. Arts. 1996**[83] *et seq.,* on good faith and the measure of damages on the basis of the good or bad faith of an obligor and, still, **LSA-C.C. Art. 2002,**[84] on the duty of an obligee to mitigate the damage caused by the obligor's failure to perform. All of these code articles, and many more, are specific examples of the overriding principle of good faith, which governs the law of the Civil Code.

B. The same is true of the sub-duty of cooperating in good faith whenever parties are legally bound to each other. Illustrations abound. Consider, for example, **LSA-C.C. Arts. 485** and **486**[85] imposing a duty of cooperation in order to avoid an unjust enrichment by one party at the expense of another; **LSA-C.C. Arts. 496** and **497**[86] lay down rules built on the same duty of cooperation between an owner and a possessor; **LSA-C.C. Art. 1860**[87] requires that an obligor act in good faith and out of a duty of cooperation in the performance of an obligation to deliver a thing, not one of the best but not one of the worst, whenever the quality of that thing has not been agreed upon; **LSA-C.C. Art. 1867**[88] requires that an obligee-creditor act in cooperation with the obligor when the latter fails to impute a payment to one of his debts; the duty of warranty imposed on a seller is nothing but a legal transposition of the moral duty of good faith and cooperation between parties to a synallagmatic contract of sale[89]; the same is true of the obligation of the lessor to deliver the thing in good condition;[90] an accipiens is also held to a duty of good faith and must cooperate with the solvens under **LSA-C.C. Arts. 2302–2305.**[91]

The merits of **LSA-C.C. Arts. 1758** and **1759** reside mostly in their formal existence and visibility at the beginning of the law of "Obligations in General." It is meant to give them, and their substance, greater authenticity, more legal weight and greater control over the whole law of obligations in Book III of the Civil Code

---

[80] LSA-C.C. Art. 96: see Appendix.

[81] LSA-C.C. Art. 215: see Appendix.

[82] LSA-C.C. Art. 576: see Appendix.

[83] LSA-C.C. Art. 1966: see Appendix.

[84] LSA-C.C. Art. 2002: see Appendix.

[85] LSA-C.C. Art. 485; Art. 486: see Appendix.

[86] LSA-C.C. Art. 496; Art. 497: see Appendix.

[87] LSA-C.C. Art. 1860: see Appendix.

[88] LSA-C.C. Art. 1867: see Appendix.

[89] LSA-C.C. Art. 2475.

[90] LSA-C.C. Art. 2684;

[91] LSA-C.C. Art. 2302; Art. 2305: see Appendix.

and, beyond, the whole law of the Civil Code, particularly as regards the obligation of "good faith."

Chapter 2

KINDS OF OBLIGATIONS LSA-C.C. ARTS. 1763 TO 1785

Behind these words "Kinds of Obligations," and others of the same type such as for example "Division of Things," [1] there is a particular and original characteristic of a civilian or civil law jurist way of thinking which is to "classify," or to "organize" by "systematically regrouping together the homogenous or heterogeneous elements of a whole in a rational chart composed of a major division based on a single dominant criterion and sub-divisions based on different combined criteria (part. by genus, kind or species) in order to submit an elaborated reference to an abstract analysis."[2] The civilian jurist excels at classifying because a classification provides him with a general framework of reference that enables him to easily make quick connections and distinctions between the component parts of one classification and the component parts of other classifications. The following classification of obligations according to their "kinds" will serve as a very good illustration of the civilian mind at work and justify the importance of a classification in explaining the effects that follow from classifying one "obligation," as being of one kind as opposed to another kind.

For purposes of clarity and simplification we will gather, and classify, the existing different kinds of obligations in the Louisiana Civil Code under two headings. In Section I, we will present the legal regime of "Patrimonial Obligations" to be subdivided into "Real Obligations" and "Personal Obligations" and in Section II, we will look at the most important "Modalities," which affect either the very existence of an Obligation or only its exigibility.[3]

ARTICLE 1

PATRIMONIAL OBLIGATIONS

The legal concept of "patrimony" is very civilian in its essence. Its Latin origin is that of "*patrimonium*," or estate inherited from one's father or *pater*. Patrimony is thus connected to "pater," father. In plain legal terms a patrimony is "the aggregate of the assets, claims, obligations on one person (that is to say, his rights and charges which can be valued in money); both the assets and liabilities, considered as forming a universality of right, a whole including not only a person's

---

[1] LSA-C.C. Articles 448–475.

[2] *Dictionary of the Civil Code*, — word: classification, p. 102.

[3] From the latin verb "exigere" to refer to a debt the payment of which can be demanded, acted upon because it is liquidated and demandable and, thus, immediately due; it is exigible. We have fashioned the word "exigibility" to distinguish this stage of an obligation from its existence.

present assets but also his future assets."[4] Only persons, natural or legal, have a patrimony because only persons can incur liabilities toward others and claim rights against others. Such is the meaning of **LSA-C.C. Articles 3133** and **3134**, in which we need only substitute the word "patrimony" to the word "property":

> **"Whoever is personally bound for an obligation is obligated to fulfill it out of all of his property, movable or immovable, present and future."** (Art. 3133).

> **"In the absence of a preference authorized or established by legislation, an obligor's property is available to all his creditors for the satisfaction of his obligations, and the proceeds of its sale are distributed ratably among them."** (Art. 3134).

The Louisiana Civil Code, in **Article 26**, attaches a patrimony to "an unborn child" as it "shall be considered as a natural person for whatever relates to its interests from the moment of conception. If the child is born dead, it shall be considered never to have existed as a person, except for purpose of actions resulting from its wrongful death." Although the legal concept of "patrimony" is used almost exclusively in relation with the word "right," so as to form the notion of patrimonial right, there is no reason not to look at the opposite side of the legal relationship that includes a right on one side and its counterpart, which is called an obligation on the other side. Thus, a right can be said to be the active component part of a patrimonial relationship in the sense that the holder of the right has the benefit of the action against an obligor. Conversely, an obligation can be said to be the passive side of a patrimonial relationship since the obligor may wait "passively" until asked to perform. Whether reference is made to a patrimonial right or to a patrimonial obligation, either one is susceptible of monetary evaluation and, for that reason, forms part of a person's patrimony. In contrast, some rights and obligations are said to be extra-patrimonial, or outside the patrimony, because they are not susceptible of monetary evaluation; practically speaking they bear no price-tag. One could mention the right to enter into a contract of marriage (**LSA-C.C. Art. 86** *et seq.*) or the right of a husband to disavow **"paternity of the child by clear and convincing evidence that he is not the father . . ."** (**LSA-C.C. Art. 187**). Such rights belong to the person herself as a "subject of law" and cannot be given any monetary value. They are "personal" and not "patrimonial" and no creditor, who is seeking some monetary compensation, can claim to have the right to exercise such rights.

The concepts of a patrimonial right and patrimonial obligation are further classified and sub-divided into a *real right* and *personal right* on the one hand and a *real obligation* and *personal obligation* on the other hand.

The first distinction, a *real right* and *personal right*, goes back to Roman law and its intricate formulary procedure where an *actio in personam* gave a plaintiff a right of action against an individual (hence, personal right), whereas an *actio in rem* represented a plaintiff's claim over a thing (hence, real right from the Latin "res" meaning "thing"). In modern civil law, the concept of real right has been preserved to refer to a right one holds directly over a thing, whereas a personal right is a right that a person has to bring an action against another person. The *Dictionary of the*

---

[4] *Dictionary of the Civil Code,* — word: patrimoine, p. 423.

Civil Code defines a real right (droit réel) as a "right bearing directly on a thing (jus in re) and giving the holder of that right all or part of the economic usefulness of the thing."[5]

As regards the notion of *real obligation*, it is very seldom written about in civil law treatises, except in Toullier, who is said to have developed the concept and inspired the drafters of the Louisiana Civil Code.

The Louisiana Civil Codes of 1825 and 1870 defined a real obligation as one attached to real property, (immovable property, said *Article 1997 of the Code of 1870*) and Professor Yiannopoulos elaborated on the subject when writing that *real obligations* are always duties incidental and correlative to real rights. They are *obligations* in the sense that they are duties imposed on a particular person who owns or possesses a thing subject to a real right, and they are *real* in the sense that, as correlative of a real right, these obligations attach to a particular thing and are transferred with it without the need of an express assignment or subrogation.[6] They are also *real* in the sense that the responsibility of the obligor may be limited to the value of the thing. In this light, it appears that the use of the term *real obligation* is confusing and should be avoided.[7] Nevertheless, the concept of real obligation has been preserved in the Louisiana law of obligations.

The personal obligation, being the counterpart of the personal right, refers to an obligation or a duty a person owes to another person who holds the right *in personam*.

§ 2.1.1.   REAL OBLIGATIONS.

The Louisiana Civil Code describes the concept of real obligations and provides broadly for the effects of such obligations.

A.   Concept of Real Obligation.

On the basis of the Latin origin of this concept, **LSA-C.C. Art. 1763** defines a real obligation as a **"duty correlative and incidental to a real right."** The institutional value of this definition is very limited indeed. It purports to define the notion of a real obligation, in reference to that of a real right, but nowhere in the Civil Code is there a definition of a real right as a general concept. One can find a listing of rights in things but no definition *per se* which would parallel and supplement the attempted definition of a real obligation. It could be said in support of the lack of a definition that "*all that is definition, teaching, doctrine falls into the domain of science*"[8] and outside the domain of legislation. Be that as it may, the notion of a real obligation has been preserved, despite some inconsistencies, in order not to disrupt habits acquired since the Civil Code of 1825 and deeply

---

[5] See *Dictionary of the Civil Code*, — word: droit réel, p. 483. See *Louisiana Law of Property, A Précis*, John Randall Trahan, "b. Real Rights", p. 2–4, LexisNexis 2012.

[6] See infra the concepts of "Assignment" and "Subrogation" § 5.2.

[7] Yiannopoulos, *Louisiana Civil Law Treatise, Property*. § 115 p. 348, 349, West Publishing Co.

[8] Excerpts from a discourse on the Code Napoléon by Portalis and case-law and doctrine by A. Esmein, 18 Loyola L. Rev. 23–27 at 28 (1971–72).

imbedded in the civil law of this State. Thus, a real obligation is an obligation, or a duty, owed to a person who can claim a performance because that person is the holder of a real right, *i.e.*, a right to make a direct and immediate [fictitiously without the involvement of an intermediary person] use of a thing.

The greater or lesser use the holder of a real right can make of a thing suggests that a distinction be made between principal real rights and accessory real rights.

Principal real rights vest in their holder the broadest powers of *usus, fructus* and *abusus* because they bear directly on the very substance of the thing. The right of ownership, because it is made up of the sub-real rights of *usus, fructus* and *abusus*, illustrates this concept most perfectly. The dismemberments of the right of ownership, such as usufruct (or the addition of *usus* to *fructus*), use (or *usus*), are also real rights because their beneficiary receives the enjoyment of one or more of the sub-real rights of an owner.

Accessory real rights are so called because they bear on the representative monetary value of a thing rather that on the thing itself. They are also known as rights *propter rem* because they are related to a thing and cannot be disassociated from it. Illustrations of accessory real rights would be the institutions of mortgage,[9] pledge[10] etc. An accessory real right gives to its holder, a mortgagee for example, the right to demand payment of an obligation from the mortgagor because of the accessory real right the mortgagee holds on the thing, movable or immovable, in the hands of the mortgagor.

B. Effects of Real Obligations.

The effects of real obligations flow from two fundamental prerequisites: A) there can be no real obligation unless there is a thing in existence; B) the real obligation is transferred with the thing as its accessory.

1. Real Obligation and Existence of a Thing.

A real obligation being a duty correlative to a real right, the latter and, therefore, the former cannot exist unless there is a thing in existence from which both the real right and the real obligation derive. As stated in **LSA-C.C. Art. 1764,**[11] the thing, which at the same time justifies the existence and the extent of the right and the obligation, can be a movable or an immovable as these concepts are defined in the Civil Code. It follows that, whenever a thing is destroyed, the right of ownership over that thing which was vested in someone will cease to exist for lack of a thing over which the right can bear. Should damages be owed to the owner, the claim of the owner against the tortfeasor or insurer cannot be a real right but rather a personal right binding a debtor to a creditor.[12]

---

[9] LSA-C.C. Articles 3278 to 3337: see Arts. 3278 to 3287 and 3337 in Appendix.

[10] LSA-C.C. Articles 3141 to 3181; see also R.S. 10:9-101 to 10:9-710.

[11] LSA-C.C. Art. 1764: see Appendix.

[12] If damages are to be paid to the owner, then a "real subrogation" will take place, i.e., a thing (money) is substituted to another thing (which was destroyed or damaged). On "subrogation" see infra § 5.2.

2. Real Obligation and the Transfer of the Thing.

The existence of a real obligation is conditional upon the existence of a thing; it follows that the fate of the latter will determine the fate of the former by application of the principle *accessorium sequitur naturam sui principalis* or more succinctly stated as *accessorium sequitur principale.*[13]

In the words of **LSA-C.C. Art. 1764,** whenever the principal thing is transferred, the real obligation which is attached to it is transferred without a special provision to that effect. It follows that a real obligation cannot be transferred separately from the *carrying* thing.

The importance of these principles is emphasized by some of their practical applications. Thus, for instance, a particular successor[14] who receives a particular title to a principal thing, an immovable for example, may renounce his *real right* to the immovable by a unilateral juridical act,[15] so as not to be burdened with the real obligations attached to the immovable. **LSA-C.C. Arts 770** and **3448**[16] are illustrations of the unilateral abandonment of a predial servitude or real obligation, and of the unilateral extinction of a real right other than ownership.

This ability of a *real obligor* to unilaterally renounce a burden related to a real obligation is in sharp contrast with the situation of an obligor of a personal obligation, who will have to express his consent, for example, to a remission of his debt by his creditor. A bilateral juridical act is, therefore, necessary to extinguish a personal obligation.

Considering that a real obligation is *fictitiously* owed by a thing, and actually by a person, it follows also that an obligor of a real obligation will be liable only to the extent that the thing offers a sufficient basis for the performance of the real obligation. In other words, the *real obligor* is not *personally bound* or responsible for the debts.[17] A mortgagor will surrender the immovable in satisfaction of the real obligation owed to the mortgagee, and a purchaser of an immovable encumbered with a mortgage binds himself to a real obligation to such an extent that he may have to accept the forced sale of the immovable in order to restrict his own liability to the limited value of the immovable. It follows also, as a logical consequence, that should the principal thing be destroyed without the fault of the obligor, the real obligation would be extinguished and the obligor relieved of any *personal* obligation.

§ 2.1.2. PERSONAL OBLIGATIONS.

The second type of obligations, or rights, are those held or owned by a person *vis-à-vis* another person. The creditor or holder of such an obligation holds a right *in personam*, a right against the person of the obligor who may be under an

---

[13] *Dictionary of the Civil Code*, Index of Legal Adages, p. 659.

[14] For an understanding of the notion of particular successor, see LSA-C.C. Art. 3506 (28): see Appendix.

[15] On juridical acts, see supra § 1.1.2.

[16] LSA-C.C. Arts. 770 and 3448: see Appendix.

[17] LSA-C.C. Art. 1764: see Appendix.

obligation to give, to do or not to do something. The nature of the performance owed by the obligor leads to draw a distinction between heritable obligations, on the one hand, and strictly personal obligations, on the other hand.

A. Heritable Obligations.

LSA-C.C. Arts. 1765 and **1984** state the general rules governing the law of heritable obligations:

> Art. 1765:
>
> **"An obligation is heritable when its performance may be enforced by a successor of the obligee or against a successor of the obligor.**
>
> **Every obligation is deemed heritable as to all parties, except when the contrary results from the terms or from the nature of the contract.**
>
> **A heritable obligation is also transferable between living persons."**
>
> Art. 1984:
>
> **"Rights and obligations arising from a contract are heritable and assignable unless the law, the terms of the contract or its nature preclude such effects."**

Every obligation is thus presumed to be heritable as to both parties. This means that, being part of one's patrimony, an obligation can be transferred or passed on to one's heirs. This presumption, however, is rebuttable and can be defeated either by the terms of a contract or by the circumstances if they are such as to suggest that the nature of the legal relationship binding the parties dictates that one or both obligations are to be considered as strictly personal. In its first paragraph, **LSA-C.C. Art. 1766**[18] states: **"An obligation is strictly personal when its performance can be enforced only by the obligee, or only against the obligee."**

A heritable obligation, being part of one's patrimony, can be transferred by juridical acts *inter vivos* as well as *mortis causa*, thereby placing the heir or assign in the same legal position as was the author.

An illustration of such juridical acts is given in **LSA-C.C. Art 1886** which provides that:

> **"A delegation of performance by an obligor to a third person is effective when that person binds himself to perform.**
>
> **A delegation effects a novation only when the obligee expressly discharges the original obligor."**

Moreover, **LSA-C.C. Art. 872**[19] is extremely clear in its statement that obligations are heritable, in the true sense of the word, when it reads that:

> **"The estate of a deceased means the property, rights, and obligations that a person leaves after his death, whether the property exceeds the**

---

[18] LSA-C.C. Art. 1766: see Appendix.

[19] See also LSA-C.C. Art. 935 in Appendix.

charges or the charges exceed the property, or whether he has only left charges without any property. The estate includes not only the rights and obligations of the deceased as they exist at the time of death, but all that has accrued thereto since death, and the new charges to which it becomes subject."

B. Strictly Personal Obligations.

The full extent of **LSA-C.C. Art. 1766** defines a strictly personal obligation in these terms:

"An obligation is strictly personal when its performance can be enforced only by the obligee, or only against the obligor.

When the performance requires the special skill or qualification of the obligor, the obligation is presumed to be strictly personal on the part of the obligor. All obligations to perform personal services are presumed to be strictly personal on the part of the obligor.

When the performance is intended for the benefit of the obligee exclusively, the obligation is strictly personal on the part of that obligee."

An obligation that is classified as strictly personal is, therefore, an obligation which, either, can be performed only by the obligor because of "who" he is, or can be performed exclusively for the benefit of the obligee-creditor because of "who" he or she is. Such obligations are said to have been entered into *intuitus personae* or in strict contemplation of the "person" of either party or both of them.

LSA-C.C. Art. 1766 stipulates that an obligation can be strictly personal as to the obligor, and it is presumed to be so whenever the obligor is bound to do something that requires his particular skill or qualifications. An illustration of such an obligation can be found in **LSA-C.C. Art. 2766** which provides that:

"Contracts for hiring out work are canceled by the death of the workman, architect or undertaker, unless the proprietor should consent that the work should be continued by the heir or heirs of the architect, or by workmen employed for that purpose by the heirs."

Since a workman, an architect or an undertaker binds himself to provide personal services on the basis of his own personal qualifications he will fall under the general presumption laid down in the second paragraph of **LSA-C.C. Art. 1766**, which makes an explicit reference to a performance that requires the special skill or qualification of the obligor. The Code, however, only establishes a rebuttable presumption as illustrated in **LSA-C.C. Art. 2766**.

An obligation can also be strictly personal as to the obligee where he would be the only party to have an interest in the performance of the obligation (**LSA-C.C. Art. 1766-3**).[20] Such would be the case of a party to a contract with a transportation company whereby the latter would be bound to ferry the former from his home to

---

[20] LSA-C.C. Art. 1766: see Appendix.

his office every working day. The services provided by the transportation company are owed only to the customer-obligee who is to benefit from the services. The contract will therefore terminate automatically with the death of the customer, for example.

LSA-C.C. Art. 1766 leaves one question unanswered which former **LSA-C.C. Art. 2004**[21] had addressed. Can an obligation be strictly personal as to both parties (obligor *and* obligee, where Art. 1766 reads obligee *or* obligor) at the same time? Although LSA-R.S. 9:2785 provides a positive answer by restating the contents of former Civil Code Article 2004, it is possible to argue, by a reasoning *a fortiori ratione* (from the lesser to the greater), that **LSA-C.C. Art. 1766** does contemplate strictly personal obligations as to both parties. Indeed, when the article provides that an obligation can be strictly personal as to either party, the reason which explains the strictly personal nature of one obligation explains, *a fortiori*, that an obligation can be personal to both parties in a bilateral legal relationship. For example, a contract involving an artist and a producer, or a contract binding a writer to an editor, can easily be considered as creating strictly personal obligations on both sides.

In addition, **LSA-C.C. Art. 3024** specifically provides an example of an obligation strictly personal as to the obligor and obligee where it states that: "**both the mandate and the authority of the mandatary terminate upon the: (1) Death of the principal or of the mandatary.**" The rights and obligations deriving from the contract of mandate are not heritable and the death of either party will put an end to the legal relationship. Is there any doubt that where "**married persons owe each other fidelity, support, and assistance**" (**LSA-C.C. Art. 98**) each party to the marriage is both "obligee and obligor" of strictly personal obligations?

The question raised as to the scope of application of **LSA-C.C. Art. 1766** can now be easily answered: since there exists in the Civil Code several examples of strictly personal obligations on both parties, Article 1766 can only be read *a fortiori ratione.*

ARTICLE 2

MODALITIES AFFECTING THE EXISTENCE OR THE

EXIGIBILITY OF AN

OBLIGATION

Under normal circumstances a civil obligation, i.e. an obligation that vests in a party the right to demand specific performance of the obligation or the right to demand damages in lieu of specific performance, should be considered as a pure and simple obligation. It means that as soon as the obligation comes into existence its performance should be carried out right then and there. The obligation should carry with it the general legal effects, which are described in **LSA-C.C. Art. 1758**.[22] However, some alterations to this immediacy of the effects of an obligation can be the result either of legislation or of the will of the parties themselves. There are two basic types of legal modalities, devices or features that may affect an obligation in

---

[21] Former LSA-C.C. Art. 2004: "An obligation to pay an annuity to a certain person during the life of the obligor, is personal as to both, and is extinguished by the death of either."

[22] LSA-C.C. Art. 1758: see Appendix.

one of its constitutive elements or modifies its normal and ordinary effects. These two modalities are the *term* and the *condition*.

Although the Louisiana Civil Code, and the French Civil Code, cover *conditional obligations* first (**LSA-C.C. Art. 1767** to **1776**)[23] and *obligations with a term* second (**LSA-C.C. Art. 1777** to **1785**),[24] for dogmatic and didactic reasons we have preferred to reverse the order of presentation and analyze the term before the condition.

ARTICLE 2: SUBSECTION A
THE TERM

Parties to an obligation may determine its scope of application in time, be it a particular time in the future or a period of time to come. They may decide, by the insertion of a *term*, when the obligation will be demandable/exigible or they may provide for a *term* tied to the duration of performance of the obligation. In either case, the parties are not tampering with the *very existence* of the obligation in question; they are only focusing on the *timing of the performance* of the obligation. A *"term"* therefore is tied to the *performance* of an obligation and not the existence of that obligation. There lies the main difference between a term and a condition, as will be explained in the next paragraph.

After a survey of the concept of term we shall consider its effects and its waiver or forfeiture.

§ 2.2-A.1. CONCEPT OF TERM.

LSA-C.C. Art. 1778 describes the *term* in these words:

> **"A term for the performance of an obligation is a period of time either certain or uncertain. It is certain when fixed. It is uncertain when it is not fixed but is determinable either by the intent of the parties or by the occurrence of a future and certain event. It is also uncertain when it is not determinable, in which case the obligation must be performed within a reasonable time."**

A term is, therefore, a future and certain event in the sense that it is an event which will definitely occur and which, when it occurs, may either delay the performance of an obligation, as suggested by an *a contrario sensu* reasoning on **LSA-C.C. Art. 1777-2**,[25] or bring an end to the performance of an existing obligation, such as put an end to a lease, for example.

In the above definition, it is possible to distinguish between two broad classifications of the term, each classification being, in turn, susceptible of sub- classifications or qualifications.

---

[23] LSA-C.C. Arts. 1767 to 1776: see Appendix.

[24] LSA-C.C. Arts. 1777 to 1785: see Appendix.

[25] LSA-C.C. Art. 1777: see Appendix.

A. Suspensive Term and Extinctive Term.

Although these technical expressions are not used in the body of any code article, they are well known in civil law doctrine in general and some comments to articles of the Louisiana Civil Code do reference them.[26] Although these comments are not part of the law of the Code, because they do not detract from the substance of the law on this concept of term, we believe it is acceptable to refer to them.

1. Suspensive Term.

A term is *suspensive* whenever it suspends or delays the right to demand the performance of an obligation until the term occurs. It means, therefore, that as long as the term has not occurred, the performance of the obligation cannot be demanded by the obligee, even though the obligation itself does exist.

Two simple illustrations will explain fully. First, it is common business practice that a buyer will be given thirty days to pay his vendor; second, it is a local custom that a rent is due on the first day of the month. In these two examples, the obligor (buyer in the sale/lessee in the lease) cannot be compelled to pay until the occurrence of the term. In other words, the performance of the obligation to pay the price of the sale or the rent of the lease is suspended or delayed for thirty days or until the first of the month.

2. Extinctive Term.

An extinctive term is one which, when it occurs, brings an end to the performance of the obligation in the future. Once the event selected as the extinctive term occurs, the obligation that existed until then ceases to exist *ex nunc*, prospectively; the extinction has no retroactive effect. What happened in the past until the extinctive term occurred remains in existence. It is common, for example, for a lease to terminate after one year; thereafter, the lessor cannot demand payment of the rent since the lessee's obligation to pay has been terminated.[27] **LSA-C.C. Art. 2746** provides another example of an extinctive term where it stipulates that "[a] man can only hire out his services for a certain limited time, or for the performance of a certain enterprise." Once the limited time has expired or once the performance is completed, the obligation ceases to exist with the performance having come to an end.

B. Sub-Qualifications/Classifications of the Term.

A term, in addition to being either suspensive or extinctive, may be certain or uncertain. Besides, the source of a term may be a contract, the law or a court decision. Lastly a term may be stipulated in favor of either party or both parties to an obligation.

---

[26] It must be stressed here that "comments" in the Civil Code have "no" force of law. See R.S.1:13 Headings and ancillary information, not part of law.

[27] LSA-C.C. Art. 2720: see Appendix.

1. Certain and Uncertain Term.

The term, as a definite event bound to occur in the course of time, and the issue of certainty or uncertainty of the term can only be raised with respect to the exact date or period of time of occurrence of the event selected as the term of the obligation.

A term is *certain* whenever the period of time preceding the occurrence of the event has been fixed. **LSA-C.C. Art. 1778** provides that "a term . . . is certain when it is fixed." One can select as a certain term, a religious event (Christmas day), a personal event (a birthday) or a set period of time (the 25th of this month, one month, a calendar year . . .).

A term is said to be *uncertain* only when the period of time preceding the occurrence of the definite event or term "is not fixed but is determinable either by the intent of the parties or by the occurrence of a future and certain event. It is also uncertain when it is not determinable, in which case the obligation must be performed within a reasonable time."[28] As an example of an uncertain term or event bound to occur although it is not possible to set a precise time, we could select the timing of a certain person's death. Gaius could, for example, agree to pay Paul upon Modestinus' death. The reference to Modestinus' death would be an uncertain term. Indeed, although it is a certainty that Modestinus will die, one cannot say with certainty when his death will occur. Selecting the "end" of a tennis match is choosing an event that will occur (one way or the other), but one cannot say, in advance, because of the "uncertainty" of the timing of the end of the match, exactly when it will end.

This notion of certainty of the timing of occurrence of the event raises some difficulties, at times, in distinguishing an uncertain term from a condition. The difficulty of the matter may be multiplied whenever a term is scheduled to occur within a condition, as will be explained below.

2. Conventional, Legal, and Judicial Term.

Although **LSA-C.C. Arts. 1777, 1778,** and **1779**[29] may convey the impression that a term may only be expressly stated in or implied from a contract or agreement, there are instances where a term may be imposed by law or by a judicial decision.

A conventional term is a term or certain event expressly or impliedly agreed upon between the parties to a contract (**LSA-C.C. Art. 1777**).

An express conventional term is one which is specifically stipulated by the parties to an agreement and which requires that the performance take place or end by the date selected or within the period of time upon which the parties agreed. To help solve the problem of computation of the term, **LSA-C.C. Art. 1784**[30] specifies the rules for figuring out the time period involved.

---

[28]   LSA-C.C. Art. 1778: see Appendix.

[29]   LSA-C.C. Arts. 1777, 1778, 1779: see Appendix.

[30]   LSA-C.C. Art. 1784: see Appendix.

An example of an express conventional term would be found in a lessor granting his lessee until the 15th of the month to pay the rent, even though the lessee occupied the premises on the first of the same month. Another example of a conventional term is one which must be included in an option to purchase, as is required by **Article 2620** which states, in part, that **"an option to buy, or an option to sell, is a contract whereby a party gives to another the right to accept an offer to sell, or to buy, a thing within a stipulated time."**

An implied conventional term is one that may be *reasonably implied* from the nature of the contract or the circumstances. Such an implied term necessarily involves an obligation that cannot be performed instantaneously and one that would require that the obligor do something over a period of time. In a contract of mandate, the principal may confer authority on his mandatary to transact one or more affairs in the principal's interest. Once the mandatary has completed his management of the affairs of the principal over the proper amount of time, the mandate will come to an end.[32]

A legal term is a term granted or imposed by law.

Thus, for example, **LSA-C.C. Art. 2595** provides that **"the action for lesion must be brought within a peremptive period of one year from the time of the sale."**

Another illustration of a mandatory legal term can be found in the contract of sale with the right of redemption: **LSA-C.C. Art. 2568** states: **"the right of redemption**[33] **may not be reserved for more than ten years . . . ."**

One could also mention the term of *seventy-two hours* that must elapse between the time a marriage license is issued and the performance of the ceremony (LSA-R.S. 9:241).

A judicial term, also called a period of grace, is a term granted by a court to a debtor who is sued by his creditor seeking performance of the obligation. The court may grant or deny this term of grace in consideration of the particular situation of the debtor. Article 2013, (2nd paragraph) offers an illustration of such a concept: **"In an action involving judicial dissolution, the obligor who failed to perform may be granted, according to the circumstances, an additional time to perform."**

It should be pointed out, though, that a court does not always enjoy this discretionary power when faced with a conventional term or, *a fortiori*, with a legal term. Thus, for instance, in the case of a sale with the right of redemption **"the period for redemption is peremptive and runs against all persons including minors. It may not be extended by the court."**[34]

---

[32] LSA-C.C. Art. 2989.

[33] LSA-C.C. Art. 2567: see Appendix.

[34] LSA-C.C. Art. 2571.

3. Interest Protected by the Term.

Since a term is meant to delay the performance of an obligation, or extinguish an existing obligation, it is most likely that a term will be protective of the interests of the obligor who is to perform the obligation. This likelihood of the effects of the term is only a presumption, and one can point to instances where the term is actually stipulated either in favor of the obligee or in favor of both parties. The scope of the effects of the term will vary greatly depending on whose interests are protected by the term.

The Civil Code provides for a rebuttable presumption as follows: "**A term is presumed to benefit the obligor unless the agreement or the circumstances show that it was intended to benefit the obligee or both parties**" (**LSA-C.C. Art. 1779**). This presumption is most reasonable and shares the same legal justification with **LSA-C.C. Art. 2057-1**, which provides: "**In case of doubt that cannot be otherwise resolved, a contract must be interpreted against the obligee and in favor of the obligor of a particular obligation.**" This legal presumption can be rebutted since it merely assumes that, because of their silence, the parties have implicitly agreed that the term would protect the obligor.

Thus, for example, in a contract of loan with the payment of interest, the lender, or obligee, will want the interest to be paid for as long a period of time as possible and it will not be rare to read in the contract that the interest will be paid first before reimbursement of the capital or that the borrower-obligor will be penalized should he repay his loan by anticipation. Another illustration can be found in the contract of loan for *consumption* or *mutuum*.[35] If no term has been stipulated, this loan is then "exigible at will" although "a reasonable term is implied."[36] The obligee-lender is then in control of the occurrence of the implied term which is protective of his interest.

It is conceivable that a term could exist in favor of both parties to a contract. In a loan, it is not unusual to find a provision inviting the parties to negotiate should the borrower want to reimburse the loan in anticipation of the term. In such a case, the term can be said to be in favor of both parties.

§ 2.2-A.2. EFFECTS OF A TERM.

Once a term, express or implied, is a component part of an obligation, it is most important to determine the rights and obligations of the parties involved in relation to the interest protected by the term. Thus, the actual effects of the term will vary, on the one hand, on account of the type of term considered and, on the other hand, according to whether the period of time involved precedes or follows the occurrence of the event selected as the term.

---

[35] LSA-C.C. Arts. 2904–2912.

[36] LSA-C.C. Art. 2909.

A. Effects of an Extinctive Term.

The function of an extinctive term is to bring an end to the performance of an existing obligation. Therefore, before the happening of the extinctive term, the obligation is immediately enforceable as any pure and simple obligation would be. The parties may seek enforcement of their rights and be compelled to perform their duties as they had bound themselves when entering into their contract. A lessor may demand payment of the rent[37] and the lessee demand that the lessor maintain the thing in a condition suitable for the purpose of which it was leased.[38]

However, these rights and duties are not meant to last. Indeed, when the event selected as the term occurs the obligation ceases to exist from then on, *ex nunc* prospectively. Whatever legal status or legal position was obtained by each of the parties at the [**LSA-C.C. Art. 2683**] time of occurrence of the term will remain. It is important to stress that an extinctive term has no retroactive effect in the sense that the "past" remains as it is and only the future is concerned.

B. Effects of a Suspensive Term.

The function of a suspensive term is to delay the performance or execution of an existing obligation until a certain time after that obligation has come into existence. In other words, the effects of the existing obligation are "suspended" until the term occurs. It follows that the parties are, for a while, subjected to a dual legal status: one which relates to that period of time before the occurrence of the suspensive term and the other which concerns the period of time that follows the happening of the term.

1. Effects While the Term is Pending.

It is most important to stress that, although the execution or performance of the effects of the obligation is delayed until the term occurs, the obligation itself is born and does exist in the sense that it has created rights and obligations in the parties. However, these rights and obligations are "in suspense"! There follows a series of legal consequences:

(a) the creditor-obligee cannot demand performance of his obligation from his debtor-obligor in whose favor the term is established. The obligor enjoys the benefit of a defense or exception based on the suspensive term, which protects him. Thus, where a vendor has given his purchaser thirty days to pay the price, the vendor cannot claim payment of that price from his purchaser before the expiration of the term, i.e. thirty days.[39]

(b) because a creditor-obligee cannot compel an obligor protected by a suspensive term to perform his obligation before the happening of the term, prescription

---

[37] LSA-C.C. Art. 2683.

[38] LSA-C.C. Art. 2682.

[39] LSA-C.C. Art. 1781 and LSA-C.C.P. Art. 423; see Appendix; see *Dictionary of the Civil Code*, Index of Legal Adages, p. 659.

cannot run against the right of action of that creditor: "*contra non valentem agere non currit praescriptio.*"[40]

(c) since a suspensive term merely delays the performance of his existing obligation by the obligor, should that obligor choose to perform before the occurrence of the term meant to protect him, his performance will be valid and binding.[41] Indeed, such a performance before the expiration of the suspensive term is not made in fulfillment of a non-existing obligation but, rather, in actual compliance with an existing and binding obligation, the performance of which was delayed as a benefit to the obligor. Therefore, the anticipated performance, the performance before the happening of the term, is not one related to the *payment of a thing not owed.*[42] The performance was due but not demandable until the occurrence of the suspensive term.

A statement made in a "Revision Comment" appearing under Article 1781 requires a necessary discussion or, rather, "constructive criticism." This Comment (b) states that "a performance rendered before the expiration of the term governing it must be rendered voluntarily, that is, out of free will not vitiated by duress, error, or fraud, or it is recoverable . . . ." One can easily understand why such a performance could be recovered where it had been made as a result of duress or fraud.[43] The obligor was, then, not acting out of his free will; he truly was not "willing" to perform; rather, he was induced or coerced by someone else to perform.

Such is not the situation, in our opinion, when an obligor performs by anticipation and yet under *error*. In this instance we are not dealing with a performance or a payment not due in any manner; we are not concerned here with "the discharge of an obligation that does not exist."[44] and the obligor was neither under "duress-violence" nor the subject of "fraud" in making his payment. That payment, that performance was due on account of an existing obligation although the performance could not be required from the obligor. Yet the creditor is entitled to that performance; he has the right to the payment. The obligor who performed ahead of time, albeit under error, can be said, in a sense, to have waived the benefit of the term that protected him.[45] Indeed isn't anyone held to some degree of care in the management of his own affairs? Furthermore, if we followed the reporter's suggestion under comment (b) to **LSA-C.C. Art. 1781**, to-wit, that an anticipated payment made under error before occurrence of the term is recoverable because not *voluntarily* made, we might then be faced with a serious conflict when we reason *a pari ratione* on **LSA-C.C. Art. 1761**.[46] Indeed, according to this latter article, when a performance has been *freely* undertaken in compliance with a

---

[40] LSA-C.C.P. Art. 423: see Appendix.

[41] LSA-C.C. Art. 1781: see Appendix.

[42] LSA-C.C. Art. 2299: see Appendix. Reasoning *a contrario sensu* on Art. 2301, see Appendix.

[43] On Fraud and Duress, see LSA-C.C. Articles 1953–1958 and 1959–1964.

[44] LSA-C.C. Arts. 2299 and 2300: see Appendix.

[45] See *Droit civil, Les obligations*, François Terré, Philippe Simler, Yves Lequette, Dalloz 11th ed.2013, # 1210 a) L'obligation existe. See also *Les obligations*, Philippe Malaurie, Laurent Aynès, Philippe Stoffel-Munck, Defrénois 2003, #1221, Exigibilité.

[46] See LSA-C.C. Art. 1761 in Appendix.

natural obligation, it may not be reclaimed. Comment (b) to this same **Article 1761** advises us that freely *"means that the performing party must have acted without outside compulsion by fraud or violence; it does not mean, however, that [the] performance cannot have been induced by error."* In Comment (d) to **Article 2299**, "[p]ayment of a thing not owed," we read: "Under **Article 2299**, a person who knowingly or through error has paid or delivered a thing not owed may reclaim it from the person who received it." Reasoning **a contrario**, when an obligation is "owed," albeit not demandable yet, payment of that obligation as a result of error should not be recoverable. If an obligor performing under error cannot recover a performance made where a mere natural obligation exists, it is obvious that the same obligor acting under error should not be able to recover his performance that is "owed" under an existing civil obligation.

Lastly, we would argue that it is not reasonable to apply the same legal regime to an obligor under a suspensive term and to an obligor under a suspensive condition.[47] An obligor under a suspensive condition owes nothing to his "would be obligee" because no obligation exists yet and none might ever exist should the suspensive condition fail to occur. It is reasonable, and logical, then to allow an obligor under a suspensive condition to recover a performance made under error because that obligor owes nothing at all, not even *"naturally."* The reasons which justify the right of such an obligor under a suspensive condition to recover his performance made under error do not exist in the case of an obligor under a suspensive term. The law, therefore, should treat these two different obligors differently and deny an obligor under a suspensive term the right to recover a performance undertaken under error.[48] Furthermore, it should be pointed out that **LSA-C.C. Art. 2301** states that **"a thing is not owed when it is paid or delivered for discharge of an obligation that is subject to a suspensive condition."** Reasoning *ratio legis stricta* and *a contrario sensu* on this article, it is reasonable to state that the principle of **Article 2301** cannot be extended to performances which *are due* on a certain day or on the occurrence of an event which is certain to happen, in other words when a suspensive term is attached to the performance of an obligation.

(d) Whenever the object of the obligor's obligation is a determinate thing, the delivery of that thing can be merely delayed by a suspensive term, whereas the ownership of the object/thing has passed to the buyer as soon as there was an agreement on the thing and the price was fixed or determinable.[49] However, when the effects of a contract or obligation are not of public order, in the sense that parties to a contract may be allowed to alter the "legal" effects of a contract, a term can be attached to such effects. Nowhere in the Louisiana Civil Code is it said that the effects of a contract of sale are of public order and that parties to a sale cannot modify these effects and tailor them to their needs. It would be perfectly acceptable for parties to a sale to include in their contract a suspensive term that would delay

---

[47] On Condition, see infra § 2.2-B.1.

[48] Under the civil law theory on sources of law and their ranking, "comments" to Articles of the Civil Code, to legislation therefore, have no legal force and are not binding sources of law. They may be considered to have a merely "persuasive" role.

[49] LSA-C.C. Art. 2456: see Appendix.

the transfer of ownership from the seller to the buyer at some future time, the end of the month for example.

(e) The existence of a suspensive term in favor of an obligor will prevent the creditor from claiming the benefit of *compensation* under **LSA-C.C. Arts. 1893** *et seq.*[50] Under the law of *compensation*, the existence of a term prevents an obligation from being demandable, that is to say *presently due*, until the term happens. It follows, then, that a suspensive term will stand in the way of a creditor who might attempt to use the benefit of compensation as a mode of extinction of an obligation he, himself, might owe his obligor. However, when a term consists in a delay of grace, whether judicial or conventional, there will be no obstacle to a claim of *compensation*. The reason can easily be found in the fact that a delay of grace is only meant to suspend a legal action against the obligor, whereas *compensation* is, actually, a mode of a reciprocal extinction of two obligations being performed simultaneously and somewhat fictitiously. It would be unreasonable and illogical to maintain a right to a legal action when the debt could easily be extinguished by compensation. Thus, a delay of grace is no obstacle to compensation.

(f) In those instances where the term is explicitly stipulated in favor of the creditor-obligee, there will follow, as a legal consequence, that the obligor could not compel his creditor-obligee to receive his performance before the occurrence of the term. The creditor-obligee is entitled to receive the benefits of his right such as, for example, collecting interest on the principal debt over the whole stretch of the agreed period of time or term. The longer the term in favor of a lender of money, the more interest he is entitled to collect. He should not be deprived of that benefit without his consent.

(g) Regardless of whether the term is in favor of one party or the other, the fact that an obligor owes a performance to his obligee and, furthermore, because that performance will have to take place at some point in time, the law grants to the obligee the means of protecting his right to that performance. While the term is pending, the obligee should have the right to resort to any conservatory act protective of his right to the expected performance of his obligation by the obligor.

Actually, **Article 1783** in fine provides for such a protection of the right of the obligee: "**The obligee may take all lawful measures to preserve his right.**"[51] It is perfectly legitimate to recognize to an obligee under a suspensive term the same opportunity as is provided to an obligee under a suspensive condition.[52] Indeed, under the legal regime of the suspensive condition an obligee is only a "may-be-obligee," whereas under the legal regime of the suspensive term an obligee is an "actual obligee," who is only waiting for a performance that will happen. Therefore, the obligee under a suspensive term should enjoy as much, if not more, of a right to "take all lawful measures to preserve his right" as a "may-be-obligee" is enjoying under **LSA-C.C. Art. 1771.**[53]

---

[50] LSA-C.C. Art. 1893: see Appendix.

[51] LSA-C.C. Art. 1783, 2nd sentence: see Appendix.

[52] On Condition, see infra § 2.2-B.

[53] LSA-C.C. Art. 1771: see Appendix.

Among those measures an obligee should be able to resort to a writ of attachment or of sequestration.[54]

The distinction between juridical acts of conservation of one's rights and juridical acts of execution is not always an easy one to make. Yet it is a fundamental one. Thus, for instance, should an obligee under a term be allowed to bring a pauliana or revocatory action to annul an act of his obligor?[55] Should the same creditor be allowed an oblique action?[56]

The question that must be answered at this point is whether an obligee under a suspensive term is *an obligee* under **LSA-C.C. Art. 2036** or *the obligee* as described in **LSA-C.C. Art. 2044?**[57] These two articles do not qualify or characterize the legal status of an obligee as being a pure and simple obligee, or one under a term or a condition. Through an interpretation a *generali sensu*,[58] we could easily conclude that an obligee under a term is an obligee under the two articles cited on the ground that where the code articles make no distinction we are to make none. Furthermore, after considering the *raison d'être* of these two actions, it is possible to conclude that, since they both contemplate a situation where the obligor would act or omit to act so as to cause his insolvency or increase his insolvency, the obligee under a term should definitely enjoy the benefit of these actions. In a sense, **LSA-C.C. Art. 1782**[59] provides the answer: since the insolvency of the debtor carries the effect that "the term is regarded as nonexistent," an obligee under a term becomes, automatically and by law, *an obligee* or *the obligee.* That obligee ought to be recognized the right to bring either a revocatory or an oblique action against the acts of his obligor when those acts occurred after the right of that obligee came into existence and caused or increased his obligor's insolvency.

2.   Effects Upon Occurrence of the Term.

Whenever a term is not a specific date (July 4th, for example) but a period of time, it may become important to ascertain both the beginning day and the ending day of that period of time. **LSA-C.C. Article 1784** sets some guidelines:

> **"When the term for performance of an obligation is not marked by a specific date but is rather a period of time, the term begins to run on the day after the contract is made, or on the day after the occurrence of the event that marks the beginning of the term, and it includes the last day of the period."**

Upon occurrence or happening of the suspensive term, the obligor's performance becomes due, and the obligee may then demand that performance. It is important to state again that *the occurrence of a term has no retroactive effect;* in other words, the past relationship between the parties is unaffected by the occurrence of a term.

---

[54] LSA-C.C. P. Art. 3501 *et seq.*; see Art. 3501 in Appendix.

[55] LSA-C.C. Arts. 2036 *et seq.*; see Art. 2036 in Appendix.

[56] LSA-C.C. Art. 2044: see Appendix.

[57] LSA-C.C. Art. 2044: see Appendix.

[58] Where the text of the law makes no distinction, we are to make none.

[59] See LSA-C.C. Art. 1782 in Appendix.

On the other hand, as we shall see below, the occurrence of a condition does have retroactive effect.[60]

Until the major reform of the law of obligations in 1984, the long established principle was that the mere occurrence of the term did not put the obligor in default.[61] In other words, upon occurrence of the term the obligee had to put the obligor in default to urge him to perform or else to have to pay moratory damages at least.

Following the legislative reforms, **LSA-C.C. Art. 1990** has reverted to the old Roman law principle that time is of the essence in the performance of obligations and that, therefore, the mere occurrence of the term that is fixed or clearly determinable automatically puts the obligor in default.[62] The principle now controlling under Louisiana law is known as *dies interpellat pro homine* or, literally, "the day interrupts on behalf of man." As a consequence, the prescriptive period applicable to the obligee's right will begin to run from the time of occurrence of the term.

§ 2.2-A.3. WAIVER AND FORFEITURE OF THE TERM.

The party for whose exclusive benefit the term has been stipulated may renounce or waive that benefit.[63] However, when the term is deemed to be for the benefit of both parties, they both must agree in order to bring any change to the stipulation governing the term.

There are instances where an obligor may lose, prematurely, the benefit of the term even though it was established in his favor. Such would be the case where an obligor would have been judicially declared insolvent in circumstances where the performance of the obligor's obligation would require his solvency.[64] Another instance of forfeiture of the term would occur when the obligor would fail to provide the required security or where that security would become insufficient to guarantee the performance of his obligation.[65] When faced with such situations the obligor could prevent forfeiture of the term by furnishing additional security so as to protect his obligee's rights.

ARTICLE 2: SUBSECTION **B**
THE CONDITION

As a legal modality or legal feature or device of an obligation, the concept of condition, as it is referred to in the Civil Code must be understood in a very particular sense. On the one hand, it can be understood as "an element of a juridical act . . . upon which the validity or effectivity of the act depends. Ex. capacity is a

---

[60] On the retroactivity of conditions, see infra § 2.2-B.2.

[61] On Putting in Default, see LSA-C.C. Articles 1989–1993 in Appendix.

[62] LSA-C.C. Art. 1990: see Appendix.

[63] LSA-C.C. Art. 1780: see Appendix.

[64] LSA-C.C. Art. 1783: see Appendix.

[65] *Id.*

condition of validity for a contract."[66] However and on the other hand, the same word condition will be here a more specific meaning as being "a modality of the obligation making its formation or its rescission conditional upon the occurrence of a future and uncertain event."[67] A condition is, therefore, the occurrence or non-occurrence of an "uncertainty," i.e. whether or not a future event will happen or not. As such, this uncertain event may either suspend the coming into existence (suspensive condition) or cause the resolution (resolutory condition) of a contract or of an obligation. Thus, a conditional obligation is one whose fate is uncertain, indefinite.

An analysis of the concept of condition and its different forms will logically lead to distinguishing between the nature of the condition, as being suspensive or resolutory, and the effects of these two different kinds of conditions.

§ 2.2-B.1. CONCEPT OF CONDITIONAL OBLIGATIONS.

Following in the path of the civilian tradition, which considers that *definitions* are for scholars to formulate and not for legislation to impose, the law of "obligations" in the Civil Code does not give a definition of the concept of *condition*. Hence, **LSA-C.C. Art. 1767**, instead of defining a condition *per se*, gives a definition of a *conditional obligation* and outlines the two broad categories of existing conditional obligations.

Although it is perfectly true that the word condition is often used indiscriminately to mean *charge, term, clause*, etc. . . . it remains, however, that subsequent code articles do refer to *condition* (**LSA-C.C. Art. 1768**) or *suspensive condition* (**LSA-C.C. Art. 1776**) without always associating together the words *obligation* and *condition*. It might be proper and justified, therefore, albeit for academic purposes only, to attempt to give a description of the concept of *condition* before describing the different kinds of conditional obligations.

A. Definitions of "Condition" and "Conditional Obligation."

LSA-C.C. Art. 1767 defines a conditional obligation as one dependent on an uncertain event. In this limited context, one can also define a condition as being an uncertain event, which may or may not occur in the future. The contrast can now be clearly marked with the *term*, which is defined in **LSA-C.C. Art. 1778** as a period of time either certain or uncertain but, in all circumstances, as a period of time bound to occur in the future and in the course of nature.

The uncertainty of the event amounting to a condition must bear on the occurrence of that event itself, so much so that one cannot ascertain whether or not that event will definitely occur. In the course of nature, the very occurrence of that event must be questionable. For our purposes, therefore, a condition can be defined as an *uncertain* event that may or may not occur, in contrast with a term, which is an event certain to happen.

---

[66] *Dictionary of the Civil Code*, — word: condition, 2. Element of a juridical act a/, p. 124.

[67] *Dictionary of the Civil Code*, — word: condition, 2. Element of a juridical act b/, p. 124.

Must a condition be also defined as a *future* uncertain event in the same way as a term is a future event?

A parallel between the two concepts would so require, as would a contrast between their respective legal regimes. In addition, the legal essence of the concept of condition also suggests that a condition be defined as a future uncertain event. And, yet, it is reported in a comment (e) to **LSA-C.C. Art. 1767** that *"a condition need not be a future event,"* and the same comment goes on to cite former **LSA-C.C. Art. 2043** as stating that a condition need be merely depending on an uncertain event (although not future).

Actually, a mere reading of the descriptions of a suspensive condition and of a resolutory condition in **LSA-C.C. Art. 1767** indicates that the event contemplated in both instances can only be a future one. Indeed, a suspensive obligation cannot be enforced until the uncertain event occurs and an obligation under a resolutory condition will come to an end when the uncertain event occurs. Furthermore, if an event that has already occurred is considered by uninformed parties to an obligation as a condition for that obligation, then the uncertainty exists really only in the parties' minds and not at all, as is required by the concept of condition, in the actual reality of the past or present circumstances.

If, unbeknownst to the parties, the event selected as the condition has already occurred, then the obligation must be considered as having been pure and simple from the outset and the parties need only bear the burden of proof of occurrence of the past event. In a sense, that proof will be very much like bringing forth the evidence of the occurrence of a term which merely delayed the enforcement (and not the existence) of the obligation in question.

B. Kinds of Conditions.

There are two kinds of conditions, suspensive or resolutory, and additional legal qualifications can be attached to such conditions.

1. Suspensive or Resolutory Conditions.

(a) An obligation is subjected to a *suspensive* condition when it may not be enforced until the uncertain event occurs (**LSA-C.C. Art. 1767**). Actually, the uncertain and future event causes the very creation or existence of the obligation to be dependent upon its occurrence.[68] Although **LSA-C.C. Art. 1767** refers to an obligation not being enforceable until the uncertain event occurs, legal regime of a suspensive condition has a much more drastic effect than just suspending the enforcement of the obligation. The suspensive condition actually suspends the very existence of the obligation between the parties until the uncertain event occurs. The non-enforcement or the "suspended enforcement" of the obligation is consequently explained by the fact that there is "no" obligation in existence until and if the suspensive condition occurs. Although the bond of law has been formed and a contract has been entered into, no obligation has been created by the bond of law or the contract. Such is the case, for example, of an insurance contract on a home

---

[68] *Dictionary of the Civil Code*, word — Condition suspensive, p. 124.

for protection against fire, flooding or other disasters. The insurance company will not be called upon to indemnify the homeowner until the house has been damaged or destroyed. There is no obligation in existence for the insurance company, although the insurance contract has been entered into. Likewise, under the law of the quasi-contract of *negotiorum gestio*, an owner or principal will not have to comply with the engagements contracted by the manager-gestor unless his business has been well managed (**LSA-C.C. Art. 2295, 2297**); in other words, the court will have to decide whether the event of *good management* has occurred and, thus, whether the suspended obligation of the owner to comply with the engagements of his manager has come into being.

LSA-C.C. Art. 1562-1 provides another example of a suspensive condition. It states: "**If a donation is subject to a suspensive condition, the donation is dissolved of right when the condition can no longer be fulfilled.**

If a donation is subject to a resolutory condition, the occurrence of the condition does not of right operate a dissolution of the donation. It may be dissolved only by consent of the parties or by judicial decree."

(b) An obligation is subject to a *resolutory* condition if it "**may be immediately enforced but will come to an end when the uncertain event occurs . . .**" (**LSA-C.C. Art. 1767**).

It follows that a resolutory condition brings an end to an existing bond of law. Thus, for example, a vendor who has reserved to himself the right of redemption has the right to take back the thing from the buyer (**LSA-C.C. Art. 2567**). The exercise of this right by the vendor is tantamount to the occurrence of an event which brings about the disappearance of a bond of law created by the contract of sale.

Another illustration can be found in **LSA-C.C. Arts. 1556** *et seq.*, which contemplates the dissolution of donations *inter vivos*, that is to say the extinction of existing bonds of law, for reasons or events which are illustrative of as many types of resolutory conditions. Thus, for example, **LSA-C.C. Art. 1560** states that "**[i]n case of revocation for ingratitude, the donee shall return the thing given. If he is not able to return the thing itself, then the donee shall restore the value of the thing donated, measured as of the time the action to revoke is filed.**"

The donation that took place is now dissolved, and the parties are returned to the situation they were in before the donation took place (*status quo ante*).

2. Additional Legal Qualifications of a Condition.

(a) Whether suspensive or resolutory, a condition can be "expressed in a stipulation or implied by the law, the nature of the contract, or the intent of the parties." (**LSA-C.C. Art. 1768**).

A condition is expressed when it is specifically referred to by the parties as they can do under **LSA-C.C. Art. 1744**, which states in part:

"**A person may make a donation *inter vivos* to his future or present spouse in contemplation of or in consideration of their marriage in accordance with the provisions of this Chapter. Such a donation shall**

be governed by the rules applicable to donations inter vivos in general, including the rules that pertain to the reduction of donations that exceed the disposable portion, but only insofar as those general rules are not modified by the following Articles . . . ."

A condition may be implied by the law as, for example, in **LSA-C.C. Arts. 2604** and **2605**, which gives a buyer a reasonable opportunity to inspect the things he bought and to reject nonconforming things within a reasonable time.

The nature of a contract may also help imply the existence of a condition as is suggested in **LSA-C.C. Art. 2460: "When the buyer has reserved the view or trial of the thing, ownership is not transferred from the seller to the buyer until the latter gives his approval of the thing."**

A condition may also be implied from the intent of the parties to a contract whenever the circumstances are clearly indicative of their consent (**LSA-C.C. Art. 1927**).

(b) A Condition Cannot Be Unlawful, Impossible, or Immoral.

A condition would be unlawful or immoral whenever it would violate the specific prohibition of **LSA-C.C. Art. 7** and, in addition, as is otherwise stated, here and there, throughout the Civil Code, for example in **Articles 1519, 1968, 2030**, etc.

An impossible condition would involve the occurrence of an event which could absolutely not take place, as would most probably be the case of a person who would agree to *"long jump"* over the Grand Canyon.

It is conceivable that a condition, possible and lawful at the time the parties enter into a bond of law, could become unlawful or impossible subsequently in the course of time. The principle of the immediate and obligatory effect of a law (**LSA-C.C. Art. 5**) will determine the extent to which the whole bond of law or the condition should be declared nonexistent.

By and large, and subject both to a proper interpretation of the will of the parties and to a court's own power of interpretation of a contract, the legal consequences flowing from the existence of an immoral, unlawful or impossible condition can be summarized as follows:

(i): should an onerous juridical act be involved, the nullity of the suspensive condition will usually carry with it the nullity of the whole juridical act or obligation; it **"makes the obligation null." (LSA-C.C. Art. 1769)**. The effects are the same as those prescribed by Civil Code **Articles 2030 and 2033.**[69] However, it is generally agreed that when a condition is one not to do something impossible, only the condition will be declared void, whereas the obligation itself will remain in existence.

Nevertheless, it must be acknowledged that the courts, relying both on the theory of cause and on the presumed intent of the parties, have the power to interpret a contract so as to give only an *accessory* role to the condition and, as such, as having little or no effect on the validity of the obligation as a whole.

---

[69] See Arts. 2030, 2033 in Appendix.

When a condition is resolutory and unlawful or impossible, *"the policy reasons calling for nullity [of the obligation] are absent,"* states comment (a) to **LSA-C.C. Art. 1769.** It is generally considered that, whenever a resolutory condition can be separated from the rest of the obligation, only the condition will be considered as not written, whereas the remaining existing obligation will continue to be binding.

(ii): should a gratuitous juridical act be under consideration, the nullity of the condition, whether suspensive or resolutory, does not render void the whole obligation. **LSA-C.C. Art. 1519** states very explicitly: **"In all dispositions *inter vivos* and *mortis causa* impossible conditions, those which are contrary to the laws of morals, are reputed not written."** Here again it should be recalled that the concept of cause, as "the reason why a party obligates himself" (**LSA-C.C. Art. 1967**), may be resorted to by a court to bring about the nullity of the whole juridical act instead of striking out only the condition.

(c) Casual, Potestative, and Mixed Conditions.

Whereas the pre-1984 law of obligations included a series of code articles clearly outlining these concepts, the new articles of the Civil Code provide no guidance. It does not mean though that, because of the absence of code articles on this matter, these types of conditions can no longer be part of the general framework of a legal relationship. They are too much part of our civilian heritage, as illustrated by the many writings of civil law scholars, to be totally disregarded or dismissed from this general presentation of the law of obligations under the artificial pretext of the silence of the law of the Louisiana Civil Code of today. It remains that **LSA-C.C. Arts. 1767** and **1770** can be used to some extent in describing here these three types of conditions.

(i) Casual Condition.

A condition, whether suspensive or resolutory, expressed or implied, can be *casual.* Former **LSA-C.C. Art. 2023** defined the casual condition as "that which depends on chance and is no way in the power of either the creditor or of the debtor." The *Dictionary of the Civil Code* defines such the casual condition in these terms: *"A condition which depends on chance and which is in no way within the power or control of the creditor or the debtor."*[70] An illustration of this type of condition would be one where a party to a contract would agree to buy from another an umbrella *should it rain tomorrow.* The event, *i.e.* raining tomorrow, is beyond the control of any of the parties to bring about or to hinder and can be said to depend on chance. It is a casual condition.

(ii) Potestative Condition.

Nowhere in **LSA-C.C. Arts. 1767** to **1776** can one find the notion of *potestative condition.* The reason for this omission is clearly stated in comment (e) to **LSA-C.C. Art. 1770:** *"this article eliminates the expression potestative condition because the Louisiana jurisprudence has been plagued by misinterpretations of it."*[71] Instead

---

[70] *Dictionary of the Civil Code,* word — Condition casuelle, p. 124.

[71] Yet, LSA-C.C. Arts. 1563 and 1566 one can read the word "power" which is close to the latin word "potestas" (which became "potestative") and quite different from the words "will" and "whim."

of using the standard civil law technical words "potestative condition," **LSA-C.C. Art. 1770** now reads:

> **"A suspensive condition that depends solely on the whim of the obligor makes the obligation null.**
>
> **A resolutory condition that depends solely on the will of the obligor must be fulfilled in good faith."**

Although we now have only one article, where we used to have at least four (former **LSA-C.C. Arts. 2024, 2034, 2035, and 2036**), the essence of the law is not, for that matter, made any clearer as evidenced by the fact that many odd, at times, and extensive comments were needed to help explain this single **Article 1770**. Whereas the comments to a code article are not part of the law of the article and might (should) soon be forgotten, it is nevertheless a proper method of interpretation at civil law to interpret a new code article in light of pre-existing concepts. Moreover, we wonder whether the use of the word *whim* in **LSA-C.C. Art. 1770** will suffice to remedy all the evils and *cure* the jurisprudence of its *plague*? It is very doubtful that the jurisprudence (since it has been apparently singled out and distinguished from legal scholars!) will find in **LSA-C.C. Art. 1770** the clear-cut distinctions that, we believe, the very concepts of *whim* and *will* cannot possibly convey. In order to guide the jurisprudence, the comments to **LSA-C.C. Art. 1770** offer a series of illustrations of what is to be understood by the words *whim*, on the one hand, and *will*, on the other hand.

One comment states: "an event which is left entirely to the obligor's <u>whim</u> is one whose occurrence depends entirely on his will such as his wishing or not wishing something." In another comment, whim is described as being the "exercise of mere unbridled discretion or arbitrariness." Such general and legal descriptions used to encompass and refer to the juridical concept of a purely potestative condition which presupposed a whimsical, arbitrary manifestation of the will or the performance of an act so trivial and petty as to amount to no impediment at all. The legal labels may have changed but, as the comments themselves acknowledge, the new **Code Article 1770** has not changed the pre-1984–1985 law. Therefore, the legal regime of what used to be known and described as a purely potestative condition remains today what it was before the 1984 revision of the law of obligations. A purely potestative condition is defined in these terms: "One that depends solely on the will (or whim) of one party and which, because it amounts to a lack of commitment when it is left to the total discretion of the obligor/debtor, brings about, in this case, the nullity of the obligation involved."[72]

The same is true of the other kind of potestative condition which, for lack of a proper concept in **LSA-C.C. Art. 1770**, we shall name under its pre-1984 label: *simply potestative condition.*

This kind of condition is described in a comment, again, of **LSA-C.C. Art. 1770**. This comment reads as follows: "an event is not left to an obligor's whim when it is one that he may or may not bring about after a considered weighing of interests, such as his entering a contract with a third party." Another comment further

---

[72] '*Dictionary of the Civil Code.* — word: condition purement potestative, p. 438.

explains that the opposite of whim, for purposes of conditions, is a "judgment or exercise of a considered and reasonable discretion." Since **LSA-C.C. Art. 1770** does not change the substance of the law, what the comments call judgment or reasonable discretion can just as well be referred to just as simply as potestative condition. The latter can then be defined as a condition "that depends on an event, the occurrence of which is no doubt voluntary on the part of one of the parties, but following a decision which is dependent on contingencies."[73] An example of this type of condition would be the promise made by an owner that he would sell his home should he leave town. Besides the fact that the owner would have to make the decision to leave town and be in the proper state of mind to freely make that decision, there exist many uncontrollable factors (employment, school, location, family, etc. . . .) which may have a serious, and even determinant impact on the decision and the ability to leave town.

Whatever the labels, old or new, we might decide to attach to these kinds of conditions, their effects would remain the same today as they were yesterday.

Under **LSA-C.C. Art. 1770-1**, whenever a suspensive condition depends solely on the whim of the obligor, the whole obligation would be null. Likewise, whenever an obligation was entered into under a purely potestative suspensive condition on the part of the obligor, the obligation was considered null (former **LSA-C.C. Art. 2034**). The reason for this nullity of the obligation can be found in that an obligor who would agree to be bound under such a condition would not really be bound, since he would be in full and arbitrary control of "his" decision and would merely intend to deceive the other party.

Reasoning *a contrario sensu* on **LSA-C.C. Art. 1770 § 1**, it is proper to say that, whenever a suspensive condition would depend solely on the whim of the obligee, the obligation would then be valid. The reason is to be found in the fact that the obligor himself would be bound by his own-unilateral promise. A simple illustration of this promise would consist in a promise of a loan of $1,000 made by Cicero to Titus, should Titus want the loan; whenever Titus, the obligee or creditor, would ask for the loan, the obligation contracted by Cicero, the obligor-debtor, would come into being. Cicero has previously bound himself to issue that loan upon Titus' demand, and he was fully aware of the potentiality of that demand.

According to **LSA-C.C. Art. 1770 § 2**, whenever a resolutory condition depends solely on the will of the obligor it must be fulfilled in good faith. The word will has been substituted here to the word whim and a comment explains, "*once performance of an obligation starts, it does not seem realistic to say that termination is dependent on the whim of a party. No doubt some practical considerations are bound to inform his will, especially if the obligation arises from a bilateral contract.*" Under the former law, an obligation contracted under a purely potestative resolutory condition on the part of either party was valid (former **LSA-C.C. Art. 2036**). The reason for the validity of the obligation is simply that, since a bond of law is in existence between the parties and binds them to the performance of their obligations, there is no reason to undo whatever has been performed. However, **LSA-C.C. Art. 1770 § 2** adds an important additional require-

---

[73] *Dictionary of the Civil Code*, — word: condition simplement potestative, p. 438.

ment, which was not part of the former law: that requirement is that the obligor must be in good faith. The obligor must be motivated by good faith when bringing about the fulfillment of the condition.

This requirement definitely changes the legal nature of the resolutory condition, as it was previously understood. **LSA-C.C. Art. 1759** now pervades the whole law of obligations and gives the court a power of control over an obligor's will to rescind an obligation. The right that the obligor reserved to himself to terminate an obligation solely on his will is now almost emptied of its original legal meaning. That party must now *"consider . . . the hardship to which the other party will be subjected because of the termination . . . ; likewise, termination because of purely personal rather than business reasons could constitute bad faith . . . ; the court may grant damages to the party harmed by the termination."*[74] One may therefore conclude that such a resolutory condition does not really depend solely on the will of the obligor. In a certain manner, **LSA-C.C. Art. 1770** has introduced the concept of "abuse of right" in the law of conditional obligations and, *a fortiori ratione a minori ad maius* (from the lesser premise to the greater premise), in the whole law of obligations as the essence of **LSA-C.C. Art. 1759** should dictate.

(iii) Mixed Condition.

A mixed condition, a concept nowhere described in the law of obligations, was previously defined as one depending "at the same time on the will of one of the parties and on the will of a third person, or on the will of one of the parties and also on a casual event."[75] There is no reason to believe that such a condition would not be entitled, today, to full legal recognition since there exists neither any express law prohibiting it nor any policy reason to reject it. Actually, when **LSA-C.C. Art. 1770-2** combines the requirements of the expression of one's will with that of good faith, it very much describes, in practical terms, what a mixed condition is in fact. Indeed, the requirement of good faith compels a party to take into account events over which that party would have no real control as illustrated by "the hardship to which the other party will be subjected because of the termination."[76] Such a situation combining these two requirements could have been described as a mixed condition under the former law of obligations. We suggest, therefore, that a mixed condition be understood as a *"future and uncertain event the occurrence of which depends both on the will of one of the contracting parties and on the will of a third party."*[77]

§ 2.2-B.2.   EFFECTS OF CONDITIONAL OBLIGATIONS.

Since a condition triggers many important effects in the relationship between parties to an obligation, it is necessary to determine, first, at which point in time this condition can occur before considering; second, the status of the rights and obligations that may be existing between the parties while the condition is pending;

---

[74]   LSA-C.C. Art.1770, comment (f).

[75]   Former LSA-C.C. Art. 2025.

[76]   LSA-C.C. Art. 1770, comment (f).

[77]   *Dictionary of the Civil Code,* — word: condition mixte, p. 380.

and third, the effects actually triggered by the fulfillment of the condition will be examined.

A.   Time of Fulfillment of the Condition.

LSA-C.C. Arts. 1773 and **1774** deal specifically with the issue of the time of fulfillment or occurrence of the condition. Following a perfect symmetry in drafting, **LSA-C.C. Art. 1773** contemplates the occurrence of a positive condition, that is to say an event which ought to occur, whereas **LSA-C.C. Art. 1774** is concerned with a negative condition or an event which ought not to occur. In addition, the law provides in **LSA-C.C. Art. 1772** for instances where a condition might be fictitiously considered as fulfilled as a result of the behavior of one party or another.

1.   Positive Condition.

In the words of **LSA-C.C. Art. 1773-1**, if the condition is that an event shall occur within a fixed time and that time elapses without the event having occurred, the condition is considered to have failed. We are concerned here with the necessary occurrence of a positive condition within an express term, or fixed time. If that condition fails to occur within the agreed time it is then considered that the condition can no longer occur. Under the specific circumstances, a court should have no right to extend the express term and, thereby, make it possible for the condition to occur.

In those instances where no time has been fixed for the occurrence of the event, the condition may be fulfilled within a reasonable time (**LSA-C.C. Art. 1773-2**). This second paragraph of **Article 1773** is an innovation and a welcomed change from the former law of conditional obligations. It is fully justified by an analogy to the law of term, as it appears in **LSA-C.C. Arts. 1777** and **1778**, and it answers the same practical needs.

Lastly, whether or not a time has been fixed, the condition is considered to have failed once it is certain that the event will not occur (**LSA-C.C. Art. 1773-3**). This rule of law is but the transposition of a rule of reason and merely further serves as an illustration of the same policies which justify the first two paragraphs of this same article.

2.   Negative Condition.

LSA-C.C. Art. 1774 contemplates the fulfillment of a condition consisting in an event, which should not occur so as to give rise to or rescind a bond of law. The policies justifying the provisions of this article are the same as those, which explain **LSA-C.C. Art. 1773**, and the rules of law are parallel to those governing the concept of the positive condition. For example, if parties to an obligation had agreed that they would be bound if it did not rain for the next two days following their agreement, and it did not rain, then the bond of law would be created after the term of two days has elapsed. Likewise, if it is certain that the event selected as the condition can absolutely not occur either within the agreed term or within a reasonable term then, obviously, the negative condition would be regarded as fulfilled and the bond of law would either be created or maintained.

3. Anticipatory Fulfillment of a Condition.

To the extent that the fulfillment of a condition is within the reach of a party to bring about or to hinder, that is to say, whenever a condition is potestative or mixed, it may happen that the party in question will attempt to prevent the happening of the event. If, for example, a buyer intentionally fails to apply for a loan so that he will be financially unable to buy a home, that buyer can be said to have acted so as to prevent the casual component part of the mixed condition from happening. In such an instance the condition will be regarded as fulfilled because it failed to occur as a result of the party with an interest contrary to the fulfillment of the condition (**LSA-C.C. Art. 1772**).

4. Failure of the Condition.

LSA-C.C. Art. 1773-3 states, in part, "**the condition is considered to have failed once it is certain that the event will not occur.**" The impact of the failure of the condition differs with the type of condition involved.

A suspensive condition suspends the existence of rights and obligations between the parties and, therefore, its failure will definitely prevent these rights and obligations from ever existing. The result is that the failure of the suspensive condition leaves the parties in the same situation they would have been in had they not contracted with each other. Should the parties, or one party, have begun to perform in anticipation of the condition occurring and while it was pending, each party will then have to take back his performance and return to the other whatever he received from him since the failure of the condition amounts to making their performances without cause (**LSA-C.C. Art. 1967**).

Whenever a resolutory condition fails to occur, the obligation which has been in existence becomes pure and simple; the parties are in the same situation as they would have been had they been bound, *ab initio*, from the beginning, by a pure and simple obligation.

B. Rights and Obligations of the Parties "Pendente Conditione."

It is necessary here to distinguish between the suspensive condition, on the one hand, and the resolutory condition, on the other hand.

1. Legal Status of the Parties While the Suspensive Condition is Pending (Pendente Conditione).

As long as the occurrence of the uncertain event has not taken place, and for whatever length of time its fulfillment is pending, the suspensive condition prevents the bond of law created between the parties to have any effect; it is as if the bond of law has been frozen or paralyzed. Therefore, no rights and no obligations can come into existence. Although a juridical act or bond of law has been formed, as stated in **LSA-C.C. Arts. 1771** and **1775**, that juridical act or bond of law is, to a large extent, without any effect. The parties must wait for their rights and obligations to be born, their expectations are "suspended" with the "suspensive condition."

At the risk of stretching a comparison a little too far, there is, nevertheless, an analogy that can be made between the occurrence of a suspensive condition and the birth of a child.

Under the Civil Code, a child is not vested with all the rights attached to one's personality until that child is born alive and if he is born alive.[78] While in his mother's womb, though, that child will enjoy the benefit of some rights, albeit under the condition that he be born alive.[79] In other words, the actual birth of the child is an event which will trigger, retroactively to the time of conception, the existence of rights and obligations. Conception and actual birth of a child are, theoretically speaking obviously, very much like the formation of a contract and the occurrence of a suspensive condition.

A series of legal consequences flow from the standstill position the parties are in while the suspensive condition is pending.

(a) A creditor under a suspensive condition cannot demand performance from his obligor since he is only a conditional creditor and may never actually become a pure and simple creditor. When **LSA-C.C. Art. 1771** allows a conditional creditor to exercise lawful measures of preservation of his right (as a conditional creditor), the same article also provides, *a contrario sensu* and *ratione legis stricta*, that the same creditor may not exercise any right of administration or disposition. Furthermore, an analogy with **LSA-C.C. Arts. 1782** and **1783** on the concept of term would lead to the same conclusion.

Considering that a conditional creditor may never become a pure and simple creditor, it follows that, should the debtor-obligor ever perform before the fulfillment of the condition, he must be entitled to claim his performance back on the ground that he made a payment of a thing not due, or not "owed."[80] This right of the obligor should be recognized with respect to any performance carried out as a result of error, fraud or duress/violence. However, if the same obligor under a suspensive condition has performed *freely* (**LSA-C.C. Art. 1761**) or *voluntarily* (**LSA-C.C. Art. 1781**), that is to say in full awareness that he owed nothing to the conditional creditor, his juridical act of performance might then take on a special character-ization so as to become, either a deposit, or a pledge, or even a gratuitous act . . . provided that the requirements for the validity of such juridical acts have been met.

(b) Prescription cannot run against the creditor since there is no right yet against which prescription could run.[81]

(c) If there is any financial risk of loss attached to the performance of the conditional obligation, that risk is on the party who is the owner of the thing that perishes while the condition is pending. The other party will then suffer the risk of

---

[78] See LSA-C.C. Arts. 26, 954, 956.

[79] See LSA-C.C. Arts. 26, 940, 1474.

[80] See LSA-C.C. Art. 2301.

[81] See LSA-C.C.P. Art. 423.

not being able to acquire the ownership of that same thing.[82]

The obligee-creditor of that conditional obligation to transfer the property of a thing may attempt to protect his conditional right by taking some measures of conservation as contemplated in **LSA-C.C. Art. 1771**.

(d) As long as the rights and obligations of either or both parties are conditional, no right of compensation can occur since none of the performances is *presently due*.[83]

Yet, as long as the condition is pending, one cannot ignore the fact that a juridical act has been formed, and that there is, at least, the *hope* that the suspensive condition will be fulfilled. This hope must be protected since it may have a monetary value and, as such, be part of the parties' patrimonies.

(i) The conditional creditor may take all lawful measures to preserve his right (**LSA-C.C. Art. 1771**). As an illustration of the types of measures that may be taken, a conditional creditor may obtain a mortgage on his debtor's property (**LSA-C.C. Art. 3293**). The justification for the availability of such rights to the creditor is two-fold: on the one hand, there is the fact that the conditional creditor might become entitled to a performance by the obligor and, on the other hand, the occurrence of the condition triggers this *fictional* effect proper to the condition and known as *retroactivity* which will be explained thereunder.[84]

(ii) Because the right of the conditional creditor may have a monetary value and, thus, fall into his patrimony, this *conditional* right may, like a hope, be the object of a transaction *inter vivos* or *mortis causa*, whether gratuitous or onerous.[85]

2. Legal Status of the Parties While the Resolutory Condition is Pending (Pendente Conditione).

An obligation under a resolutory condition is fully in existence as soon as it has been entered into and performances are due, whether unilaterally or bilaterally. The obligation should be considered, to a large extent, as if it were pure and simple. However, the presence of a resolutory condition in a bond of law raises the question of whether that bond of law will remain in existence in the future and continue to justify having all its effects.

The broad language used in **LSA-C.C. Art. 1771** requires that we interpret this article *a generali sensu*; it should apply to the resolutory condition as it applies to the suspensive condition. Actually, we could say that depending on which side of a juridical act we look at, a condition may be described, at first sight and "on the surface," as suspensive for one party and resolutory for the other. Two examples will help illustrate this point:

---

[82] See LSA-C.C. Art. 2467.

[83] On Compensation, see LSA-C.C. Arts 1893–1902; see below Extinction of Obligations: Compensation § 7.5.

[84] See below § 2.2-B.2(C).

[85] See LSA-C.C. Arts. 1984, 2451; LSA-C.C.P. Art. 3542.

Let us assume a donation of a movable from the donor to the donee under the condition that the donee will no longer smoke cigarettes.

Example No. 1: If the donation has not actually taken place, if no delivery of the movable has occurred, the condition must then be considered as suspensive because the legal status of the parties and their relationship *vis-à-vis* the movable have not changed. The donor remains owner of the movable until (and if) the condition is fulfilled. In some respect, therefore, and as far as the donor is concerned, the condition can be looked upon as resolutory because that donor's legal right over the movable might be dissolved should the condition occur. If we consider, now, the legal status of the donee and his relationship *vis-à-vis* the movable, it is possible to say that the donee will not receive any rights in the movable until the condition occurs; in other words, his rights are suspended.

Example No. 2: If the transfer of the movable has taken place and the donee is now in possession of it, obviously the position of the parties in relation to the movable has changed. The donee is to be considered as the owner of the movable and should remain the owner . . . unless he should resume smoking cigarettes (if that is the condition). It appears, therefore, that the donee is, in some way, an owner under a resolutory condition: he will have to return the movable to the donor if he should ever resume smoking. Conversely, the donor might become the owner of that movable once again should the condition occur; he can, therefore, look at the condition as a suspensive one.

Does this mean that a condition necessarily carries two labels depending on the side of the bond of law from which it is examined? Absolutely not. A condition is either suspensive or resolutory; it is one or the other, according to whether or not the original legal relationship (or lack thereof) existing between the parties has been modified or not. If that relationship remains as it was until (and if) the condition is fulfilled, then the condition is suspensive. If that relationship has been modified by a juridical act and is susceptible of being erased or dissolved should a condition occur, then that condition is necessarily resolutory. This analysis explains why **LSA-C.C. Art. 1771** uses no adjective where it refers merely to a conditional obligation.

C. Rights and Obligations of the Parties Upon Fulfillment of the Condition.

The principle governing the fulfillment or occurrence of the condition is that of the retroactivity of the effects of the condition. This principle, however, suffers some exceptions.

1. Principle of Retroactivity.

The *Dictionary of the Civil Code* describes as follows the effect of the retroactivity of a condition: "Retroactive effect attached to a fulfilled condition in such a way that the effects of a juridical act are considered to have actually existed back at the time the juridical act was entered into and not from the time of fulfillment of the condition; the effects are either resolutory or creative."[86] **LSA-C.C. Art. 1775** expresses the general principle in these terms: "Fulfillment of a condition has effects that are retroactive to the inception of the obligation . . . ."[87] Thus, unless the parties to a conditional juridical act provide otherwise, a condition produces its retroactive effects automatically, as soon as it happens. This statement means that, fictionally and conceptually, the effects of the condition date back to the time when the juridical act with the condition was entered into. As a result, and at the risk of formulating an excessive simplification, what has been done in the meantime while the condition was pending, and thus before its occurrence, should be undone or, vice-versa, what has not been done while the condition was pending should *have* been done.

Among the general consequences attached to the retroactivity of the condition we can give the following two as illustrations: 1) Date of the contract: the contract is formed as soon as its legal requirements are met; it is therefore at that particular time that retroactively the date of the contract is to be fixed. In other words, the date of the coming into existence of the contract is not to be fixed at the date of occurrence of the condition but, retroactively, to the date the requirements for its formation had been met. The parties may, however, stipulate differently. 2) New statute: should a new statute be passed after the bond of law has been entered into but while the condition is pending, because of the retroactivity of the condition, that statute should not be applicable to the contractual rights of the parties. These rights, which were *conditional* when the obligation was entered into, should be[88] considered, now, as pure and simple as of the time the contract had been formed.

The retroactive effects of a condition are, therefore, drastic and go against the most reasonable expectations. It is the reason why the retroactivity of a condition is somewhat limited and its scope will vary with the kinds of conditions involved.

2.   Retroactivity and Kinds of Conditions.

(a) Retroactivity of the Suspensive Condition; Its Limitations.

The essence of a suspensive condition is to *suspend* the effects of an existing legal relationship and, *a fortiori*, all performances flowing from the effects of that legal relationship. Through the fiction of retroactivity, there will take place a sort of creation *ab initio* or *ex tunc* of the effects of the relationship and the resulting obligations. This fiction is considered to be what the parties had in mind when they entered into the obligation with a suspensive condition in contrast with the adoption of a suspensive term which they could have chosen instead.[89]

Some of the effects flowing from the retroactivity of the suspensive condition can be listed as follows:

---

[86] *Dictionary of the Civil Code,* — word: rétroactivité de la condition, p. 508.

[87] See Art. 1775 in Appendix.

[88] LSA-C.C. Art. 6 states, in part, that "in the absence of contrary legislative expression, substantive laws apply prospectively only."

[89] On Suspensive Term, see supra § 2.2-A.1(A). It is worth restating that a suspensive term either allows for the effects of a contractual relationship to definitely take place in the future or the term may only delay into the future a performance that may be necessary to fulfill the effects of an obligation.

(i) should the obligor have performed *pendente conditione*, therefore before any obligation had actually been created, what was then an undue performance has now become retroactively due and, thus, can no longer claimed back. Retroactively the performance has been "legally" justified.

(ii) should the obligee have, *pendente conditione*, transferred to a third party a right in the thing that is the object of the obligor's performance of his obligation, such a right becomes retroactively valid and vested although at the time of the transfer to the third party the obligee transferred a right which was not yet his.[90]

(iii) conversely, the rights granted by the obligor to a third party *pendente conditione* should be retroactively invalidated. However, this principle may not be applied to its fullest extent as a third party may have acquired rights in good faith from the obligor.[91]

There are, obviously, some reasonable limitations to the retroactive effect of the condition. On the basis either of the good faith principle or the public records doctrine, **LSA-C.C. Art. 1775** stipulates, in part, that "**fulfillment of the condition does not impair the right acquired by third parties while the condition was pending.**" As a consequence, the third parties who, in good faith, had received rights from a party to the contract while, at that time, the condition was pending, these third parties will be protected and spared the retroactive loss of their rights. Moreover, those third parties who acquired rights in immovables under the protective shield of the public records will also be spared the harsh effects of the retroactivity of the condition.

Another limitation to the retroactive effect of the condition is stated in these terms in **LSA-C.C. Art. 1775**: "**Nevertheless, that fulfillment does not impair the validity of acts of administration duly performed by a party, nor affect the ownership of fruits produced while the condition was pending.**" Illustrations of application of this rule can be found in **LSA-C.C. Arts. 486 and 2575.**[92]

Basically, these acts of administration do not affect the integrity of the right to dispose (*the abusus*) which will be acquired by the obligee following the fulfillment of the condition. Furthermore, it can be presumed that these acts of administration were undertaken with the implicit consent of the parties, as these parties could be considered as "representing" each other.[93]

(b) Retroactivity of the Resolutory Condition: Its Limitations.

The retroactive effects of a resolutory condition are basically the same as those of a suspensive condition. An interesting illustration of the impact of these effects can be found in the contract of sale with the right of redemption. Under **LSA-C.C. Art. 2567, 2572, and 2588,**[94] the vendor and original owner of the thing sold receives it back, in theory, as if the sale had not taken place.

---

[90] See as an example, LSA-C.C. Art. 3293 in Appendix.

[91] See as an example, LSA-C.C. Art. 2588 in Appendix.

[92] See LSA-C.C. Arts. 486 and 2575 in Appendix.

[93] On Representation, see LSA-C.C. Arts. 2985–2988.

[94] See LSA-C.C. Arts. 2567, 2572 and 2588 in Appendix.

The principle is, therefore, well established that the obligation which was creative of legal effects as soon as it was entered into should have all these effects wiped out, erased, by the mere occurrence of the resolutory condition.

The limitations to the retroactivity of the resolutory condition are the same as those which concern the suspensive condition. **LSA-C.C. Art. 1775**[95] is general in its wording as it makes no distinction between suspensive and resolutory conditions and, consequently, we are not to draw a distinction where the law does not provide for one (*ubi lex non distinguit nec nos distinguere debemus*).

(c) Exceptions.

The retroactivity of the condition has been described above as a fiction and, thus, as a creation of the human mind. Hence it is inevitable that such a creation of the mind operating in an abstract sphere would come into conflict with the reality of things or the material world. It is the reason why there exist exceptions to the principle of retroactivity of a condition. These exceptions are essentially two:

(i) **LSA-C.C. Art. 1776** states that "[i]n a contract for continuous or periodic performance, fulfillment of a resolutory condition does not affect the validity of acts of performance rendered before fulfillment of the condition." Contracts falling under this exception would be a contract of lease, a labor contract, a contract for the hiring of industry, etc. When such contracts, although they may include a resolutory condition (as implied in all bilateral contracts[96]), are entered into, it is obvious that any partial performance by a party has been matched, more or less, by a partial performance by the other party. For example, in a contract of lease, the lessee has enjoyed the premises in exchange for a rent paid to the lessor. Although the lessor could possibly be compelled to return to the lessee the rents he received from the latter, it would be impossible, because of the nature of things, to force the lessee to return the physical and moral enjoyment of the premises which he occupied. In such instances the resolutory condition can have only a prospective effect; it cancels the contract and brings an end to the parties' obligations in the future.

(ii) A second exception to the retroactivity of the condition concerns the so-called real contracts. A real contract is a "contract formed, perfected, by the actual delivery of a thing (re), the person receiving the thing becomes debtor only following the actual real transfer, delivery." Such would be a contract of loan, a deposit, a pledge.[97] In such contracts the occurrence of a suspensive condition takes effect without any retroactivity because, strictly speaking, there is no contract at all until, for example, the loan has been effectuated or the deposit actually made. The date of the agreement (oral or written) of the loan is not to be taken into account since there is no reimbursement owed or interests to be paid until the borrower has actually made use of his right to borrow the money and actually received the loan when he needed it. Therefore, it is not until the actual transfer of the money or asset

---

[95] See LSA-C.C. Art. 1775 in Appendix.

[96] On bilateral contract see LSA-C.C. Art. 1908 in Appendix.

[97] *Dictionary of the Civil Code*, — word: contrat réel, p. 483. On real rights and real obligations, see supra § 2.1.1.

from the lender to the borrower has occurred that the contract of loan itself has materialized, truly come into existence.

Chapter 3

OBLIGATIONS WITH MULTIPLE PERSONS LSA-C.C. ARTS. 1786 TO 1806

The most common obligation, the pure and simple obligation, binds one party to another or binds each party to the other. Such an obligation is "bilateral," when each party owes to the other an obligation. For example, in a contract of sale the seller owes the thing to the buyer and the latter owes the price to the seller; therefore each party is at the same time "obligor" and "obligee" vis-à-vis the other. The seller, as obligee or creditor, is entitled to the price and as obligor or debtor the same seller owes the thing he sold to the buyer. The buyer, in turn, is obligee of the seller who owes him the thing he bought and he is obligor of that same seller to whom he owes the price.

In some instances there may exist more than one party involved on either side of the obligation. Whatever the source of that obligation, be it a juridical act or a juridical fact, it can bind more than one obligor to one single obligee, or one single obligor to more than one obligee, or more than one obligor to more than one obligee. These broad categories of obligations with multiple persons are described in legal terms by **LSA-C.C. Article 1786** as follows: " . . . the obligation may be several, joint, or solidary."[1]

ARTICLE 1
THE SEVERAL OBLIGATION

§ 3.1.1. DEFINITION AND NOTION.

Rather unusual and of little practical importance, the several obligation is defined by **LSA-C.C. Art. 1787** in this manner: an obligation is several for the obligors "when each of different obligors owes a separate performance to one obligee." Conversely, an obligation is several for the obligees "when one obligor owes a separate performance to each of different obligees."

It follows, therefore, that an obligation is several on the part of obligors whenever each one of them is independently bound to a separate and distinct performance not owed in any manner by the other obligors. The item or items of the respective obligor's performance(s) may be to do different acts or give different things or abstain from doing something, etc. . . . . Although the source of the *several obligation* may be the same for multiple obligors, it remains that each one of these multiple obligors is a "several obligor," who owes the obligee-creditor a "separate" item of performance. Actually, one can look upon a *several obligation* as one which

---

[1] LSA-C.C. Art. 1786: see Appendix.

59

could have been the result of different and separate individual sources of obligations. Where one obligor would owe his obligee the transfer of a real right over a car (obligation to give) and a second obligor, bound under the same source of obligations, would owe the performance of servicing that car (obligation to do), a several obligation on the part of the obligors would have been created.

The relationship between the parties can be turned around and looked at from a different angle in such a way that we could have several obligees expecting separate items of performance from one single obligor. In this case, the obligation would be several on the part of the obligees.

§ 3.1.2. EFFECTS OF SEVERAL OBLIGATIONS.

The analysis of the effects of several obligations does not require any extensive treatment since a *several obligation* must be considered as being merely the gathering under one source of multiple but separate obligations creating as many different bonds of law as there are parties.[2] As **LSA-C.C. Art. 1787-3** states:" A several obligation produces the same effects as a separate obligation owed to each obligee by an obligor or by each obligor to an obligee." Therefore each several obligor is an entity separate from the other obligors and the legal regime of any one obligation may be different from the legal regimes of the other existing obligations. Thus, the insolvency or inability of one "several" obligor to perform his obligation will have no impact at all on the performances of their obligations by other obligors. The remedies or rights of action of the obligee are particular to each one of the several obligors so that the means of enforcement of each obligation are specific to each one . . .

ARTICLE 2
THE JOINT OBLIGATION

§ 3.2.1. DEFINITION AND CONCEPT.

There exists a joint obligation on the part of multiple obligors when these obligors are bound together to one performance arising from one and the same obligation. Likewise, an obligation is joint on the part of multiple obligees when, together, they are entitled to just one performance from the obligor. As **LSA-C.C. Art. 1788** states: **"When different obligors owe together just one performance to one obligee, but neither is bound for the whole, the obligation is joint for the obligors. When one obligor owes just one performance intended for the common benefit of different obligees, neither of whom is entitled to the whole performance, the obligation is joint for the obligees."** The *Dictionary of the Civil Code* defines such an obligation as "a plural obligation in which each one of multiple obligors can be pursued only for his part/share."[3]

---

[2] LSA-C.C. Art. 1787: see Appendix.

[3] See *Dictionary of the Civil Code*, — word: conjoint, ointe, 1, p. 127. In French law such an obligation is known as "conjointe."

The joint obligation is considered as the common rule or as the general principle of the law of obligations involving multiple persons. In other words, by requiring some particular legal characteristics or identifiable features from other kinds of obligations with multiple persons, the Civil Code lays down the rebuttable presumption that, *whenever multiple obligors are bound by the same obligation to undertake together just one performance, these obligors must be considered as bound jointly.*

It is unusual for multiple obligors to be bound jointly *ab initio*, that is to say, at the time of inception of an obligation. The reasons are, first of all, that a joint obligation calls for a divided performance by the joint obligors of the "one" performance and, second, the joint obligation multiplies the legal effects of these individual performances and weakens the position of the obligee by shielding and exempting each obligor from the other obligors' failure to perform.[4]

It is much more likely, therefore, that an obligation with multiple persons will be solidary or indivisible from its inception so as to ensure its full performance, minimize the potential variety of legal effects and better protect the obligee in his rights. Consequently, most cases of joint obligations will arise in the course of time upon the death of an obligee or an obligor, as illustrated in **LSA-C.C. Arts. 1416, 1420,** or upon termination of the existence of a legal entity, as exemplified by **LSA-C.C. Art. 2817.**[5]

§ 3.2.2. EFFECTS OF JOINT OBLIGATIONS.

An obligation can be joint either because multiple obligees are, jointly, entitled to one performance from one obligor or because multiple obligors owe, jointly, one performance to one obligee.

A. Joint Obligees.

Joint obligees may be two investors who, together, would decide to invest a certain amount of money in the manufacturing of some new product. The manufacturer, or obligor, would then be indebted for the whole amount invested but would owe each individual investor only his respective share of the investment. Furthermore, should only one of the two investors-obligees put the single obligor in default for not performing on time, only that one investor who put the obligor in default would derive the benefits of such an action.[6]

The same legal effects flow from an interruption of prescription. If one joint obligee interrupts prescription *vis-à-vis* the single obligor, only that obligee will benefit from his action.[7] A codal illustration of a joint obligation on the part of obligees can be found in **LSA-C.C. Art. 2600** which provides, in part, that "**if a seller died leaving more than one successor, each successor may bring an**

---

[4] LSA-C.C. Arts. 1789, 1817: see Appendix.

[5] See Arts. 1416, 1420 and 2817 in Appendix.

[6] LSA-C.C. Art. 1991: see Appendix.

[7] LSA-C.C. Art. 3503: see Appendix. One must reason *a contrario* on Art. 3503.

action for lesion individually for that share of the immovable corresponding to his right."

B.　Joint Obligors.

A joint obligation on the part of obligors is created whenever multiple obligors are bound together to perform one obligation. However, each one of them is bound to perform only his individual share of the whole obligation; each one of them is bound *pro numero virorum*,[8] i.e. according to the number of men. Although bound together by the common identity of their performance, the obligors remain independent from each other so that each one owes only part or portion of the performance. It follows that a *"person shall be joined as a party in the action when either: (1) In his absence, complete relief cannot be accorded among those already parties. (2) He claims an interest relating to the subject matter of the action and is so situated that the adjudication of the action in his absence may either: (a) As a practical matter, impair or impede his ability to protect that interest. (b) Leave any of the persons already parties subject to a substantial risk of incurring multiple or inconsistent obligations."*[9]

Should the creditor-obligee interrupt prescription *vis-à-vis* one joint obligor, this interruption of prescription will have no effect against the other joint obligors. The same is true of the effects of a putting in default of one joint obligor and not the others.[10]

The plurality of links or bonds of law between the obligee and the joint obligors has this consequence that the joint obligors will not necessarily be bound to the obligee under the same legal regimes. Each bond of law may be vested with a particular legal identity so that, for example, some defenses available to one obligor may not be available to the others.[11] The same reasons explain why the insolvency of a joint obligor is a risk for the obligee and cannot be ascribed to another joint obligor. The obligee is entitled only to his share from each one of his joint obligors who are to assume no greater burden than they are presumed to accept under the law or under the contract and that burden is a *virile* share.[12] Thus, the obligee of an insolvent joint obligor must suffer the loss that the non-performance of that part of the obligation will inevitably entail.

Whenever a joint obligation is indivisible in its performance, in the sense that the item of performance owed by the joint obligors is not susceptible of being divided in parts (**LSA-C.C. Art. 1789**), the rules of solidarity (**LSA-C.C. Arts. 1790**

---

[8] LSA-C.C. Arts. 1788, 1789: see Appendix. "Pro numero virorum" means "according to the number of 'men' i.e. heads."

[9] LSA-C.C.P. Art. 641: see Appendix.

[10] LSA-C.C. Art. 1989, *et seq.*; see Arts. 1989 and 1991 in Appendix.

[11] LSA-C.C. Art. 1801; reasoning *in pari materia and a fortiori ratione.*

[12] A virile share is that part of the totality of an indebtedness as divided by the number of obligors. The same is true of the virile portion of an obligee. The *Dictionary of the Civil Code* (p. 434) defines "portion virile"/virile portion in these terms: "Share of an undivided aggregate of assets obtained by dividing this aggregate by the number of entitled beneficiaries."

et seq.) and those of indivisibility (**LSA-C.C. Arts. 1815** *et seq.*)[13] will apply.

ARTICLE 3
SOLIDARY OBLIGATIONS OR IN SOLIDO OBLIGATIONS

§ 3.3.1.   DEFINITION AND NOTION.

Solidarity must be understood both as a legal fiction and as a practical necessity. It is defined in the *Dictionary of the Civil Code* as follows: *"Within a legal relationship of an obligation, specific bond between the obligation's passive subjects (debtors) or active subjects (creditors).More precisely, a contractual or statutory modality of an obligation involving multiple parties which prevents the division of an obligation."* In essence, solidarity is an obstacle, a bar to the division of an obligation as a result of a particular feature attached to the bond of law binding together multiple persons. These persons can be, either multiple obligees [active solidarity], or multiple obligors [passive solidarity].

The obstacle that solidarity erects against the division of an obligation among its multiple parties amounts, to a large extent, to consider these multiple parties as being fictitiously one and the same person on account of the personal link that has been established between them. Each party can make his the motto *"all for one and one for all."*[14]

The burdensome legal effects that passive solidarity will impose on a solidary obligor explains why the sources of solidarity are few and restrictive. No burden or risk is to be imposed on an average reasonable person unless she has agreed to assume it or unless the law has ordered it. Conversely, the dangers and inconveniences that active solidarity creates for each solidary obligee by placing each one at the mercy of any other, explains why the law has not provided for instances of this type of solidarity although it can be created by contract.

§ 3.3.2.   SOURCES OF SOLIDARITY.

The far-reaching, harsh and aleatory effects of solidarity are the reason why "solidarity of obligation shall not be presumed. A solidary obligation arises from a clear expression of the parties' intent or from the law" (**LSA-C.C. Art. 1796**). The two sources of solidarity are, thus, the law and contract. The fact that there may be two different sources of solidarity of an obligation is not an obstacle to two or more obligors being held solidarily bound for that same obligation but on account of a different source of solidarity. One solidary obligor could be bound solidarily on account of a contract whereas another solidary obligor could be bound for the same obligation on the basis of a legal disposition.[15] As **LSA-C.C. Art. 1797** states; "An obligation may be solidary though it derives from a different source for each obligor." This latter code article is a legislative embodiment of a principle previously formulated by the Louisiana jurisprudence which had put an end, in a rather radical

---

[13] See Arts. 1789, 1790, 1815 in Appendix.

[14] From "The Three Musketeers" by A. Dumas.

[15] LSA-C.C. Art. 1797: see Appendix.

manner, to a then existing hybrid type of solidarity known as *imperfect solidarity* or *liability in solidum*.[16]

A. The Law.

The Louisiana Civil Code offers several examples of *passive solidarity* imposed by law. When considering the variety of these instances it is possible to gather them into two different categories on the basis of their particular rationale.

One category of instances of legal solidarity is built on the presumed intent of the parties bound solidarily. The law simply assumes that these parties would want or would agree to be bound *in solido, solidarily,* if they were given the opportunity to express their intent. Such would be the case, for example, when these parties would want to provide some type of guarantee of performance to their obligee.

Illustrations of such instances of legal solidarity can be found in a series of Code Articles. Under **LSA-C.C. Art. 227 "Fathers and mothers, by the very act of marrying, contract together the obligation of supporting, maintaining, and educating their children."** Notice that "fathers and mothers . . . contract together . . . ." **LSA-C.C. Art. 2900** provides **"when several persons jointly borrow the same thing, they are solidarily liable toward the lender"** for the return of the thing borrowed. It is most likely the only condition under which the lender would consider granting a loan for use to multiple borrowers.[17]

The same can be said of the obligation of several persons who have received the same object in deposit and are bound to return this very object (LSA-C.C. 2933). Additional illustrations can be found in **LSA-C.C. Art. 3015 and 3045.**[18] Article 3045 is quite explicit: **"A surety, or each surety when there is more than one, is liable to the creditor in accordance with the provisions of this Chapter, for the full performance of the obligation of the principal obligor, without benefit of division or discussion, even in the absence of an express agreement of solidarity."**

A second category of cases of legal solidarity can be said to amount to a form of penalty to be imposed on obligors because of their joint participation in a wrongful act.

The best illustration of this type of legal solidarity is offered by **LSA-C.C. Art. 2324-A,** which imposes a liability *in solido* on anyone **"who conspires with another person to commit an intentional or willful act,"** so that each person is **"answerable, in solido, . . . for the damage caused by such act."** Likewise, under **LSA-C.C. Art. 2318: "The father and the mother are responsible for the damage occasioned by their minor child . . . ."**

Likewise, it is possible to find an instance of legal solidarity, although not specifically posited, in **LSA-C.C. Art. 2762.**[19] The failure of a contractor to build a

---

[16] Foster v. Hampton, 381 So. 2d 789 (1980).

[17] LSA-C.C. Art. 2891: see Appendix.

[18] See LSA-C.C. Arts. 2933, 3015 and 3045 in Appendix.

[19] LSA-C.C. Art. 2762: see Appendix.

sound and sturdy building, one that would not fall to ruin in the course of ten years (. . .) should make him liable *in solido* with his subcontractors who failed to perform in a workmanlike manner. In this instance, solidary liability would be imposed as a penalty for an obligor's failure, the contractor and the subcontractors, to perform as expected.

B. Contract.

A contract is the law between the parties and, within the limitations or authorizations set by the law.[20] The parties may renounce rights granted merely for the protection of their private interests. For example, the law assumes, as a matter of principle, that the legal regime of joint obligations better protects the individual interests of obligors. Nevertheless, these same obligors are given the option of waiving that protection, which is not of public order, and can stipulate that they will be bound solidarily.

The contractual stipulation of solidarity need not be couched in express or formal terms provided solidarity "arises from a clear expression of the parties' intent"[21] (**LSA-C.C. Art. 1796**). The inclusion, in a contract, of a specifically tailored legal terminology, such as *in solido* or *solidarily*, is not necessary as long as the parties' intent can be unambiguously interpreted by a court as disclosing their informed willingness to be bound solidarily.[22] Where a definite ambiguity exists or a doubt arises as to whether a contractual obligation should be characterized as solidary or not, the presumption that the obligation is joint should control. Solidarity being an exception to the common standard type of obligations with multiple persons, that exception should be construed narrowly and strictly so as to allow the principle of joint obligations to prevail since it conveys the presumed intent of the parties that they are unwilling to take on more than their virile share unless they consent to it.

§ 3.3.3. EFFECTS OF SOLIDARITY.

The effects of active solidarity, or solidarity between obligees, are somewhat unusual, not to say dangerous for a solidary obligee, and can easily explain why it is rather uncommon to encounter this type of solidarity. Quite to the contrary, it is very frequent for passive solidarity or solidarity between obligors to exist in a variety of instances and to grow in scope and importance.

A. Effects of Active Solidarity.

The very essence of solidarity is to prevent the division of an obligation through the creation of a fictitious bond of mutual representation between the obligees. It follows, as a consequence, that each one of the solidary obligees is vested with the right to demand performance of the whole obligation and to receive the same whole

---

[20] LSA-C.C. Art. 7: see Appendix.

[21] See LSA-C.C. Art. 1796 in Appendix.

[22] See LSA-R.S. 10:3-116.

performance from the obligor. [23] An implicit assumption which helps understand the actual mechanism of solidarity is that the bond of solidarity creates a sort of implied representation or even a mandate or *de facto* representation or mandate between the obligees[24] so that each one is presumed to represent the others and to act on behalf of the others.

The practical effects of active solidarity are many. First of all, each one of the solidary obligees may demand the whole performance and when that performance has been rendered to any one of them it extinguishes the obligation and releases the obligor even though the benefit of the obligation remains to be divided among the multiple obligees.[25] A second effect is that, should a solidary obligee interrupt prescription of the action against the obligor, the other solidary obligees will benefit from such an initiative.[26] Thirdly, and reasoning *a pari ratione* on **LSA-C.C. Art. 1793**, should a solidary obligee put the obligor in default, the benefit of this action will be shared with the other solidary obligees. From that time on damages for delay in his performance by the obligor will be owed to all the solidary obligees.[27] An additional effect of active solidarity is illustrated by the fact that, should the obligor be sued by one solidary obligee or should he have been put in default by one of them, the obligor would no longer have the right to choose which obligee could receive his performance. Under **LSA-C.C. Art. 1791**,[28] the obligor enjoys the freedom of choosing the beneficiary of his performance until he has been put in default by one of them or until an action is brought against him by one of the solidary obligees.

The presumed existence of a mandate or power of representation between the solidary obligees helps explain why no single solidary obligee can act to the detriment of the others; in a sense, each one should be held accountable for the damages that may result from the non-performance of his duty.[29] Such is the foundation of the denial of the right to any single solidary obligee to remit the full debt to the obligor. A solidary obligee, acting alone, may only remit his portion of the debt, the obligor remaining bound to the other solidary obligees for the balance.[30] The same rationale leads one to conclude (reasoning *a fortiori ratione a majori ad minus*) that a solidary obligee acting alone may not novate the entire debt without the consent of his co-solidary obligees.[31] Novation being **"the extinguishment of an existing obligation by the substitution of a new one,"** each solidary obligee might suffer a prejudice if such a novation *in toto* by one of them were allowed. To the extent that a solidary obligee may agree with the obligor to substitute a new performance for the former one, such novation can only affect

---

[23] LSA-C.C. Arts. 1790, 1791: see Appendix.

[24] LSA-C.C. Arts. 2985, 2989: see Appendix.

[25] LSA-C.C. Art. 1791: see Appendix.

[26] LSA-C.C. Art. 1793: see Appendix.

[27] LSA-C.C. Art. 1990: see Appendix. See Remission of debt, infra p. 153.

[28] See LSA-C.C. Art. 1791 in Appendix.

[29] LSA-C.C. Arts. 3001, 3002, 3030: see in Appendix.

[30] LSA-C.C. Art. 1792: see Appendix. On "Remission" see LSA-C.C. Art.1888 et seq; see also below Remission § 7.4.

[31] LSA-C.C. Arts. 1879, 1881, 1882: see Appendix. See Novation, infra § 7.3.1.

that part of the obligation owed to the solidary obligee seeking a novation.

As far as the relationship between the obligees is concerned it can be said that, in general, they divide among themselves, according to their respective rights, the performance received from the obligor. Basically, in their internal and horizontal relationship, the solidary obligees cease to be *solidary* to become *joint obligees*. Each obligee is entitled to a virile share of the payment, and that share will be equal to the others unless either the parties have provided otherwise or the circumstances dictate differently.

B.   Effects of Passive Solidarity.

In light of the practical importance and highly common occurrence of passive solidarity, it is necessary to consider this form of solidarity in more details than was the case of active solidarity. Two different levels of relationships between the parties involved must be analyzed; there is, first of all, a vertical relationship binding the multiple solidary obligors to the obligee and there is, secondly, a horizontal relationship creating rights and duties among the solidary obligors themselves.

1.   Vertical Effects of Passive Solidarity in the Relationship Between the Obligee and His Solidary Obligors.

LSA-C.C. Art. 1794 states: **"An obligation is solidary for the obligors when each obligor is liable for the whole performance. A performance rendered by one of the solidary obligors relieves the others of liability toward the obligee."** This article suggests that there is, at the same time, only *one item* of performance owed, that is to say *the whole performance*, but also a plurality of obligors held personally and individually for that performance regardless of whether the object or item of performance is divisible or indivisible in its performance. Thus, solidarity creates a personal bond between the obligee and each one of the solidary obligors.

This multiplicity of bonds between the solidary obligors and their obligee carries with it many important consequences.

(a) The obligee **"at his choice, may demand the whole performance from any of his solidary obligors. A solidary obligor may not request division of the debt.**

Unless the obligation is extinguished, an obligee may institute action against any of his solidary obligors even after institution of action against another solidary obligor."[32] **(LSA-C.C. Art. 1795).**

The obligee may demand the entire performance from any one of his solidary obligors at his option and that obligor, as opposed to a simple surety or joint obligor, may not plead the benefit of division.[33] In other words, solidary obligors waive the right to demand that the obligee-creditor should divide his action so as to obtain from each obligor only his virile share of the debt. Nevertheless, when a solidary

---

[32]   LSA-C.C. Art. 1795.

[33]   LSA-C.C. Art. 1795; LSA-C.C.P. Arts. 1005, 1111.

obligor is sued by the obligee, he may raise the benefit of the dilatory exception, which has for its purpose to delay the progress of the action without tending to defeat it.[34]

(b) The multiplicity of bonds in existence suggests that the legal regime of the solidarity of one obligor may arise from a source other than the sources of the solidarity of his co-obligors.[35] The solidarity of one obligor may find its source in a statute or a contract whereas the solidarity of another may arise from a delict or quasi-delict. It follows logically that each separate source of solidarity may create a different legal regime for each bond of solidarity. In other words, one obligor may be bound differently from another obligor to perform the same thing. Indeed, one solidary obligor may be bound under a term,[36] whereas another may be bound under a condition.[37] Moreover, one solidary obligor may be entitled to plead the relative nullity of his obligation on account of a vice of consent,[38] whereas another might raise the defense of incapacity, etc.

(c) In the event the obligee does not receive the whole performance from one solidary obligor, he may demand that performance or the balance from any other solidary-obligor. Only the whole performance of the obligation will release the solidary obligors and relieve them of liability towards the obligee.[39]

(d) Solidarity is not indivisibility.[40] As a consequence, should one obligor *in solido* die before the performance of the obligation, his heirs together, and not each one individually, will *jointly* owe the performance of the obligation formerly owed by the deceased.[41] Solidarity is not heritable.

(e) As stated above, despite the multiplicity of bonds, it is possible to see in solidarity a sort of implied representation or mandate between the solidary obligors.[42] An illustration of this close relationship between the obligors is found in **LSA-C.C. Art. 1799**, which provides that **"the interruption of prescription against one solidary obligor is effective against all solidary obligors and their heirs."**[43] Reasoning *a pari ratione* on **LSA-C.C. Art. 1799** and in light of the reason (*ratio legis*) behind **LSA-C.C. Art. 1800**,[44] it is possible to say that, should a solidary obligor be put in default, the other solidary obligors themselves will, thereby, be put in default.[45] This result assumes, of course, that all the solidary obligors are bound to the obligee under the same identical circumstances or legal regimes and that

---

[34] LSA-C.C.P. Arts. 922, 926; LSA-C.C. Art. 1805.

[35] LSA-C.C. Art. 1797.

[36] LSA-C.C. Arts. 1778, 1798: see Appendix.

[37] LSA-C.C. Arts. 1767, 1798: see Appendix.

[38] LSA-C.C. Art. 1948: see Appendix.

[39] LSA-C.C. Arts. 1794, 1795: see Appendix.

[40] LSA-C.C. Art. 1820: see Appendix.

[41] LSA-C.C. Art. 1789-1: see Appendix.

[42] LSA-C.C. Arts. 2985, 2986, 2989: see Appendix.

[43] See also LSA-C.C. Art. 3503: see Appendix.

[44] See Arts. 1799 and 1800 in Appendix.

[45] LSA-C.C. Art. 1991: see Appendix.

none of them would have a strictly personal defense to defeat the obligee's action.

(f) The multiplicity of bonds and the close community of interests between the solidary obligors explain also why there exist defenses which are common to all of them while other defenses remain strictly personal to a particular obligor.[46]

The common defenses available to all the obligors against an action brought by the obligee are those which can be raised by any one of them on behalf of all of them. A solidary co-obligor who is sued by the obligee-creditor may set up all the defenses that result from the nature of the obligation, as well as those that are common to all the co-obligors. Under this heading, one would include the following defenses: a term or a condition affecting the whole obligation and, therefore, the existence or the performance of that obligation; full performance already carried out by one solidary obligor;[47] illegality of the object of the performance or nullity of the obligation because of the lack of a required formality;[48] prescription of the obligation;[49] novation;[50] impossibility of performance because of a fortuitous event.[51]

Other common defenses may be available to the solidary obligors only for part of the obligation. In these instances, it can be said that the defense is mixed or partly common and partly personal (*i.e.*, personal to the obligor who may raise it to its full extent). Under this heading, one could list: remission of debt;[52] compromise;[53] compensation;[54] confusion;[55] renunciation of solidarity in favor of one obligor.[56] In these cases, the solidary obligors who are not parties to these juridical acts or facts can only claim to be excused from that part of the performance which would subsequently be owed to them by the solidary obligor who is a party to the remission, the transaction, the compensation, etc.

Yet, in those instances where one solidary obligor party to these juridical acts or facts would also happen to be the only party concerned by the obligation and, thus, be the principal obligor alone liable for the whole obligation, it might be possible for the other solidary obligors, who then would stand only as sureties, to be completely released from any obligation.[57]

With respect to those defenses which would be characterized as strictly personal, there are those which can be raised only by that particular solidary obligor protected by one defense or another. Such would be the case of a defense based on

---

[46] LSA-C.C. Art. 1801: see Appendix.

[47] LSA-C.C. Arts. 1794, 1854: see Appendix.

[48] LSA-C.C. Arts. 2029, 2030: see Appendix.

[49] LSA-C.C. Arts. 3477, 3492: see Appendix.

[50] LSA-C.C. Art. 1885: see Appendix.

[51] LSA-C.C. Art. 1873: see Appendix.

[52] LSA-C.C. Art. 1803, 1888: see Appendix. See Remission infra § 7.4.2.

[53] LSA-C.C. Arts. 1803, 3071: see Appendix.

[54] LSA-C.C. Arts. 1893, 1898: see Appendix. See Compensation, infra § 7.5.1.

[55] LSA-C.C. Arts. 1903, 1905: see Appendix. See Confusion, infra § 7.6.2.

[56] LSA-C.C. Art. 1802: see Appendix.

[57] LSA-C.C. Art. 1804-3: see Appendix.

the particular modalities of a solidary obligor's obligation as, for example, where his own obligation would be subject to a term or a condition. The same would be true of the availability of a vice of consent protective of an identified obligor only. The immediate consequences attached to the fact that a solidary obligor could raise a strictly personal defense are that, on the one hand, this particular obligor is exempted, temporarily or permanently, from the performance of the obligation and that, as a result, the individual share of the remaining solidary obligors is increased by an equivalent proportional amount.

2. Horizontal Effects of Passive Solidarity: Relationship Between the Solidary Obligors.

Once the obligee has received the full performance of the obligation from one of the solidary obligors, the benefit of solidarity disappears with the extinction of the debt. The principle which now governs the relationship between the solidary obligors is that solidarity is not heritable; it cannot be claimed by that solidary obligor who, through his performance, extinguished the obligation.[58]

The non-heritability of the benefit of solidarity from the obligee by the solidary obligor who performed means that there will take place a distribution of the debt among the *former* solidary obligors, who have now become *joint obligors* vis-à-vis one another. The solidary obligor who extinguished the debt is given a right of contribution against his co-debtors but he must divide his action so that he can demand from each one of them no more than their share or virile portion.[59]

The division of the debt among the obligors is not necessarily made on an equal basis. There may exist some exceptions to an equal distribution:

(a) By agreement, it may have been stipulated, or by statutory disposition it may have been directed, that one obligor should carry a heavier burden than the others. It may also appear implicitly from an agreement or from the circumstances that only one of the obligors should be liable for the whole debt because he is to be considered as the principal obligor and the only one concerned.[60] In this instance, the other obligors will stand as sureties for that obligor who is the only one concerned.[61]

(b) By judgment, a court could assign a greater share of the debt to one obligor than to the others.[62]

(c) Under **LSA-C.C. Art. 1800**,[63] an obligor *in solido* who is at fault in not performing his obligation will be the only one ultimately liable for the damages he may have caused to the obligee.

---

[58] LSA-C.C. Art. 1804: see Appendix.

[59] See LSA-C.C. Art. 1804 in Appendix.

[60] See LSA-C.C. Art. 1804 in Appendix.

[61] LSA-C.C. Arts. 3035, 3037: see Appendix.

[62] LSA-C.C. Arts. 2323-A, 2324-1: see Appendix.

[63] See LSA-C.C. Art. 1800 in Appendix.

The right of contribution made available to a solidary obligor against his co-obligors is based on the fundamental principle that each obligor should bear his full share of the debt but no more.[64] This principle explains why the right of contribution finds its practical expression in a dual right of action available to the obligor who performed and why the insolvency of a co-obligor should not be assigned exclusively to the obligor seeking contribution.

Whatever is the source, or whatever are the sources of solidarity, it is fairly representative of the situation (although not necessarily *legal*) to say that the solidary obligor who performed so as to extinguish the obligation acted either as a mandatary-representative or as a gestor for his co-obligors. Whether we rely on representation[65] or mandate[66] or resort to *negotiorum gestio*[67] (management of affairs), that solidary obligor who extinguished the obligation is entitled to a personal action to enforce his right of contribution against his co-solidary obligors.[68]

Since this action is personal, it ought to carry with it the payment of interest in the same manner as provided in **LSA-C.C. Art. 3014**,[69] which applies to a mandatary who has expended sums of money in the performance of the mandate. Reasoning *a pari ratione* and *in pari materia*, a solidary obligor who has paid the shares of his co-obligors in addition to his own should be entitled to the payment of interest on the sums he expended on behalf of his co-obligors.

The second facet of the right of contribution finds its justification in the institution of legal subrogation.[70] Whenever an obligor pays a debt he owes *with others*, he will benefit from subrogation by operation of law.[71] This aspect of the right of contribution means that the obligor who performed "**may avail himself of the action and security of the original obligee against the obligor, but [the obligation] is extinguished for the original obligee**" (**LSA-C.C. Art. 1826-A**). The obvious advantage of this particular right of subrogation is that the solidary obligor who benefits from it will be entitled to make use of the mortgage, privilege and other securities which guaranteed the payment of the debt held by the obligee against the remaining co-obligors. Actually, it is the very same action that the obligee could have exercised against his solidary obligors that the subrogated obligor brings against his joint obligors.

The nature of the right of solidarity being to create as many personal relationships as there are solidary obligors and the rationale of the right of contribution being to divide equally, in general, the debt among the obligors, it is therefore understandable that the risk of insolvency of one solidary obligor is to be spread proportionately among the remaining solvent obligors. Unless all his

---

[64] LSA-C.C. Art. 1805: see Appendix.

[65] LSA-C.C. Art. 2985–2988.

[66] LSA-C.C. Arts. 2989–3032.

[67] LSA-C.C. Arts. 2292–2297.

[68] LSA-C.C. Arts. 1805, 2297, 3010: see Appendix.

[69] LSA-C.C. Art. 3014: see Appendix.

[70] On Subrogation, see infra § 5.2.1.

[71] LSA-C.C. Art. 1829: see Appendix. On Subrogation see infra § 5.2.1.

solidary obligors are insolvent, an obligee-creditor will be paid *in toto* by one of them or in parts by all of them. Once that obligee-creditor has been paid, it might remain to deal with the impact of the insolvency of one or more obligors on the right of contribution vested in one of them. **LSA-C.C. Art. 1806** stipulates that:

> **"A loss arising from the insolvency of a solidary obligor must be borne by the other solidary obligors in proportion to their portion.**
>
> **Any obligor in whose favor solidarity has been renounced must nevertheless contribute to make up for the loss."**

The rationale for the second paragraph of this code article can be found in the principle that, by their personal contractual relationship, the obligee-creditor and the solidary obligor in whose favor solidarity has been renounced may not increase the burden or the virile share of the remaining obligors.[72] Therefore, a solidary obligor who benefited from a renunciation of solidarity by the obligee[73] cannot hide behind this benefit in his relationship with his co-obligors so at to shift the burden of insolvency of one of his co-obligors on the others. Originally he had bound himself towards them to bear his virile share of the debt and the insolvency of one of them will have the consequence of increasing, *pro tanto*, his own share.

What should be the legal consequences resulting from the **"remission of debt by the obligee in favor of one obligor"**? (**LSA-C.C. Art. 1803**). One consequence is that this remission will benefit **"the other solidary obligors in the amount of the portion of that obligor"** [*id*]. It means actually that, by the remission of debt to one solidary obligor, the obligee has transformed his solidary obligation into a joint obligation between, on the one hand, the obligor whose debt he has remitted and, on the other hand, all the remaining obligors. The latter, however, remain bound solidarily among themselves for the balance of the debt. It follows that one of the remaining solidary obligors sued for the payment of the balance will have the right of contribution against his co-obligors for their respective share of the balance.

If we assume, now, that one of these solidary obligors who remain liable for the balance of the debt is insolvent, the important question is then raised as to who should bear the risk of loss resulting from the inability of that solidary obligor to pay his share. Should the loss be borne by the solidary obligor who happens to be sued by the obligee for payment of the balance? Should that loss be spread among the remaining solvent solidary obligors liable for the balance? Must we add to these solidary obligors the obligor whose debt had been remitted by the obligee? Why shouldn't the obligee himself be assigned a share of the loss?

An application of the principles referred to above leads to one conclusion which is both rational and equitable.

It is of the nature of a remission of debt granted by an obligee to one obligor *in solido* to amount to an extinction of that obligor's share of the debt. That obligor is relieved of any further additional obligation and, thereby, exempts or relieves his co-obligors *in solido* of a payment up to the amount of which he, himself, has been

---

[72] LSA-C.C. Arts. 1978, 1983, 1985: see Appendix.

[73] LSA-C.C. Art. 1802: see Appendix.

remitted.[74] Thus, a remission of debt should have no detrimental effects against the remaining co-obligors *in solido* because they are not parties to that remission, they are third parties to it, and they should not see their own obligation increased without their consent.[75] Since, in our example, one solidary obligor had his debt remitted and since the other co-obligors cannot have their share of the debt increased beyond the normal application of the mechanism of solidarity, it follows that in the event an obligor *in solido*, who is liable for the balance of a debt, has become insolvent before the obligee has claimed payment of the balance, the burden of his insolvency will have to be distributed between the remaining solvent solidary obligors and the obligee himself. What happens is that the obligee will, fictitiously, take the place of the "remitted" obligor and assume the share of the insolvency which, before the remission of the debt, should have befallen that obligor now protected by the remission. In other words, the obligee is the one who is to suffer for having given up a right he had to full payment when he remitted part of the debt and he should not, now, be allowed to shift the burden of loss of recovery of a share of the debt on the remaining obligors. The remission of the debt automatically released the beneficiary obligor from any further liability towards his co-obligors, thereby depriving the latter of a right of contribution they would have had against their former co-solidary obligor.

---

[74] LSA-C.C. Art. 1803: see Appendix.
[75] LSA-C.C. Arts. 1983, 1985: see Appendix.

Chapter 4

OBLIGATIONS WITH MULTIPLE OBJECTS LSA-C.C. ARTS. 1807 TO 1820

An obligation may bear on one, two, or more objects or items of performance. The obligor may, indeed, bind himself towards his obligee in different ways. He may, for example, owe an obligation which requires him to carry out multiple items of performance for the benefit of his obligee. In such a case, the obligation created will be characterized as a conjunctive obligation.[1] On the other hand, the obligor and the obligee may have agreed to the performance of one item to be chosen out of other possible items. That selection of one item can be made by one party or the other. In this case the obligation will be referred to as an alternative obligation.[2] It may also happen that an obligor will bind himself to the performance of one principal item and, yet, reserve to himself the *faculty* of substituting a secondary item to the principal one. Although this kind of obligation is not specifically covered in the Civil Code, it has been identified as a "facultative obligation." Lastly, it may happen that the object(s) or item(s) of the obligor's performance of his obligation cannot be divided in its actual performance; such an obligation is then characterized as either divisible or indivisible.[3]

ARTICLE 1
CONJUNCTIVE OBLIGATIONS

An obligor may bind himself to **"multiple items of performance" (LSA-C.C. Art. 1807)** in such a manner that he cannot be said to have performed his obligation and extinguished it until all the multiple items have been fully carried out. The conjunctive obligation is defined in the *Dictionary of the Civil Code* as "an obligation by virtue of which the debtor is cumulatively bound to carry out multiple obligations."[4] The obligation thereby created may involve either several different or identical items of performance which are bound in such a way as to form a universality of things.

1: In the first instance, an obligor may owe a performance involving the delivery of an animal and another performance requiring that he render some services; he could also owe a third performance requiring that he abstain from competing with his obligee. The three different items of performance (deliver, render, abstain) must be tied together in such a manner as to reflect the obligor's intent to fulfill them all. Although each item of performance can be regarded as the object of a separate

---

[1] LSA-C.C. Art. 1807: see Appendix.

[2] LSA-C.C. Arts. 1808–1814: see Appendix.

[3] LSA-C.C. Arts. 1815–1820: see Appendix.

[4] *Dictionary of the Civil Code*, — word: conjonctif, ive (2), p. 128.

obligation, it remains that the obligor is bound to perform them all.[5] A conjunctive obligation is therefore an obligation comprised of multiple items of performance. Fictitiously each item of performance could be looked at as the object of a constituent obligation.

Each constituent obligation may be subjected to a particular legal regime which may vary from one constituent obligation to another. In the example given above, it is obvious that an obligation to do (render) will be governed by rules different from those governing an obligation not to do (abstain). The prescriptive period applicable to one may vary from that applicable to the other, etc. . . . Yet, the intent of the parties is that each constituent obligation is but a part of a whole, an element of a single entity, the conjunctive obligation, which provides the true *raison d'être* of each of its component parts.

This unusual structure of the conjunctive obligation is best illustrated by the fact that the obligor may be in breach of the whole conjunctive obligation itself, and not only of a constituent obligation, should he fail to perform any one of the items involved and expected of him. The breach of one item might trigger the obligee's right to demand immediate performance of all the remaining items of performance gathered together under a conjunctive obligation. According to **LSA-C.C. Art. 1807-2, "[t]he parties may provide that the failure of the obligor to perform one or more items shall allow the obligee to demand the immediate performance of all the remaining items."**

2: The second instance of a conjunctive obligation deals with the obligor's performance of identical items, all gathered under one single universality. The difficulty, here, is in finding a means of distinguishing such a particular kind of conjunctive obligation from an indivisible obligation which is also concerned with a universality of things. Since an extensive analysis of indivisible obligations follows in this same chapter, it will be sufficient to refer, here, only to the conjunctive obligation.

A universality of identical things or items will become the object of a conjunctive obligation when all these things or items are distinctively listed or enumerated and still bound together by a connecting link which brings them all under one single universality.[6] Such would be the case, for instance, where an obligor (let us assume a lessee) would agree to pay his obligee (the lessor) an amount of money (the rent or universality) in four separate installments spread over a certain period of time. Each quarterly installment can be looked upon as the item of performance of a separate constituent obligation, each one subjected to its own prescriptive period beginning at maturity. However, the *whole* rent is eventually owed, as a lessee may quickly discover should the lease include an acceleration clause. The effect of such a clause is to trigger an anticipated maturity of the remaining installments or items of performance upon the lessee's failure to perform, i.e, to pay one installment on time. As stated above, **"the parties may provide that the failure of the obligor to**

---

[5] LSA-C.C. Art. 1807: see Appendix.

[6] Such an illustration must be distinguished from an item or an object of performance made up of multiple identical things but referred to as a single item under a general name: examples would be a "library," a "flock of sheep," etc.

perform one or more items shall allow the obligee to demand the immediate performance of all the remaining items" (LSA-C.C. Art. 1807-2).

ARTICLE 2

ALTERNATIVE OBLIGATIONS

"Alternative," in common parlance, obviously means that a choice is to be made between two or more items. Thus, an alternative obligation requires that a choice be made between two or more items of performance, so that the obligor will be released from his obligation whenever he will have carried out one of those items of performance.[7] The essence of an alternative obligation is to place two (or more) items of performance on the same plane so that they are all *principal* items. No single item is accessory or secondary to another. If the obligation deals with two objects, both objects are equally due and the performance of either one will be sufficient to extinguish the whole obligation. Either one releases the obligor when carried out.

As an illustration, there would be an alternative obligation in the event an obligor would agree to give something in payment to his obligee[8] or to pay him a certain amount of money. Likewise, there would exist an alternative obligation for a roofer who would bind himself either to personally repair a roof or to have it repaired by someone else and pay for the repairs.

These examples must be distinguished from a very close and parallel situation where a choice between performances must be made but where there exists, actually, only one object to an obligation. This situation is descriptive of facts where, for example, an obligor would have to choose between two different currencies to make one single payment, to carry out one single performance. Whether the choice is between a payment in U.S. dollars or one in Japanese yens, there is still only one single obligation owed, one single performance due. There does not exist here two obligations with two different objects. The issue in this case is only one of modalities, or means of payment, or means of performing, and not an issue of choice between alternative objects or items of performance.

It is possible to see in an alternative obligation a sort of insurance granted to an obligee-creditor, a kind of guarantee of payment assuring him that at least one item of performance out of two or more will be conveyed to him. The feeling of security of an obligee-creditor will be lesser or greater depending, first, on which party, the obligee himself or the obligor, has the right to choose an item of performance over another and, second, on whether the items or objects are susceptible of specific performance or not at the time the choice is exercised.

---

[7] LSA-C.C. Art. 1808: see Appendix.

[8] LSA-C.C. Art. 2655: see Appendix.

§ 4.2.1. CHOICE OF ONE ITEM OF PERFORMANCE.

A fundamental principle governs this issue of choice: whether the choice of selecting the performance of one item over another is left with the obligor or with the obligee, either party must exercise that choice in good faith.[9]

A. Choice Belongs to the Obligor.

It is a presumption of the Louisiana law of obligations that, in an alternative obligation, **"the choice of the item of performance belongs to the obligor."**[10] This particular presumption finds its rationale in, and at the same time is a mere application of, a broader rule of contracts which provides, as illustrated in this article, that **"in case of doubt that cannot be otherwise resolved, a contract must be interpreted against the obligee and in favor of the obligor of a particular obligation."**[11] By and large, the Civil Code tends to favor that party to an obligation who carries a "burden," such as the burden of performing and who, in general, may be the weaker of the two parties, the less informed.[12]

B. Choice Belongs to the Obligee.

The presumption that the choice belongs to the obligor is a rebuttable legal presumption since it merely protects the interest of private parties. Consequently, it is conceivable that the choice of the object of the obligation be "expressly or impliedly granted to the obligee."[13]

C. Choice to Be Exercised in Good Faith.

Either party who is given the choice must make that choice in good faith.[14] This requirement means that, for example, the party who has the choice may not exercise it until the particular modalities affecting the alternative obligation have materialized. As an illustration, an obligor who is given the right to choose one branch of the alternative or the other, may not select one object over another until the term stipulated in favor of the obligee has occurred.[15] On the other hand, an obligee who may choose the item of performance he wishes to receive may not demand performance from the obligor until the suspensive condition which could be attached to the obligation does happen.

A specific codal application of this principle of good faith appears in **LSA-C.C. Art. 1810: "When the party who has the choice does not exercise it after a demand to do so, the other party may choose the item of performance."** Thus,

---

[9] LSA-C.C. Art. 1759: see Appendix.

[10] LSA-C.C. Art. 1809: see Appendix.

[11] LSA-C.C. Art. 2057-1.

[12] See, for example, the rules on warranty in a contract of sale; see also the rules on capacity to enter into a contract, or the giving of consent under duress.

[13] LSA-C.C. Art. 1809: see Appendix.

[14] LSA-C.C. Art. 1759: see Appendix.

[15] LSA-C.C. Art. 1779: see Appendix.

unless extenuating circumstances exist, such as a fortuitous event,[16] the obligee who suffers from the delay in the exercise by the obligor of the choice should be entitled to make his own choice of the item of the performance to be carried out by the obligor.

D.   Consequences Attached to the Choice.

Whenever the choice of one item of performance has been made by the proper party, and in due time, that item is owed in its entirety. Once selected the item becomes the only object of an obligation which, from alternative, has now become pure and simple. The exercise of the choice extinguishes the alternative feature of the obligation. There follow some legal consequences:

1. The obligor cannot perform part of one item and part of another; although a choice must be made between the items, each one remains an entity and is not susceptible of partial performance.

2. Should the items of performance of the alternative obligation be involved, one a movable and the other an immovable, the movable or immovable nature of this item and, therefore, the legal regime of the obligation, will not be determined until the choice has been exercised. Until a choice has been made, no item of performance has become the object of a pure and simple obligation. Hence the forms and modalities of transfer of ownership of the item will vary according to the nature of the object selected to be delivered by the obligor.

3. At which point in time is the right of ownership of an item passed from one party to the other? Is it at the time when the choice is made, which actually means when the obligation becomes pure and simple? Or is the ownership transferred retroactively back to the time when the parties entered into the alternative obligation? Our preference would be to consider the exercise of the choice as tantamount to the occurrence of a suspensive condition (either potestative or mixed) and to state, therefore, that there ought to be retroactivity of the effects of the exercise of the choice.[17]

§ 4.2.2.   NON-PERFORMANCE OF AN ALTERNATIVE OBLIGATION.

Although it offers a greater chance of being performed than a pure and simple obligation because the alternative obligation creates at least two chances, rather than one, of an obligation being performed, an alternative obligation may still be caught up in circumstances which might prevent it from being performed in its totality (*in toto)* or even in part.

---

[16]   LSA-C.C. Art. 1873 *et seq.*; on fortuitous event and impossibility of performance, see infra § 4.2.2.

[17]   On Conditions, see supra § 2.2-B.1; on the effects of the occurrence of a suspensive condition, see supra § 2.2-B.2.

A. Total Impossibility of Performance (*In Toto*).

If the two items which were contemplated as potential objects of the performances of the alternative obligations have been destroyed by fortuitous event before the obligor was put in default to perform and in the absence of any fault on his part, the whole alternative obligation will be extinguished *regardless of which party had been granted the choice.*[18] Under these circumstances, the obligor is excused from any performance and the obligee must bear the risk of loss of either performance in this sense that he can no longer demand that the obligor perform. As far as the financial risk of loss is concerned, if there is one, it is obviously for the obligor to bear since he can no longer transfer any of the destroyed items to the obligee.

The same legal consequences will follow if the items of performance were to become unlawful, by the enactment of a new statute for example, before the choice had to be made by either party.[19]

On the other hand, if the two items contemplated in the alternative obligation have been destroyed or, somehow, have become impossible through the fault of the obligor, different rules of law will control.

1. If, under these circumstances, the choice belonged to the obligor he will be **"liable for the damages resulting from his failure to render the last item that became impossible."** (**LSA-C.C. Art. 1814-1**). In other words, the obligor will owe at least the value of the second item which he destroyed and, possibly, the profit of which the obligee was deprived.[20] The reason for this rule is that the second item had become, through the obligor's destruction of the first one, the single object of the obligation which, as a consequence, had become pure and simple; it is as if that remaining item of performance of the obligation had been the only one in existence from the beginning.

2. If, under these same circumstances, the choice belonged to the obligee, it can be said that the obligee has been prevented from exercising his choice between the items of performance of the obligation because of the obligor's fault. He ought to be given a *new* choice between the values of the two original items. There occurs what can be referred to as a "real subrogation" where a thing (value) is substituted to another thing (the original item of performance). Moreover, reasoning *a fortiori ratione* on **LSA-C.C. Art. 2467,**[21] which deals with destruction by fortuitous event, the obligee should also be granted the additional right to recede from the contract.

3. In the event the choice of items belonged to the obligor and the impossibility of performing one or more items was caused by the obligee's fault, the obligor who has, thereby, been deprived of his right to choose between the items may not be compelled to deliver any remaining item.[22] The obligation has been extinguished.

---

[18] LSA-C.C. Art. 1813: see Appendix.

[19] LSA-C.C. Art. 1813.

[20] LSA-C.C. Art. 1995: see Appendix.

[21] LSA-C.C. Art. 2467: see Appendix.

[22] LSA-C.C. Art. 1814-2: see Appendix.

B.   Impossiblity of Performance in Part.

When an alternative obligation gives the obligor the right to choose the item of performance, should one of the contemplated items be destroyed either by fortuitous event or by the obligor's own fault, the remaining item must be tendered to the obligee. The risk of loss of one item is for the obligor to bear and since the obligee had not been given the right to make the choice, the obligee must accept the performance of the remaining item.[23]

However, when the obligee was given the choice of items and one of them is destroyed by a fortuitous event, he must accept the performance of the remaining item or choose one from the remaining items should the choice be between more than two items. Yet, if one of the two items has been destroyed by the fault of the obligor who, thereby, prevented the obligee from exercising his choice, this same obligee may choose to accept the remaining item or elect to demand damages representing the value of the item that was destroyed by the obligor. The damages may exceed the value of the item destroyed since they **"are measured by the loss sustained by the obligee and the profit of which he has been deprived." (LSA-C.C. Art. 1995).**

ARTICLE 3
FACULTATIVE OBLIGATIONS

The Louisiana Civil Code does not include any article dealing specifically with this concept of facultative obligations. Yet it is a well-known institution of the civil law dating back to Roman law. Moreover, there are remedies provided for in the Civil Code which can be explained only in reference to this kind of obligation. An analysis of this concept will show its usefulness and lead to distinguishing it from similar types of obligations.

§ 4.3.1.   CONCEPT OF FACULTATIVE OBLIGATION.

In the *Dictionary of the Civil Code*, a facultative obligation "is said of an obligation whereby the obligor is bound to a single object (in contrast with a conjunctive obligation and an alternative obligation), but with the right for that obligor to free himself by providing another specified object."[24] Thus, an obligation is facultative when an obligor owes one particular and principal item of performance and when, at the same time, he may be released of that performance by tendering another item as a substitute item, which will take the place of the principal item of performance. The facultative obligation is thus characterized by the existence of a principal item which is the only one truly due under the obligation (this item is said to be *in obligatione*) but, to that item the obligor, at the moment of performing may, of his own volition, substitute another item for his performance (this item is said to be *in facultate solutionis*).

---

[23] LSA-C.C. Art. 1812-1: see Appendix.

[24] *Dictionary of the Civil Code*, — word: facultatif, ive (3), p. 233.

Although one could easily devise examples of contractual facultative obligations to illustrate the practical importance of the concept, it is more relevant to point out the actual existence of this type of obligation through examples taken from the Civil Code.

1. **LSA-C.C. Arts. 2589** and **2591**[25] grant the seller of an immovable the right to ask for the rescission of the sale "**for lesion when the price is less than one half of the fair market value**" of that immovable (**LSA-C.C. Art. 2589**). In response to this right of action of the seller, "**the buyer may elect to return the immovable to the seller, or to keep the immovable by giving to the seller a supplement equal to the difference between the price paid by the buyer and the fair market value of the immovable . . .** " (**LSA-C.C. Art. 2591**).

One may notice two important characteristics of the seller's remedy otherwise known as action in lesion.[26] The first characteristic to point out is that only the obligor (buyer) has a choice between carrying out one item of performance (return the immovable) or another (make up the just price and keep the thing). The second important characteristic is that the plaintiff-seller has only one ground of action, which is his right to demand the rescission of the sale. In other words, the seller does not have the right to demand the just price in lieu of the rescission of the contract of sale. The reason is that only one obligation is owed to the seller by the purchaser and that obligation is the return of the immovable. The substitute or facultative obligation cannot be the grounds for a law suit by the seller, since he is only entitled to the rescission of the contract of sale. The purchaser may lawfully offer a substitute performance, make up the just price and compel the seller to receive it.

2. **LSA-C.C. Art. 234** offers another example of a facultative obligation. Under this article a father, or a mother, who owes alimony to a child "**may offer to receive, support and maintain the child, to whom he or she may owe alimony, in his or her house . . . .**" The principal obligation imposed on the father or the mother is to pay alimony for the support of the child; the substitute facultative obligation available to the father or the mother is to receive the child in his or her own home. This facultative obligation is available to the father or the mother in response to the child's only right to alimony payments.

3. A promise to sell made with the payment of earnest money creates a facultative obligation for the benefit of both parties who are considered, then, as obligors.[27] Under **LSA-C.C. Art. 2623**,[28] a promise to sell gives each party the right to enforce specific performance, that is to say, to compel the other party to finalize the sale. This right of action to seek specific performance of the principal obligation still remains the only available remedy to either party in the event the promise to sell has been made with earnest money. However, under **LSA-C.C. Art. 2624**, "**either party may recede from the contract, but the buyer who chooses to recede must forfeit the earnest money, and the seller who so chooses must**

---

[25] LSA-C.C. Arts. 2589, 2591: see Appendix.

[26] See Précis on Louisiana Law of Sale and Lease § 2.5.1.

[27] LSA-C.C. Art. 2624: see Appendix.

[28] LSA-C.C. Art. 2623: see Appendix.

return the earnest money plus an equal amount." The *faculty*, the option here granted to each party, is tantamount to the freedom of offering a certain amount of money to get out of the contract by offering to perform a less burdensome item, which it is in the discretion of either party to choose.

§ 4.3.2.   FACULTATIVE OBLIGATIONS DISTINGUISHED FROM OTHERS.

A facultative obligation can be distinguished from other similar kinds of obligations on the ground, mainly, of its peculiar effects. These effects are determined by the essential feature of the facultative obligation, which is that it is concerned with one object or item of performance, the only one being *in obligatione* because it is intended to be performed as an effect of the bond of law existing between the parties.

1. A comparison between an alternative obligation, on the one hand, and a facultative obligation, on the other hand, will reveal that these two kinds of obligations differ with respect to the risk of loss of an item destroyed by fortuitous event.

Indeed, should one of two items of an alternative obligation be destroyed, the remaining item then becomes the object of a pure and simple obligation. That object can be demanded from the obligor. On the contrary, if the principal object of a facultative obligation is destroyed by a fortuitous event, no *alternate* item is owed by the obligor. The substitute or facultative item or object does not enter the realm of the obligation and cannot be demanded by specific performance. For example, should an immovable bought at a lesionary price be destroyed by fortuitous event while in the hands of the purchaser and without any fault on his part, that purchaser will not owe anything to his vendor. Therefore, the risk of loss is for the creditor-obligee, who may not obtain any other item of performance, not even, and most importantly, the full price. On the other hand, should the principal object of a facultative obligation, the immovable for example, be destroyed by the fault of the obligor, the latter may be sued by the obligee for the equivalent value of the immovable which can no longer be returned to the seller-obligee. The latter will be entitled to the payment of damages for the loss he has sustained and the profit of which he has been deprived.[29] Still, in response to this suit for the payment of damages, the obligor may offer, instead, the *facultative item*, which he always had the right to convey, instead of the principal object, the immovable.

2. The legal nature and regime of a facultative obligation are determined by the nature of the principal object of the obligation. Under **LSA-C.C. Art. 2624**, the movable or immovable nature of the obligation is controlled by the immovable or movable nature of the thing, object or item of the transaction. Therefore, the legal regime of the obligation is defined at the outset as soon as the facultative obligation is formed since only one item of performance is owed under that obligation. Such is not the case, on the other hand, of an alternative obligation, since its legal regime

---

[29] LSA-C.C. Art. 1995: see Appendix.

is not determined or fixed until the choice of the item of performance has been made by one party or the other.

3. A facultative obligation should not be analogized with a penal clause or a provision for stipulated damages.[30] The latter is "**a secondary obligation for the purpose of enforcing the principal one**" (**LSA-C.C. Art. 2005**). The legal regime of this latter kind of obligation is such that, in case of non-performance of the principal obligation, the obligee-creditor may still sue for specific performance of that principal obligation and, in the event it cannot be performed, the stipulated damages will then be owed. It can be said that the parties have planned ahead of time for a "real subrogation" in the event of non-performance of the principal item of the obligation. In a word, there is no room for a choice to be made by the obligor. On the contrary, when a facultative obligation exists, it gives the obligor the ability to recede *freely and willingly* from the contract with the full knowledge and consent of the obligee. A facultative obligation is not a means of pressure in the hands of an obligee to compel his obligor to perform the principal obligation, as stipulated damages can, on the contrary, be looked at.

How, then, can a facultative obligation be distinguished from the closest related obligation, the alternative one? Broadly stated, a facultative obligation can be identified by the combination of the following criteria:

(a) a facultative obligation gives the obligor, and the obligor only, the unrestricted freedom to choose between at least two items of performance where *one is less burdensome than the other.*

(b) a facultative obligation places a different emphasis on the two items involved; *one item is considered as the principal* and only object of a primary obligation. An alternative obligation places the two items or objects on the same level.

(c) in a facultative obligation the *obligee has a right of action only for the performance of the primary obligation;* the obligee does not have the right to demand performance of the facultative obligation.

(d) a facultative obligation will most often show a more or less important *disparity in the values* of the items of performance. The *facultative item,* will bear a value usually inferior to that of the item of the principal or primary performance. The discrepancy in the values of the items is well illustrated in the examples of the lesionary sale and the promise to sell with earnest money. Hence, a facultative obligation, by its original nature, protects the obligor in granting him the right to "pay a modest price" for his freedom not to perform a more demanding obligation.

ARTICLE 4
DIVISIBLE AND INDIVISIBLE OBLIGATIONS

Although this subject matter has always been surrounded with an aura of obscurity, it is possible to reduce it to simple and practical concepts. This goal was in large partly achieved by the 1984–85 revision of the Civil Code articles on

---

[30] LSA-C.C. Arts. 2005 *et seq.*

obligations. An analysis of the concepts of divisibility and indivisibility is necessary before examining the sources and effects of these kinds of obligations.

§ 4.4.1.   CONCEPTS OF DIVISIBLE AND INDIVISIBLE OBLIGATIONS.

The rationale and the essence of these notions are dictated primarily by the characteristics of the nature of the object of the obligation or item of performance, and secondarily, if it is the case, by the number of parties involved in the performance of that obligation. Fundamentally, an obligation is indivisible when the object of the performance, because of its nature or because of the intent of the parties, is not susceptible of division either materially or intellectually.[31] The *Dictionary of the Civil Code* describes indivisibility as the "*condition of that which cannot be divided in one particular respect (esp. that which cannot be admitted or supplied only in part), and which must be considered as a whole or pair in totality, even (if a debt is involved) as regards the heirs of a debtor (each one being held responsible for the whole . . . ".*[32]

However, whenever an obligation, even divisible in its performance, pits one obligee against one obligor only, the single obligor must perform the whole obligation as if it were indivisible.[33] Indeed, **"an obligee may refuse to accept a partial performance"** (**LSA-C.C. Art. 1861-1**). Therefore, whenever an obligation is of concern to one obligee and one obligor only, there is, *a priori*, no reason to wonder whether the obligation is divisible or indivisible; the presumption of law makes the performance indivisible. Nevertheless, this legal presumption is rebuttable as will be explained below under the sources of indivisibility.

The issue of divisibility or indivisibility of obligations becomes of paramount importance when multiple obligees or multiple obligors are parties to one and the same obligation. This may occur from the time of inception of the obligation or from the time one party dies leaving at least two heirs who become obligees or obligors of the obligation previously in existence. Should indivisibility be the legal regime of that obligation, it will stand as an obstacle to the application of the general principle governing obligations with multiple parties according to which such obligations are to be considered as *joint.*[34] It is a fundamental principle of the law of obligations involving multiple obligors that:

> **"When different obligors owe together just one performance to one obligee, but neither is bound for the whole, the obligation is joint for the obligors.**

> **When one obligor owes just one performance intended for the common benefit of different obligees, neither of whom is entitled to the**

---

[31] LSA-C.C. Art. 1815: see Appendix.

[32] *Dictionary of the Civil Code,* — word: indivisibilité (2), p. 306.

[33] LSA-C.C. Art. 1816: see Appendix.

[34] On Joint Obligations see supra § 3.2.1. See LSA-C.C. Arts 1788, 1789.

whole performance, the obligation is joint for the obligees." (LSA-C.C. Art. 1788)

It is essential, therefore, to ascertain how an obligation can become indivisible either between obligees (active indivisibility) or between obligors (passive indivisibility).

§ 4.4.2. SOURCES OF INDIVISIBILITY.

LSA-C.C. Art. 1815 states in very simple terms that:

> **"An obligation is divisible when the object of the performance is susceptible of division.**
>
> **An obligation is indivisible when the object of the performance, because of its nature or because of the intent of the parties, is not susceptible of division."**

Consequently, the indivisibility of an obligation may be due to the nature of the object of the performance, the obligation or the contractual stipulations binding the parties to an obligation. The sources of indivisibility are, thus, either nature or the intent of the parties.

A.   Nature as a Source of Indivisibility.

There exists a natural indivisibility of an obligation when its object "because of its own nature, cannot be divided either materially (obligation to deliver a live animal safely), or rationally (obligation owed to a lessee to warrant his peaceful enjoyment of the premises), or conceptually/intellectually because of the purpose or goal it was intended to have (obligation to build a home) . . . "[35]

The natural indivisibility of an obligation can be described in these terms: absolute or relative.

1.   Absolute Natural Indivisibility.

Absolute natural indivisibility is dictated, first of all, by the law of nature and appears as the only authentic and unquestionable kind of indivisibility of an obligation. It can also be created by legislation thereby making the indivisibility "fictitiously or conceptually" natural. Whether actual or fictitious/conceptual, absolute natural indivisibility refers to an object of an obligation which, in its performance, cannot possibly be divided in parts.

Let us consider the following obligations:

(a) A vendor of a live animal is to transfer its ownership and to deliver it to the buyer. In addition, the vendor is under the obligation to warrant that the animal is free of vices.

---

[35] *Dictionary of the Civil Code,* — word: indivisibilité naturelle, p. 306.

Under these broad facts, the vendor is bound to three different obligations: an obligation to give (transfer the right of ownership) and two obligations to do (deliver the possession of the live animal and provide a warranty against vices). In performing his obligation to give, the vendor could easily transfer the right of ownership of the animal to two or more buyers. Indeed the right of ownership, as an object of an obligation, may be divided into "shares" and each share could be vested in a different person. The obligation to give a real right, such as the right of ownership, may be divided.

On the other hand, the delivery of possession of the animal or the obligation of the vendor to surrender the actual physical control of the live animal cannot be divided into parts without endangering the physical integrity, the life, of the animal. Obviously, if the buyer or buyers wish to purchase a live animal, the obligation to deliver the animal alive cannot be divided.

With respect to the obligation of warranty, the vendor's obligation is to make sure that the buyer will be able to enjoy the use of the animal in exchange for the price the buyer paid. Obviously, this obligation of warranty would be breached if the animal were affected by some disease or illness which would prevent the buyer-owner from making use of it. In other words, this obligation to do, warrant against vices, illnesses, is not susceptible of division because its very object, the warranty, is itself not susceptible of being divided. It either exists or it does not. In this respect, it should not be confused with the coverage of the warranty. The latter may be greater or lesser but the warranty itself, regardless of its coverage, is a whole not susceptible of division.

(b) A buyer gives his vendor a mortgage on the immovable he just bought and agrees to grant a servitude of passage for the benefit of the vendor's estate.[36] Moreover, the buyer promises not to engage in any competitive business activity against his vendor for the next five years.

The granting of a mortgage[37] or of a predial servitude is the giving of a real right. As a matter of principle, real rights are susceptible of division as is the case of the fundamental right of ownership.[38] There are, however, two exceptions to the divisibility of real rights: they are mortgages and predial servitudes.

LSA-C.C. Art. 3280 states that:

> **"Mortgage is an indivisible real right that burdens the entirety of the mortgaged property and that follows the property into whatever hands the property may pass."**

Hence, the nature of a mortgage is made, by law, an item of performance not susceptible of division. The first mortgagee-lender has a mortgage over the "whole" house of the buyer and a second mortgagee also has a mortgage over the same "whole" house. The mortgage is not divisible "into a certain number or type of rooms" in the house!

---

[36] LSA-C.C. Arts. 646, 697, 705: see Appendix.

[37] LSA-C.C. Art. 3278: see Appendix.

[38] LSA-C.C. Art. 477-A: see Appendix.

The same is true of predial servitudes. **LSA-C.C. Art. 652** provides that:

"A predial servitude is indivisible. An estate cannot have upon another estate part of a right of way, or of view, or of any other servitude, nor can an estate be charged with a part of a servitude.

The use of a servitude may be limited to certain days or hours; when limited, it is still an entire right. A servitude is due to the whole of the dominant estate and to all parts of it; if this estate is divided, every acquirer of a part has the right of using the servitude in its entirety."

It follows that, although the right to the predial servitude is an entity which, by law, is not susceptible of division, (*i.e.*) it is vested as a whole or it is not, several beneficiaries could actually make use of that servitude and do it to the fullest extent: the advantages resulting from a predial servitude may be divided, if they are susceptible of division.[39] Our buyer would, therefore, grant his vendor the entirety of the right of way, although the use or advantage of that same right could be granted in full to several persons.

With respect to the buyer's obligation not to compete with his vendor, he has bound himself to an obligation not to do.[40] Obligations not to do are, in principle, naturally indivisible. Indeed, either one abstains from doing something or does something, even so slightly, in breach of that obligation not to do.

The above two examples of absolute natural or legally created natural indivisibility help in formulating some general rules or presumptions regarding this particular kind of indivisible obligation.

The first presumption one can lay down is that obligations to give are, as a matter of principle, divisible in their performance unless the nature of the item of performance makes the obligation indivisible and unless it is one of the two exceptions created by law: mortgages and predial servitudes.

The second presumption governing the subject matter is that obligations not to do are not susceptible of division.

The third presumption involves obligations to do and, with respect to them, it is fair to say that they are frequently divisible, particularly when they spread over a period of time. However, there are also those obligations which are often made indivisible by the intent of the parties.

2. Relative Natural Indivisibility.

An obligation is relatively indivisible whenever its object, although susceptible of material or intellectual/conceptual division, must be considered as being indivisible in relation to, or in light of, the *natural* objective/goal/purpose pursued by the parties. The goal or purpose intended to be achieved by the obligor's performance is the fulfillment of an indivisible object.

Two examples will help illustrate this notion of relative natural indivisibility:

---

[39] LSA-C.C. Art. 653.

[40] On obligations "to do" and "not to do" see supra § 1.2.1.

(a) Suppose that two writers agree to combine their talent and efforts to write a book with their names to appear on the cover page as co-authors. It is expected that these two writers will, somehow, divide the task among themselves and that each one will be responsible for some parts of the book. Yet they mutually owe each other an indivisible obligation of result, to wit: the obligation of completing the task assigned. Furthermore their publisher expects, and has contracted for, a manuscript of a book which will represent the product and result of the writers' commitments. In light of the objective pursued, the publication of a book, it is obvious that the writers' obligation is one of relative indivisibility. Either the book is written or it is not.

(b) Suppose a person enters into a building contract with a builder for the construction of a swimming pool. The material stages in the building of the pool could easily be divided into as many parts as different trades or skills will be involved. Yet the owner is most likely to be concerned exclusively with acquiring the ultimate finished product of the builder's obligation: the pool. The natural objective or purpose of the contract is a completed swimming pool and that objective controls the characterization of the builder's obligation as being an indivisible one.

B.   Conventional Indivisibility.

LSA-C.C. Art. 1815 provides, in part, that "**an obligation is indivisible when the object of the performance (. . .) because of the intent of the parties, is not susceptible of division.**"

By their contract, the parties may provide for an *artificial, fictitious*, or *conceptual* indivisibility of an obligation which, otherwise, would be naturally divisible. The intent of the parties may be to make the *object* of the obligation or *item of performance* indivisible in its fulfillment. Conventional indivisibility strives to conceptually and artificially attach to an object a legal feature which only nature would normally create. Regardless of the number of parties involved, the item of performance cannot be divided between them because their will, their intent, has made it indivisible.

Conventional indivisibility often stands as an exception to the principle that obligations are presumed to be joint whenever multiple parties are involved.[41] Should two obligors be bound to one obligee, the assumption which prevails is that the existing obligation is joint between the obligors, each obligor performing his part of the whole obligation. However, as seen above, the freedom of contract, within the limits of **LSA-C.C. Art. 7,**[42] allows parties to agree to turn the joint obligation into a solidary one.[43] Parties to a contract may also turn a joint obligation involving multiple obligors into an indivisible one; in this sense the intent of all the parties involved is to focus on the item or object of the performance so as to make it indivisible, thereby preventing the obligors from engaging in partial performances. No obligor may merely perform his virile share in the hope of being

---

[41] On Joint Obligations see supra § 3.2.1.

[42] See LSA-C.C. Art. 7 in Appendix.

[43] LSA-C.C. Art. 1796: see Appendix.

released; only performance of the whole, as intended and meant to be indivisible, will extinguish the obligation.

The above analysis referred both to solidarity and indivisibility and may have given the impression that a parallel can easily be drawn between these two institutions of indivisibility and solidarity. Actually **LSA-C.C. Art. 1789-2** appears to call for such a parallel where it provides that "**when a joint obligation is indivisible, joint obligors or obligees are subject to the rules governing solidary obligors or solidary obligees.**"

Although there does exist a definite resemblance between these two twin institutions, it remains that indivisibility and solidarity should be kept separate and distinct one from the other as "**a stipulation of solidarity does not make an obligation indivisible**" (LSA-C.C. 1820). As a survey of the effects of indivisibility will now show, it might be advisable (and it is our advice) to combine these effects with those of solidarity by stipulating that an obligation which is solidary by law or by contract will also be conventionally indivisible; or, vice versa, that an obligation naturally indivisible will also be made solidary by the contractual intent of the parties.

§ 4.4.3.   EFFECTS OF DIVISIBLE AND INDIVISIBLE OBLIGATIONS.

The legal effects of divisibility or indivisibility are governed by the fact that the item of performance may or may not be divided between the multiple obligees of one obligor or between the multiple obligors of one single obligee.

A.   Effects of Divisible Obligations.

The legal regime of a divisible obligation resembles that of a joint obligation whenever the former involves either more than one obligee or more than one obligor.

The principle remains that, as long as one obligee is entitled to an item of performance by one obligor, the latter must perform the obligation as if it were indivisible. [44] However, if the obligee should die, his successors will be considered as multiple obligees and looked upon as joint obliges, each one being entitled to a partial performance. Likewise, should the obligor die, his successors will be presumed to be joint obligors. Under these circumstances, it will become very important to determine whether or not the object of the obligation can be divided between the single obligor's successors, in light of the nature of the obligation or on account of the intent of the original parties to the obligation. In other words, an obligation that was indivisible when entered into initially may become joint and divisible if multiple obligors should take over from the originally single obligor or should the originally indivisible object of an obligation be transformed, by real subrogation, into a divisible object.

---

[44] LSA-C.C. Art. 1816: see Appendix.

The divisibility of an obligation may, therefore, be set *ab initio*, from the beginning, or result from events that may occur over the existence of the obligation. For example: "**A divisible obligation must be divided among successors of the obligor or of the obligee. Each successor of the obligor is liable only for his share of a divisible obligation. Each successor of the obligee is entitled only to his share of a divisible obligation.**" (**LSA-C.C. Art. 1817**).

The divisibility of an obligation among joint obligors presents, obviously, a danger for the obligee. The latter may demand only his share from each one of his joint obligors. It is particularly so after the death of the original obligor since, under the law, that obligor's successors will be bound jointly only. Thus, the obligee may have to bear the risk of loss should one joint obligor be unable to perform. To circumvent this potential future risk, an obligee may demand some type of security to guarantee the payment of the whole obligation. He may also request that the object of the obligation be considered as indivisible until fully performed. Conventional indivisibility may thus be stipulated between the original parties to an obligation so as to prevent, in the future, the divisibility of the item of performance between the successors of the original "single" obligor or the successors of an obligor who was solidarily bound with others, since the bond of solidarity cannot be "inherited," in the sense that it cannot be transferred to the successors of a solidarily bound obligor, so as to bind them in the absence of their consent.

B.   Effects of Indivisible Obligations.

LSA-C.C. Art. 1818 provides that "**an indivisible obligation with more than one obligor or obligee is subject to the rules governing solidary obligations.**" It follows that, whenever an obligation is indivisible, we ought to apply to that obligation the same rules as those which govern the effects of solidary obligations.

The reverse, however, is not true: "**a stipulation of solidarity does not make an obligation indivisible.**" (**LSA-C.C. Art. 1820**). It is important, therefore, to draw the distinction between solidarity and indivisibility and to preserve their particular identity.

1.   Effects of Active Indivisibility or Indivisibility on the Part of Obligees.

Regardless of the source of indivisibility, whenever multiple obligees are owed an indivisible obligation, the item of performance can be claimed in its entirety by any one of the multiple obligees.[45] The bond of law (*vinculum juris*) binding the obligor to indivisible obligees is such that the obligor owes to each individual obligee the performance of the whole object of the obligation. The obligor may not give each obligee a part of an indivisible object. However, once the entire performance has been received by an indivisible obligee, it is incumbent upon that obligee to divide the object of the obligation (if it can be divided) among his co-obligees. The *commodum* (or advantage, opportunity) becomes divisible in the horizontal rela-

---

[45] LSA-C.C. Art. 1790, *a pari ratione*: see Appendix.

tionship between the obligees whereas the *vinculum*, or vertical bond of law between the obligor and his indivisible obligees, is not.

The indivisibility of the *vinculum* leads to the following legal consequences:

(a) should an indivisible obligee interrupt prescription against the obligor, that interruption will benefit all his co-indivisible obligees.[46]

(b) should an indivisible obligee put the obligor in default, that action will benefit all his co-obligees.[47]

(c) an indivisible obligee may not remit the entire debt or novate the whole obligation without the consent of all his co-obligees.[48]

Active indivisibility is a very rare thing. The fact that it enables one obligee to receive the entire performance from the obligor creates a risk that the other co-obligees may not receive their share of the performance should the first obligee somehow fail in his duty to divide the *commodum* among all of them. The same observation can obviously be made about active solidarity which explains why it is as unusual a situation as active indivisibility.

2.   Effects of Passive Indivisibility or Indivisibility on the Part of Obligors.

Passive indivisibility can be looked at as a security device *naturally* or *contractually* given to an obligee by one or more obligors. Passive indivisibility vests in an obligee at least the same rights against his indivisible obligors that passive solidarity would grant him against solidary obligors.[49] Essentially, passive indivisibility entitles the obligee:

(1) to demand the whole indivisible performance from any one of his indivisible obligors,

(2) to interrupt prescription against one indivisible obligor and, thereby, interrupt prescription *vis-à-vis* all of them,[50]

(3) to put in default one of them so as to put in default all of them.

All in all, "**an indivisible obligation is subject to the rules governing solidary obligations**" (**LSA-C.C. Art. 1818**), both with respect to the vertical relationship created between the obligee and the indivisible obligors and with respect to the horizontal relationship existing between the indivisible obligors themselves. And, yet, "a stipulation of solidarity does not make an obligation indivisible" (**LSA-C.C. Art. 1820**). Where, then, is the difference?

---

[46] LSA-C.C. Art. 762, *in pari materia* and *a pari ratione:* see Appendix; Art. 1793, *in pari materia* and *a pari ratione:* see Appendix.

[47] LSA-C.C. Art. 1793, *in pari materia* and *a pari ratione*: see Appendix.

[48] LSA-C.C. Art. 1792, *in pari materia* and *a pari ratione*: see Appendix; LSA-C.C. Art. 1881 a pari ratione: see Appendix; on Novation see infra § 7.3.1.

[49] On Solidarity, see supra § 3.3.1.

[50] LSA-C.C. Art. 3503: see Appendix.

3.   Heritability: Distinguishing Feature Between Indivisibility and Solidarity.

The distinction that must be preserved between indivisibility and solidarity finds its rationale in the different sources of the bonds of law which are created.

Indivisibility finds its *raison d'être* in the object of the obligation, the item of performance, whereas solidarity is related to the number of parties or persons to an obligation. Thus, solidarity is a matter of number of persons/parties to an obligation; indivisibility is a feature of an obligation triggered by the object of the obligation, the item of performance. This difference in the origin of these two types of obligations explains at least one fundamental distinction between them and, possibly, a secondary distinction.

(a) The fundamental difference between these two concepts is that solidarity is not heritable whereas indivisibility is. Any and each heir of an obligee of an indivisible obligation may demand the whole performance of that indivisible obligation. Heirs of a solidary obligee become joint obligees. An heir of an indivisible obligee cannot alone remit the totality of the debt and he cannot, alone, agree to a novation of the object of the obligor's obligation.[51] Should an heir of an obligee of an indivisible obligation remit the debt owed by the obligor,[52] (assuming the "debt" is divisible) his co-heir(s) obligee(s) will be able to demand performance of the indivisible object/item after deducting the share received by the co-heir obligee who remitted the debt.

As regards obligors, solidarity does not prevent the division of a debt between the successors of a solidary obligor. Because solidarity is not heritable the successors of an obligor *in solido* will be held to be joint obligors and each one will be liable for only a share of the obligation.[53]

Indivisibility, on the other hand, prevents the division of the object of an obligation among the successors of the obligor or obligors. The reason is that indivisibility is an inherent legal feature of the object, regardless of whether there is one obligor or multiple obligors. Thus, it is somewhat misleading to state, as broadly as **LSA-C.C. Art. 1818** does, that "**an indivisible obligation . . . is subject to the rules governing solidarity obligations.**" On the other hand, it is quite accurate to state, at least in this respect, that "**a stipulation of solidarity does not make an obligation indivisible.**" (LSA-C.C. Art. 1820).

(b) A secondary distinction between solidarity and indivisibility could arise in the event of a change in the nature of the object of an indivisible obligation.

Let us suppose that two obligors-vendors owe an obligation to deliver a live animal, a horse for example, to their obligee-buyer. The nature of the item of the performance is such that the obligation is indivisible; any one of the two obligors-vendors could be asked to deliver the whole animal. How would this contractual relationship be changed in the event the horse was to die as a result of the fault of

---

[51]   On Novation, see infra § 7.3.1.

[52]   On Remission of debt, see infra § 7.4.1.

[53]   LSA-C.C. Arts. 1789, 1794: see Appendix.

one of the two indivisible obligors-vendors? Dismissing here the issue of legal solidarity between joint tortfeasors,[54] it remains that damages will have to be paid to the obligee-buyer in lieu of the delivery of the animal. The payment of damages is the transfer of a sum of money which, in itself and by nature, is a divisible object. Thus, previously bound to deliver an indivisible object, the horse, the obligors must now deliver a divisible thing, money.

The question which arises, then, is the following: have the formerly indivisible obligors of the obligation to deliver an animal remained indivisible obligors for the payment of the damages or have they been transformed into solidary obligors or, still, have they become joint obligors?

Several possible answers can be suggested:

(i) A first answer would consist in saying that the previously indivisible obligors have become "**solidarily liable for the resulting damages**" (**LSA-C.C. Art. 1800**). This answer would find its justification in **LSA-C.C. Art. 1818**,[55] which states that an indivisible obligation is governed by the rules of solidarity. Thus, by operation of law, the indivisible bond that nature had imposed on the obligors because of the kind of item of performance involved (the animal), has been transformed into a personal relationship of solidarity for the payment of damages.

(ii) A second conceivable answer would be to state that indivisibility would survive the disappearance of the original indivisible object. Such secondary indivisibility could be justified either on the ground that the obligors, rather than the obligee, should bear the consequences of the fault of one of them or on the ground that there took place a sort of legal *real subrogation*, whereby a thing is substituted to another thing and takes on the legal feature of the original object.[56]

(iii) A third answer would take into account the fact that the obligation to pay damages is a naturally divisible obligation between joint obligors. Each joint obligor would then owe his share of the damages. Such a suggestion would eventually place the risk of loss on the obligee, who might not be able to recover the damages from one of the two obligors, and it would compel the obligee to divide his right of action between the two joint obligors. All in all, this third answer might turn out to be detrimental to an obligee who, at the outset, enjoyed an advantageous position under the form of an indivisible obligation owed by his obligors.

In conclusion, it appears to us that, under the factual circumstances given, the first answer should be preferred over the others because it rests on sound rules of law without violating recognized principles of equity. Furthermore, in order to avoid and prevent these kinds of situations from occurring, it is advisable for an obligee to secure the benefits of solidarity and indivisibility by contractually stipulating that the performance of the obligation will be considered altogether "*solidary and indivisible*" regardless, either of the nature of the item of the performance or of the number of obligors involved at the time the obligation is entered into.

---

[54] LSA-C.C. Art. 2324.

[55] LSA-C.C. Arts. 1800, 1818: see Appendix.

[56] LSA-C.C. Art. 1825, *a pari ratione*: see Appendix.

Chapter 5

TRANSFER OF OBLIGATIONS LSA-C.C. ARTS. 1821 TO 1830

An obligation has been defined as a legal relationship binding a person to render a performance [either to give or to do or not to do something] in favor of another.[1] This very same legal relationship creative of an obligation can, itself, become the object of new obligation. In other words, an existing obligation can become a thing or an object of a juridical act such as a contract.[2]

As an example one can cite the contract of novation[3] which has for its object "**the extinguishment of an existing obligation by the substitution of a new one**" (**LSA-C.C. Art. 1879**). In this particular instance, there is creation of a conjunctive[4] obligation which binds the parties to extinguish an existing obligation and to create another one different from the former.

The fact that an obligation may become the object of another obligation suggests that parties may enter into juridical acts for the purpose of transferring an obligation from one party to another party or, even, to a third person. Such a transfer of obligations may occur in many ways, three of which will be studied here. A transfer of obligations may take place by an assumption of obligations or by means of subrogation or, still, by way of an assignment of credit.

ARTICLE 1

ASSUMPTION OF OBLIGATIONS

An assumption of an obligation is a juridical act which involves three parties at least. Two of these parties are already bound to each other when a third one agrees to take upon himself the debt or obligation of one of the original two parties. After an analysis of the concept of assumption and its purposes, we shall discuss the two different kinds of assumption governed by the Civil Code.

---

[1] LSA-C.C. Art. 1756: see Appendix.

[2] The ambiguity of the language of LSA-C.C. Art. 1977, and the use of the word "obligation" in particular, can be interpreted to refer to an existing obligation becoming the object of another "obligation": see Appendix.

[3] On Novation, see infra § 7.3.1.

[4] On Conjunctive Obligations, see supra Chapter 4.

§ 5.1.1. CONCEPT AND PURPOSES OF AN ASSUMPTION OF OBLIGATIONS.

Two examples will help illustrate this concept. At the same time, they will provide a justification for its existence and usefulness as a means of transfer of obligations.

> Example 1: Let us suppose, first, that Paulus is indebted to Ulpian; we assume, then, that Paulus obtains from Gaius the commitment that Gaius will pay Ulpian the debt originally owed by Paulus.

Paulus will be considered as the obligor, Ulpian will be the obligee and Gaius will be the third person-obligor. Paulus and Gaius have entered into an assumption whereby they have agreed that Gaius will assume the role of obligor held by Paulus originally.[5]

> Example 2: Let us suppose that, initially, the same three persons are involved so that Paulus is the obligor, Ulpian is the obligee and Gaius is the third person. The second assumption contemplates that Ulpian obtains from Gaius that he will commit himself to perform, for the benefit of Ulpian, the obligation originally owed by Paulus.

> The obligee, Ulpian, and Gaius, the third person, have agreed on "an assumption by the latter [Gaius] of an obligation owed by another [Paulus] to the former [Ulpian] . . . " (**LSA-C.C. Art. 1823**).

These two examples, illustrative of the two basic forms of assumptions of obligations, show very clearly that an assumption may serve two important and different purposes: first of all, an assumption of an obligation may provide a creditor-obligee with a kind of surety, where he may have had none before, since he may now call on two different obligors (the original obligor and the third person who assumes the obligation) to perform the same obligation. The second purpose of an assumption of an obligation is that, depending on the circumstances, it may be used to extinguish a <u>preexisting</u> obligation that binds the obligor and the third person. It is, indeed, quite conceivable that the third person (Gaius) might be indebted to the obligor (Paulus) on the basis of a preexisting obligation and that, through an assumption by Gaius of Paulus' obligation *vis-à-vis* his own obligee Ulpian, the third person (Gaius) might wish to extinguish his own prior debt *vis-à-vis* Paulus.

§ 5.1.2. ASSUMPTION OF AN OBLIGATION BY AGREEMENT BETWEEN AN OBLIGOR AND A THIRD PERSON.

A. Requirements for a Valid Assumption Between the Obligor and the Third Person.

The first paragraph of **LSA-C.C. Art. 1821** provides that "**an obligor and a third person may agree to an assumption by the latter of an obligation of the former. To be enforceable by the obligee against the third person, the**

---

[5] LSA-C.C. Art. 1821: see Appendix.

agreement must be made in writing."

1. The Parties and the Requirements for a Valid Assumption.

To be binding between the obligor and the third person, the juridical act of assumption must meet all the requirements for a valid contract. [6] The requirements of capacity to enter into a juridical act and of cause, or reason for binding oneself by a juridical act, are particularly important here. The third person who agrees to assume an obligation binding on somebody else must have the capacity to dispose of his own patrimony or assets; that third person must enjoy more than the mere capacity to administer his own affairs. The reason is that an assumption of obligations will make the third person liable under the same conditions as the obligor is liable, and if the latter must have the capacity to dispose of her assets, so must the third person.

As to the cause of the agreement of assumption between the obligor and the third person it must be lawful.[7] The cause of that agreement, or the apparently objective reason for it, will normally be the intent to extinguish the debt owed by the obligor to his obligee. On the face of it, this is what the third person binds herself to do on behalf of the obligor and, as a matter of principle, there is nothing unlawful about such a cause.[8]

One must however inquire beyond this objective reason or cause and investigate the subjective motive, reason or intent of the parties.

The subjective and real reason or motive prompting the third person to assume the obligor's obligation vis-à-vis the obligee might actually be that the third person is herself indebted to the obligor on account of a prior legal relationship. By agreeing to assume the obligor's obligation vis-à-vis the obligee, the third person will, at the same time, extinguish that obligor's obligation vis-à-vis the obligee and her own obligation vis-à-vis that same obligor who is also her own obligee. Two obligations will be simultaneously extinguished by one performance.

Another reason or cause which might prompt the third person to assume the obligor's obligation, so as to extinguish it, might be a gratuitous one. Quite simply stated, the intent of the third person to make a donation to her obligor by agreeing to perform the latter's obligation towards the obligee can be a valid cause. In this instance, the element of cause must be carefully scrutinized to ascertain its lawfulness. Indeed, the obligor and the third person could not do indirectly by an agreement of assumption of obligations what they might otherwise be prohibited by law from doing directly, *i.e.*, donate to each other.

Although the agreement of assumption is entered into between the obligor and the third person, it is necessary that the instrument be in writing so that the agreement of assumption can be submitted to the obligee to be enforceable by him

---

[6] LSA-C.C. Arts. 1915 *et seq.*

[7] LSA-C.C. Art. 1966: see Appendix.

[8] LSA-C.C. Art. 1855: see Appendix.

against the third person.[9] In a sense, the obligee becomes a party to a contract, or agreement, that includes a stipulation for the benefit of another.[10] The agreement is submitted to the obligee for his consent so as to vest in him the benefit of having now two obligors on whom he may call, and who, in addition, are bound *in solido*.[11]

2. Form of the Agreement of Assumption.

Article 1821 of the Civil Code requires that this agreement of assumption be in writing in order to be enforceable by the obligee against the third person. This requirement parallels the broader requirement of a writing needed to prove a promise to pay the debt of a third person.[12] An assumption of an obligation is tantamount to a promise to pay such a debt of another.

Would the lack of a writing cause the assumption to be *non-existent* to the point of barring the creation of any right whatsoever in the obligee? Would the third person be relieved of any obligation at all? Reasoning *a pari ratione* on **LSA-C.C. Art. 1762**[13] and in *pari materia* on paragraph 3 in particular, it is possible to make the argument that the absence of a writing would not prevent a natural obligation, at least, from arising from the circumstances so that the third person might feel bound by a moral duty to render the expected performance[14] which, under the "circumstances," could amount to a natural obligation. That same natural obligation could then become the onerous cause of a subsequent contract, binding the third person to perform the obligation owed by the obligor to the obligee.[15]

B. Effects of an Assumption Between the Obligor and the Third Person.

Two sets of effects result from this form of an assumption of obligations: the first set of effects concerns the relationship between the third person and the obligor, whereas the second set of effects flows from the relationship between the third person and the obligee.

1. Effects Between the Obligor and the Third Person [Assuming Obligor].

This bilateral relationship gives rise, actually, to two sub-sets of effects, some taking place between the third person and the obligor and others occurring in the relationship between the obligee and the obligor.

(a) As far as the third person and the obligor are concerned, the former may have entered into the assumption in order to extinguish a debt he himself owes to

---

[9] LSA-C.C. Art. 1821-1: see Appendix.

[10] LSA-C.C. Art. 1978: see Appendix.

[11] See Effects of an Assumption Between the Obligor and the Third Person infra, § 5.1.2.

[12] LSA-C.C. Art. 1847.

[13] See Art. 1762 in Appendix.

[14] LSA-C.C. Art. 1760; see Natural Obligations supra § 1.3.1.

[15] LSA-C.C. Art. 1761: see Appendix.

the latter on account of some prior juridical act or fact. It is obvious, then, that the extinction of this debt between the third person and the obligor will depend on the legal regime of that debt as well as be contingent upon the contents of the new contractual agreement made necessary by the assumption itself.

Let us suppose, for example, that the obligation owed by the third person-assuming obligor to the original obligor was subject to a suspensive term,[16] which has not yet occurred when the assumption agreement is entered into. In this situation, the assumption agreement might provide that the third person-assuming obligor is waiving the benefit of the term stipulated in his favor so that compensation, in full or in part, could take place.[17] On the other hand the third person-assuming obligor may not wish to waive the benefit of the term stipulated in his favor because the obligation that his own original obligor owes him, should he perform the primary obligation *vis-à-vis* the original principal obligee, might have some tax advantages for him.

An additional effect flowing from the relationship between the third person-assuming obligor and the original obligor centers around the existence, *vel non*, of that third person-assuming obligor's right of contribution. In this respect, we believe that it is somewhat misleading to state, in a broad manner, that *"if the assuming obligor is also a debtor of the original obligor, he has no right to contribution, after performing the obligation, by analogical application of the principle of revised C.C. Art. 1804."*[18] Actually, the absence of a right to contribution might be explained by Art. 1822-1[19] in circumstances where the assuming obligor is bound only to the extent of his own debt to the original obligor or to the extent of the debt he is willing to assume.

In contrast with the above situation wherein the third person-assuming obligor is himself a debtor of the original obligor, it may happen that an assumption of obligation will be entered into by the third person-assuming obligor in order to make a donation to the original obligor. The agreement of assumption may amount to a donation by the assuming obligor to the original obligor by means of the performance undertaken directly by the assuming obligor for the benefit of the obligee. This tripartite agreement of assumption will find its cause or reason in the gratuitous intent of the third person-assuming obligor, now the donor, vis-à-vis the obligor, now the donee. To the extent that this gratuitous motivation or cause is lawful, the agreement of assumption itself will be valid.

(b) The second sub-set of effects of this form of assumption illustrates the originality of this means of transfer of obligations. This assumption of an obligation does not release the original obligor of his own debt *vis-à-vis* the obligee.[20] An assumption does not amount to a remission of debt,[21] nor is it the equivalent of a

---

[16] LSA-C.C. Art. 1777 *et seq.*: see Appendix; see Term supra, § 2.2-A.1.

[17] LSA-C.C. Art. 1893 *et seq.*; see Art. 1893 in Appendix.

[18] Comment (c) of LSA-C.C. Art. 1821; see Art. 1821 in Appendix; see Art. 1804 in Appendix.

[19] LSA-C.C. Art. 1822: see Appendix.

[20] LSA-C.C. Art. 1821: see Appendix.

[21] LSA-C.C. Art. 1888 *et seq.*; on Remission of Debt, see infra § 7.4.1.

novation.[22] The original obligor remains bound to his obligee. The agreement of assumption he entered into with the third person-assuming obligor amounted to providing the obligee with an additional obligor with whom he is bound solidarily vis-à-vis the obligee.

2. Effects Between the Obligee and the Co-Obligors (Original and Assuming Obligors).

It is in this particular relationship that an assumption has its most important effects and where, actually, one can best grasp the *raison d'être* of this institution.

The third person-assuming obligor agrees to take upon himself the obligation of the original obligor and to stand as an obligor vis-à-vis the obligee. Moreover, this third person-assuming obligor becomes, by law, solidarily liable with the original obligor. **"The unreleased obligor remains solidarily bound with the third person"** states **LSA-C.C. Art. 1821-3**.

This general reference to solidarity[23] and its application to an assumption of obligations are qualified, however, by particular rules governing an assumption between obligors. These rules are such that they appear to establish, or revive rather, a distinction which used to be made between perfect solidarity and what was called, once upon a time, imperfect solidarity.[24]

The first particular and relevant rule is stated in **LSA-C.C. Art. 1822-1**: **"A person who, by agreement with the obligor, assumes the obligation of the latter is bound only to the extent of his assumption."** This rule stands in sharp contrast with the rule stated in **LSA-C.C. Art. 1794**: **"An obligation is solidary for the obligors when each obligor is liable for the whole performance. A performance rendered by one of the solidary obligors relieves the others of liability toward the obligee."** It follows from the *sui generis* rule of Art. 1822-1 that the third person-assuming obligor is not bound towards the obligee beyond the amount of his own obligation towards the original obligor, barring, of course, any agreement to the contrary.

One additional consequence of this particular rule is that an obligation which may have been indivisible between the original obligor and the obligee may now become divisible as a result of this rule governing solidarity, hence indivisibility, in an assumption. It follows that even **LSA-C.C. Art. 1818**[25] may have to be disregarded whenever an assumption of obligations is involved. However, it can be said that a particular type of solidarity applies to an assumption of obligations between the obligor and the third person-assuming obligor because the obligee has to express

---

[22] LSA-C.C. Art. 1879 *et seq.*; on Novation, see infra § 7.3.1.

[23] On Solidarity, see supra § 3.3.1. The use of the verb "remain" in this Art. is improper. Indeed, the two obligors, original and assuming, were most likely not "initially" bound solidarily. They became bound by the contract of assumption, and it is this contract that creates the bond of solidarity between them. So, instead of "remains," we should have "is" and the sentence should read: "The unreleased obligor is solidarily bound . . . ."

[24] See supra Solidarity § 3.3.1; since the Louisiana Supreme Court did away with this concept of imperfect solidarity, it will not be discussed here.

[25] See LSA-C.C. Art. 1818 in Appendix.

his consent to the agreement of assumption. When expressing his consent the obligee acquires the benefit of solidarity between two obligors, although they may not be bound to the same extent, whereas he had only one obligor from whom to claim the performance before the assumption was entered into.

A second particular rule deviating from the principle of solidarity is stated in **LSA-C.C. Art. 1822-2: "The assuming obligor may raise any defense based on the contract by which the assumption was made**." The contract by which an assumption was/is made has for its cause the contractual relationship which exists between the original obligor and the third person-assuming obligor. In other words, this contractual relationship may provide the third person-assuming obligor with defenses he could raise against the obligee on grounds which, under the rules of solidarity, could be raised only between the solidary obligors themselves.[26] A reason for this particular rule of solidarity here is that the obligee had to express his consent to the agreement of assumption thereby becoming aware of the defenses that the third person-assuming obligor could raise on the basis of the contract of assumption.

§ 5.1.3.   ASSUMPTION OF AN OBLIGATION BY AGREEMENT BETWEEN THE OBLIGEE AND A THIRD PERSON.

LSA-C.C. Art. 1823 states that "[a]n obligee and a third person may agree on an assumption by the latter of an obligation owed by another to the former. That agreement must be made in writing. That agreement does not effect a release of the original obligor."

This form of assumption involves only two parties and, because it amounts to an agreement to pay the debt of another, it must be in writing,[27] as **LSA-C.C. Art. 1823** emphasizes in this particular instance.

A.   The Agreement of Assumption: Its Parties and Its Cause.

An assumption of the original obligor's obligation by an agreement between the obligee and the third person-assuming obligor is a unilateral onerous contract between the latter two parties.[28] The involvement of the original obligor is not necessary and, actually, this form of assumption may take place without the original obligor's knowledge.

By such an agreement, the third person-assuming obligor binds himself towards the obligee to substitute his own performance to that which was to be rendered by the original obligor.[29] This agreement must, therefore, meet all the requirements for a valid contract, the requirement of cause in particular.[30]

---

[26] See LSA-C.C. Art. 1804 in Appendix.

[27] LSA-C.C. Art. 1847: see Appendix.

[28] LSA-C.C. Art. 1907: see Appendix.

[29] LSA-C.C. Art. 1855: see Appendix.

[30] LSA-C.C. Art. 1966 *et seq.*

Where is the cause of that agreement to be found? Must it be uncovered out of the contractual relationship binding the third person-assuming obligor to the obligee or must it be found in the agreement binding the original obligor to the obligee? It is important to state at this point, once again, that this form of assumption of obligation does not release the original obligor of his debt towards his obligee.[31] It follows, then, that the agreement of assumption between the obligee and the third person-assuming obligor may not have for its cause or reason to extinguish the debt between the original obligor and the obligee since the obligor will not be released by the mere existence of this agreement.

It appears, on the other hand, that the cause of the agreement of assumption can be found, in part, in the legal relationship binding the original obligor to the obligee. That cause consists mainly in the agreement of assumption becoming an accessory contract to guarantee the performance of the principal contract between the original obligor and the obligee. A further argument in support of this assertion can be found in the rule which, in the silence of the law, would state that, under this form of assumption, the third person-assuming obligor does not become a solidary debtor with the original obligor. The original obligor is not bound by a contract to the assuming obligor and in the absence of the existence of a legal bond of solidarity, only a contract could create that bond between two obligors.

Can the cause of the agreement of assumption be found in the relationship between the original obligor and the third person-assuming obligor?

That cause may be a *gratuitous* one, meaning that the assuming obligor is motivated by an *animus donandi* or intent to make a donation to the original obligor. That cause can also be an *onerous* one to the extent that the third person-assuming obligor could be indebted to the original obligor. If the cause of the agreement of assumption is to be found in the legal relationship between the original obligor and the third person-assuming obligor, it ought to follow that the validity of the agreement of assumption would be contingent upon the lawfulness of the contractual relationship existing between the assuming obligor and the original obligor. Yet, **LSA-C.C. Art. 1824-1** states that the third person-assuming obligor cannot raise against the obligee any defense based on the relationship between himself and the original obligor. An error that the assuming obligor could have made in contracting with the original obligor (error as the person of the donee-obligor, for example, if the assuming obligor meant to carry out his obligation *vis-à-vis* the obligee as a donation for the benefit of the original obligor) could not be raised as a defense in an action brought by the obligee against the assuming obligor.

It appears, therefore, that the cause of the agreement of assumption between the third person-assuming obligor and the obligee cannot be found in the relationship between the two obligors. That agreement of assumption between the obligee and the third person-assuming obligor seems to be independent from the contractual relationship existing between the two obligors. Where is, then, the cause of the agreement of assumption?

---

[31] LSA-C.C. Art. 1823: see Appendix.

It is certain that this agreement of assumption must have a cause to be a valid binding agreement although that cause need not be expressed.[32] That cause is to be found in the original and principal agreement binding the original obligor to the obligee. It is a fact that, in the absence of that original and principal agreement, the agreement of assumption would not exist or that it would take on a different name and be subject to different requirements. The cause of that original and principal agreement serves also as the cause of the agreement of assumption. It is possible, then, to understand why **"the assuming obligor may raise any defense based on the relationship between the original obligor and the obligee. He may not invoke compensation based on an obligation owed by the obligee to the original obligor."** And why **"[a] person who, by agreement with the obligee, has assumed another's obligation may not raise against the obligee any defense based on the relationship between the assuming obligor and the original obligor."**[33]

B.   Assumption of Obligations, Novation, and Assignment of Credit or Rights.

The LSA-C.C. Articles on novation[34] have done away with novation of creditors *per se* for the reason that the effects of such a kind of novation can be achieved through an assignment of right or credit.[35]

Has this new form of transfer of obligation by means of an assumption become, then, a substitute for the former institution of novation of creditors now written out of the Civil Code?

The answer appears, to us, to be in the negative, mainly because some of the requirements which governed a novation of creditors cannot be found today in an assumption of obligations. Such was the case, for example, of the requirement of consent of a debtor to a novation of creditors; that consent is not required of the original obligor in an assumption of obligations between the obligee and the third person-assuming obligor.

Is an agreement of assumption of obligations between the obligee and the third person-assuming obligor the same thing, then, as an assignment or transfer of credit?

Again, we believe that the answer should be in the negative. Indeed, if the novation of creditors was deleted from the Civil Code on the ground that its effects could be achieved just as well by an assignment of credit, it is obvious that an assumption of obligations between the obligee and the assuming obligor could not be made a substitute for a novation of obligees-creditors. It follows necessarily that an assumption of obligations between the obligee and the third person-assuming obligor must also be different from an assignment of credit.

---

[32] LSA-C.C. Arts. 1966, 1969.

[33] LSA-C.C. Art. 1824 (2-1).

[34] LSA-C.C. Arts. 1879 *et seq.* new in 1984–1985. See Appendix; see Novation infra § 7.3.1.

[35] LSA-C.C. Arts. 2642 *et seq.*

The essence of this type of agreement of assumption of obligations is to add the third person-assuming obligor to the original obligor for the benefit of the obligee. The latter party, when entering into this agreement of assumption, contracts more to obtain a *security*, a back-up obligor, than wanting to transfer or assign his credit to the assuming obligor after he has been paid by the latter. Most likely, the obligee is more concerned with the preservation of his rights against the original obligor, whom he may want to sue and can still sue for the whole performance, than with disposing of his credit at a discount, as is the case in most instances of an assignment of credit. Furthermore, an assuming obligor may raise against the obligee the defenses, which the original obligor himself could raise if sued by his obligee.[36] On the contrary, a transferee of an assignment of credit immediately becomes an obligee-creditor, and it is against him that the defenses and exceptions could be raised. It appears, furthermore, that such an agreement of assumption of obligations between the obligee and the third person-assuming obligor can take place without the consent of and without any notification to the original obligor.[37] On the other hand, an assignment of credit or of a right requires notification to the obligor.[38]

C.   The Requirement of Form.

LSA-C.C. Art. 1823 makes an agreement of assumption between the obligee and the assuming obligor a formal contract, since it requires that the agreement be in writing. The same article does not specify the type of writing required. It would seem, therefore, that either an act under private signature or an authentic act would fulfill the requirement.[39] (**LSA-C.C. Arts. 1832, 1833, 1837**).

This formality of a writing is imposed by the rules of evidence and Civil Code Article 1847, in particular. An assumption, being a promise to pay the debt of another, cannot be proven by mere oral evidence. The protection of the assuming obligor from a frivolous testimony of unreliable witnesses is best assured by this requirement of a writing.[40]

D.   Effects of an Agreement of Assumption Between Obligee and Assuming Obligor.

The effects of such an agreement must be examined from two different perspectives since the agreement of assumption will have effects with respect to three parties at least: the obligee, the third person-assuming obligor and the original obligor. It is appropriate to examine, first of all, the immediate effects of the agreement of assumption between the obligee and the assuming obligor and, second, the effects of this same agreement in the relationship between the two obligors.

---

[36] LSA-C.C. Art. 1824: see Appendix.

[37] Reasoning *a contrario sensu* on LSA-C.C. Art. 1823 and *in pari materia* with Art. 1821.

[38] LSA-C.C. Art. 2643: see Appendix.

[39] LSA-C.C. Art. 1823: see Appendix; see also Arts. 1832, 1833, 1837 in Appendix.

[40] LSA-C.C. Art. 1847, see Appendix; for an exception to this requirement see infra Proof of Obligations § 6.1.

1. Effects of the Agreement Between Obligee and Third Party Assuming Obligor.

The first negative effect or consequence of this agreement is that it does not release the original obligor.[41] The latter has not been involved in negotiations between the obligee and the assuming obligor and, therefore, his personal situation *vis-à-vis* the obligee ought not to be changed without his participation. The original obligor may be strongly motivated by a feeling of pride or honor in wanting to perform his own obligation, or he might not wish that a particular third person-assuming obligor become, in turn, a substituted obligee because he might fear being indebted to that assuming obligor turned obligee. Thus, although the agreement of assumption could eventually benefit the original obligor, he must remain free to reject that benefit if he has good reasons to object to it, so as to remain bound toward his original obligee only.

A second important negative effect of this form of agreement of assumption is that it does not make the original obligor and the assuming obligor solidarily bound to the obligee. Solidarity between the two obligors is not imposed by law in this instance, in contrast with the other form of assumption, and it cannot be presumed since the original obligor may not have been a party to the agreement of assumption. Although solidarity is rejected in this instance of assumption of obligations it remains that the original obligor and the assuming obligor owe the same thing notwithstanding that their obligations derive from different sources.[42] How to explain, then, the two provisions of Civil Code Article 1824, which incorporate some effects of solidarity? Would not it have been more appropriate to reinstitute here the concept of imperfect solidarity (*in solidum* solidarity) to preserve the principal effects of solidarity, which benefit the obligee, while doing away with its secondary effects which are protective of the interests of the obligors? Why penalize the obligee, now deprived of the benefit of solidarity, when a compromise, protective of the rights of all concerned, could have been devised by a regime of imperfect solidarity?

A third effect of the agreement of assumption between the obligee and the assuming obligor is that the agreement entitles the assuming obligor to "**raise any defense based on the relationship between the original obligor and obligee.**" (**LSA-C.C. Art. 1824-2**). This particular provision well illustrates the accessory or secondary nature of the assuming obligor's obligation and points out that his obligation is conditional upon the validity of the primary obligation binding the original obligor to the obligee. However, strictly personal defenses remain available only to a particular party. Although **LSA-C.C. Art. 1824** only mentions the personal defense of compensation as being available exclusively to the original obligor, it must be assumed (*a pari ratione*) that other purely personal defenses should be treated likewise.

A fourth effect of the agreement of assumption between the obligee and the assuming obligor is that the relationship between the assuming obligor and the original obligor is made *res inter alios acta* (a thing done between others). The

---

[41] LSA-C.C. Art. 1823: see Appendix.

[42] LSA-C.C. Arts. 1794, 1797: see Appendix.

assuming obligor cannot rely on that relationship to raise defenses against the obligee. By assuming an obligation, the third person-assuming obligor has agreed to be bound as the original obligor is bound, and it is obvious that the latter could not be permitted to enter into an agreement with a third person so as to create new defenses he could raise against his obligee. Likewise the assuming obligor cannot find in his relationship with the original obligor some excuses for not performing.

2.   Effects of This Form of Agreement of Assumption in the Relationship Between the Two Obligors.

Two different situations must be discussed here.

In the first instance, we will assume that the obligee has obtained performance from his original obligor. In such a case the original obligor is obviously released of his obligation and, with the extinction of the principal obligation, the assumed obligation also ceases to exist. The accessory contract of assumption follows, here again, the fate of the principal contract.[43]

Where, in the second instance, the obligee had to call on the assuming obligor to obtain performance of the obligation owed to him, the assuming obligor may have a cause of action against the original obligor. That cause of action will be determined by the particular nature of the legal relationship binding the two obligors. That relationship might have arisen, for example, from a sub-sale between the original obligor (sub-seller) and the assuming obligor (sub-purchaser) of the obligee-seller. On the other hand, that relationship could have been a gratuitous one should the assuming obligor have intended to make a donation to the original obligor by performing gratuitously the latter's obligation toward the obligee. A third type of relationship could arise from the assuming obligor performing the obligation of the original obligor and being subrogated into the rights of the obligee against the original obligor.[44] (**LSA-C.C. Art. 1855**).

In conclusion, the effects of the relationship between the two obligors are determined by the particular nominate or innominate, gratuitous or onerous, contract that binds them.

ARTICLE 2

PERSONAL SUBROGATION

The concept of personal subrogation, a legal fiction, needs to be described before its two different forms can be analyzed and the particular effects of each form are laid out.

---

[43] *Accessorium sequitur principale.* See: *Dictionary of the Civil Code*, Index of Legal Adages, p. 659.

[44] LSA-C.C. Art. 1855-2: see Appendix.

§ 5.2.1. CONCEPT OF SUBROGATION.[45]

LSA-C.C. Article 1825 defines subrogation in these terms: "**Subrogation is the substitution of one person to the rights of another. It may be conventional or legal**." The *Dictionary of the Civil Code* informs us that "subrogation" comes from the Latin word "subrogare," meaning to subrogate or to place someone in place of another, to elect a replacement. The following definition of "personal subrogation" follows: "In a broad sense, substitution of one person to another in a legal relationship in order to entitle the former to exercise all or some of the rights belonging to the latter."[46]

Subrogation can thus be described as a legal device meant to cause a person to be placed in the shoes of another. A legal fiction is thus created whereby an obligation or a right is declared to survive in a person other than the original party following the performance of the original obligation. This is why "subrogation" amounts to the transfer of an obligation. For example, an obligee-creditor called *subrogee-solvens* (subrogee because he is subrogated and solvens because he has performed an obligation) can be substituted to another creditor, the original *obligee-accipiens*, (accipiens because he has received the benefit of the performance of an obligation), so that the obligor is now indebted to the subrogee-solvens who extinguished the obligation owed to the accipiens by performing in the place of the original obligor. Subrogation is, therefore, both a mode of extinction of an obligation and a method of transfer of that same obligation.

A very simple illustration of this concept will help clarify its internal mechanism. Let us suppose that Gaius is indebted to Ulpian in the amount of 1,000; let us assume, also, that Paulus is a good friend of Gaius and wants to spare him the threats and harsh words that Ulpian is constantly voicing at Gaius. Paulus may be allowed to pay Gaius' debt to Ulpian and obtain from Ulpian that he (Paulus) be subrogated into Ulpian's rights against Gaius. Ulpian would drop out of the picture and Paulus would become Gaius' creditor.

This simple illustration points out that a subrogation assumes a performance made by a third party (subrogee-solvens) with the intent of seeking some form of reimbursement of his own performance from the obligor. Essential to the notion of subrogation is the *animus obligandi* (intent to bind) of the subrogee-solvens who performs the obligation of another with the intent to bind that other. It is that intent which will trigger, in part, the transfer of the obligation from the original obligee-accipiens to the benefit of the subrogee-solvens and substitute the latter into the shoes of the former.

The *raison d'être* and justification for this concept of subrogation are to be found in the shifting of the rights of action available to an obligee-accipiens to the benefit of the subrogee-solvens against the obligor. Whenever a third person pays the debt of another, unless that third person was motivated by a gratuitous intent (*animus donandi*) and meant, therefore, to make a gift to the obligor by extinguishing his

---

[45] Subrogation: from the latin *subrogare* (*sub+rogare*) meaning to choose someone in the place of another, substitute someone to another.

[46] *Dictionary of the Civil Code*, — word: subrogation, p. 537.

debt, the third person will have a right of action for reimbursement against the obligor.

This right of action for reimbursement may be justified and supported in many different ways:

1) It might be justified on the ground that the third person (solvens) acted under a *mandate* from the obligor who must, thereafter, **"reimburse the mandatary for the expenses and charges he has incurred and to pay him the remuneration to which he is entitled"** (**LSA-C.C. Art. 3012**).

2) The payment made by the third person (solvens) could also be explained by that third person's intent to manage the affairs of another, the obligor's affairs.[47]

3) A third possible justification could be found in the third person's intent to create a contract of loan between himself and the obligor by advancing the amount of the debt in paying the obligee.[48]

4) A fourth possible justification can be found in the theory of unjust enrichment (*de in rem verso*) since it could be said that the obligor has been enriched at the expense of the third person-solvens who spared him, temporarily, the payment of his debt.[49]

Whatever the justification we select to explain the right of action of the solvens against the obligor, it remains that in itself and by itself this right of action could not be secured by any surety, mortgage or privilege. On the other hand, it is conceivable that the claim that the creditor-accipiens had against his obligor was a secured claim. In that case it would be in the interest of the solvens to be *substituted, subrogated* into the guarantees, sureties, and/or security devices the creditor-accipiens had against his obligor. The ultimate purpose of subrogation is, therefore, to transfer from the creditor-accipiens to the subrogee-solvens, the rights, actions and accessory rights (mortgages, sureties etc. . . .) that the creditor held against his obligor.

A transfer of obligations by way of subrogation can occur in two ways: by contract or by law.

§ 5.2.2. SOURCES OF SUBROGATION.

Article 1825 of the **LSA-C.C.** states that **"[s]ubrogation is the substitution of one person to the rights of another. It may be conventional or legal."**

A. Conventional Subrogation.

A conventional subrogation can result from a contract between the obligee-accipiens and the third person-solvens. Such a conventional subrogation granted by the obligee or creditor is known as *ex parte creditoris*, or subrogation on the part

---

[47] Management of Another's Affairs or *Negotiorum Gestio*; LSA-C.C. Arts. 2292 *et seq.*

[48] Loan for Use, LSA-C.C. Arts. 2891 *et seq.*

[49] LSA-C.C. Art. 2298; Enrichment Without Cause; Section 1 General Principles.

of the creditor. The second type of conventional subrogation can be the outcome of a contract between the obligor-debtor and the third person; in this case, the subrogation is described as *ex parte debitoris*, on the part of the debtor.

1. Conventional Subrogation by the Creditor (Ex Parte Creditoris).

Article 1827 of the **LSA-C.C.** describes this form of subrogation in these words: **"An obligee who receives performance from a third person may subrogate that person to the rights of the obligee, even without the obligor's consent. That subrogation is subject to the rules governing the assignment of rights."**

The validity of this form of conventional subrogation is conditioned on the existence of some requirements:

(a) Express Agreement.

The agreement between the obligee-accipiens and the third person-solvens must include an express or clear reference to the right of subrogation since the obligee is not required under the law to grant it to the third person.[50] The latter has no right to being subrogated outside the specific cases of subrogation by operation of law. A third person-solvens may only request, but not demand, that the obligee agree to grant him the benefit of subrogation. Thus, if subrogation is to be granted by the obligee, both he and the third person-solvens must override any presumption that the obligee did not intend to subrogate the third person in his rights against the obligor. The agreement involved must be clear and specific with respect to the right of subrogation.

(b) Form.

No particular form or formality is required and a writing is not even necessary. Since such a subrogation is very much like an assignment of credit, consent, which is sufficient to transfer a credit, ought to be sufficient by itself to vest subrogation in the third person. It would remain, nevertheless, that the burden of proof could be a difficult one for the third person-solvens to carry. For that reason it is strongly advised to record the right of subrogation in a written instrument.[51]

(c) Timing.

The question which necessarily arises is the following: at which point in time in the relationship between the third party-solvens and the obligee-accipiens can or must subrogation be granted?

A third person-solvens may perform the obligation of another, the obligor, at any time during the existence of that obligation unless that same obligation includes some modalities which might limit the obligor's right to perform to a particular time period, as would be the case of a term or a condition. What is of paramount importance in the performance of an obligation susceptible of conventional subro-

---

[50] LSA-C.C. Art. 1855, in part: "Performance rendered by a third person effects subrogation only when so provided by law or by agreement." See Appendix.

[51] LSA-C.C. Art. 1847 would require a writing for purposes of proof; see Art. 1847 in Appendix.

gation is that it is the payment or performance itself; therefore the timing of that performance or payment which extinguishes the obligation may trigger the subrogation.[52] Indeed, in itself and by itself *subrogation* cannot exist without a support on which it can rest. It exists because it is an accessory right brought into existence by the performance of an obligation. There is no reason to be substituted into the rights of another person unless that person is willing to consent to the substitution because she has received some satisfaction or benefit, i.e. the payment or performance that person is owed. Logic and reason dictate, therefore, that subrogation could not take place before a performance or payment occurs, since subrogation would lack the necessary support or *raison d'être* for its existence. Before actually performing, a third person-solvens could merely be given a promise of subrogation from the obligee; one could then look upon the later performance as the occurrence of a suspensive term or a suspensive condition triggering the granting of subrogation.

Likewise, conventional subrogation should not be available to a third person-solvens sometime after the solvens has performed the obligation because, at that later time, no debt exists any longer, and there are no rights into which the solvens could be subrogated. The obligee-accipiens can no longer subrogate someone into something that no longer exists. The payment of performance received by the original obligee-accipiens has extinguished the obligation; with the obligation to perform having ceased to exist, there is no longer any *raison d'être* for any subrogation, since there is no longer an obligee nor an obligor.

With respect to this particular requirement of the timing of subrogation and performance of any obligation, we strongly disagree with a comment given in the West edition of the Civil Code. This comment under **Code Article 1827**, states: *"Under this Article, the agreement for subrogation may be made at any time."*[53] Such a suggestion is nonsensical, illogical and unfounded because it fails to pay due consideration. A payment may be made with or without subrogation; the latter is born out of the former and brings forth a right identical to the right extinguished by the payment. The performance and the subrogation take place concomitantly.

To state, as **Article 1827** does, that conventional subrogation by the obligee is subject to the rules governing the assignment of rights[54] does not mean that one institution is a substitute or twin of the other. Otherwise, why have both in the Civil Code? Although their overall effects are very much similar, it remains that their legal nature is different; an assignment of rights is a principal contract,[55] it could be a sale, it could be a gratuitous transfer, whereas subrogation is an accessory agreement and, thus, some of their effects can only (have to!) be different.

(d) Notice.

---

[52] LSA-C.C. Art. 1854: see Appendix.

[53] LSA-C.C. Art. 1827, Comment (f).

[54] See LSA-C.C. Art. 2642 *et seq.*

[55] LSA-C.C. Art. 2642: see Appendix.

Under the Louisiana Civil Code of 1870, it was not necessary that a conventional subrogation by the obligee be alerted to the obligor.[56] In practice, however, it was common for such a subrogation to be brought to the attention of the obligor, so that the third person-solvens would have a claim against that obligor with his knowledge. Under the principles of the new law of obligations of 1984, in particular **Articles 1758-B** and **1759,**[57] it should be recognized that the obligor ought to be notified that a payment of "his" obligation has been made by a third person and that subrogation was granted by the creditor-obligee-accipiens to that third party-solvens. After all, since subrogation is subject to the rules governing the assignment of rights,[58] Civil Code Article 2643 should be applicable by analogy (*ubi eadem ratio, idem lex*).

2. Conventional Subrogation by the Obligor (Ex Parte Debitoris).

LSA-C.C. Art. 1828 describes this type of subrogation in these terms: **"An obligor who pays a debt with money or other fungible things borrowed for that purpose may subrogate the lender to the rights of the obligee, even without the obligee's consent.**

The agreement for subrogation must be made in writing expressing that the purpose of the loan is to pay the debt."

The validity of this type of conventional subrogation is conditioned upon the existence of some requirements.

(a) Formality.

Because of the far reaching consequences of this type of subrogation which, actually, allows an obligor to dispose of a credit or right which belongs to his obligee and to transfer that credit or right into the patrimony of the third person-solvens, it is reasonable to subject it to a formality. In a sense, the obligor himself removes a right or credit from his obligee's patrimony to transfer it into the patrimony of a third person, the third party-solvens. A writing is required,[59] although it need not be in authentic form, so as to ensure as much as possible the lawfulness of the transaction entered into between the obligor and the third person-solvens.

(b) Express.

This transaction between the third party-solvens and the obligor with the benefit of subrogation into the rights of the obligee-accipiens amounts to the third party-solvens making a loan to the obligor of the amount paid to the obligee and seeking to be subrogated by the obligor into the rights of the same obligee as a sort of security device. It follows that this subrogation must, in addition to being in writing, also stipulate expressly that the purpose of the loan made by the third person was to pay off the obligor's debt[60] (**LSA-C.C. Art. 1828-2**). The reason for

---

[56] Former LSA-C.C. Art. 2160.

[57] LSA-C.C. Art. 1758-B: see Appendix; LSA-C.C. Art. 1759 see Appendix.

[58] LSA-C.C. Art. 1827: see Appendix; LSA-C.C. Art. 2643: see Appendix.

[59] LSA-C.C. Art. 1828-2, in particular: see Appendix.

[60] *Id.*

this express statement regarding the cause or reason (or destination) of the payment with subrogation is to make sure that the loan and the subrogation are lawful and free of fraud of the rights of others. In particular, this form of subrogation could not be used by the third person-solvens to acquire an illegitimate advantage over other creditors of the obligor; the loan made by the third person must be made for the specific and limited purpose of paying off a debt owed to an existing creditor, so that the subrogated third person will take the very same place occupied by that creditor and nobody else's.

(c) Obligee's Awareness.

Since the obligor is actually disposing of his obligee's right in putting someone (the third person-solvens) in the obligee's place, it might appear logical and fair to require that the obligee be notified of the agreement between the obligor and the third person-solvens. Yet, no notification of this agreement to the obligee is required under the law. The obligee remains a stranger to the subrogation because his rights are preserved otherwise. Indeed, if there is subrogation by the obligor it is either because there has been payment to the obligee at a time when the obligation was due or because the obligation was subject to a term in favor of the obligor and the latter decided to waive the benefit of that term by offering to perform before the maturity of his obligation. Either way the obligee will have received performance of the obligation due to him and should not be concerned with the subrogation granted by the obligor to the third person-solvens. There is no need, therefore, for a subrogation *ex parte debitoris* to be notified to the obligee.

B. Legal Subrogation or Subrogation by Operation of Law.

LSA-C.C. Art. 1829 lists four specific instances of subrogation by operation of law and adds a fifth "catch-all" category.[61] With this fifth category a major problem is now resolved; under the previous Code article[62] (former Article 2161) no such general provision could be found. The problem was, then, one of determining the scope of application of the article by interpreting it as being either exclusive or illustrative of any other instance of subrogation by operation of law. The new version of **Article 1829** solves the issue for the better.

The four instances of subrogation by operation of law listed in **Article 1829** can be lumped together under the following two distinct headings:

1. Subrogation by Operation of Law in Favor of a Third Person-Solvens Who Was Herself Bound as an Obligor.

(a) "Subrogation takes place by operation of law:

(1) In favor of an obligee who pays another obligee whose right is preferred to his because of a privilege, pledge, mortgage, or security interest;" (LSA-C.C. Art. 1829-1).

---

[61] LSA-C.C. Art. 1829: see Appendix.

[62] Former Art. 2161 of the Civil Code of 1870.

A creditor-obligee whose claim against a debtor is not secured or whose claim is of a lower rank than other existing claims against the same debtor, may wish to pay off a preferred, higher ranked creditor and, thereby, become subrogated into that secured creditor's right against the debtor. In such a way, an unsecured obligee-creditor or a lower ranking creditor may prevent any action against the debtor-obligor, action which could have been detrimental to his own right had that action been brought by a preferred creditor against the patrimony of their same debtor-obligor.[63]

(b) "Subrogation takes place by operation of law:

(2) in favor of a purchaser of movable or immovable property who uses the purchase money to pay creditors holding any privilege, pledge, mortgage, or security interest on the property;" (LSA-C.C. 1829-2)

In this instance the purchaser of a movable or an immovable thing who uses the purchase price to pay off his vendor's secured creditors holding real rights on the property, is subrogated by law into the rights of these secured creditors. Such a purchaser would be in a position to deter unpaid creditors from attempting to seize the property in his own hands because, by subrogation, he has acquired real security rights (privilege, pledge, mortgage . . .) on his own property. Should unpaid creditors dare to make a move against him and attempt to seize the property to have it sold in the hope that they would be paid out of the proceeds of the sale, they would still rank behind that subrogated-purchaser.[64]

2. Subrogation by Operation of Law in Favor of a Solvens Who Was Not Bound to Perform.

(a) "Subrogation takes place by operation of law:

(3) in favor of an obligor who pays a debt he owes with others or for others and who has recourse against those others as a result of the payment;" (LSA-C.C. Art. 1829-3)

The wording of this code article is so broad as to include all those legal situations where an obligee could sue a variety of obligors bound to him either as principal obligors (solidarity, indivisibility)[65] or as principal obligors and accessory obligors.[66]

(b) "Subrogation takes place by operation of law:

(4) in favor of a successor who pays estate debts with his own funds;" (LSA-C.C. Art. 1829-4)

An heir who accepts a succession under the benefit of inventory is not bound personally for the debts of the succession. Should such an heir discharge a debt of the succession out of his own personal funds for the purpose, for example, of barring a creditor of the estate from delaying its settlement and, thereby, making the

---

[63] LSA-C.C. Art. 3185 *et seq.* See Appendix.

[64] For a specific example of such a type of legal subrogation, see former LSA-R.S. 47:2105.

[65] On Solidarity see supra § 3.3.1 and on Indivisibility, see supra, § 4.4.2.

[66] LSA-C.C. Art. 3047: see Appendix; Art. 3048: see Appendix.

succession incur additional expenses, this heir will be subrogated into the rights the creditor had against the estate of the deceased. As a result of the subrogation, the heir will have the same chance of being reimbursed from the succession as the creditor had. In a sense, the *benefit* of subrogation is meant to encourage an heir under *benefit* of inventory to personally discharge a debt of the succession.

§ 5.2.3.   EFFECTS OF SUBROGATION.

Although conventional subrogation and subrogation by operation of law have the same *essential* effects consisting in placing a new obligee-creditor in the shoes of an original obligee-creditor, these same two types of subrogation carry also with them different *secondary* effects which, in one particular respect, require a separate analysis.

A.   Essential Effects of Subrogation.

LSA-C.C. Art. 1826-A reads as follows: "A. When subrogation results from a person's performance of the obligation of another, that obligation subsists in favor of the person who performed it who may avail himself of the action and security of the original obligee against the obligor, but is extinguished for the original obligee."

There are two essential effects attached to a payment with subrogation: a) a transfer of the obligee-creditor's right to the third person-solvens and b) limitations on the extent of that right.

1.   Transfer of the Obligee-Creditor's Right of Action to the Third Person-Solvens.

LSA-C.C. Art. 1826, provides that the "**obligation subsists in favor of the person who performed it who may avail himself of the action and security of the original obligee against the obligor** . . . ." Thus, the action and the security as a whole are transferred with their particular modalities, be they a term, a condition etc.

The subrogated obligee acquires the very same claim the original obligee-creditor had against the obligor-debtor. This means, for example, that the subrogated obligee could use the same arguments of procedure the original obligee-creditor himself could have used and, furthermore, that the rules of venue will be the same ones that governed the claim of the original obligee-creditor.

There is one important limitation, however, to this transfer of the original claim. Whenever it can be ascertained that strictly personal rights were attached to the person of the original obligee-creditor-accipiens, either because of their *intuitus personae* nature (strictly personal) or because the contract between that obligee-creditor and his obligor so stated, these strictly personal rights of the obligee-creditor cannot be transferred to the third person-solvens who would otherwise enjoy the benefit of subrogation. An illustration of such a strictly personal right not transferable to the third person-solvens, unless otherwise agreed upon, is the benefit of solidarity enjoyed by an obligee-creditor against his obligors.[67]

Conversely, for the same reason that the original claim or right survives in the hands of the obligee-solvens, the obligor will be in a position to raise against that obligee-solvens the same defenses and exceptions he would have been able to raise against his original obligee-creditor before the subrogation took place. For example, since compensation takes place by operation of law,[68] the obligor could oppose to the obligee-solvens the defense of compensation which he could have raised against the original obligee-creditor before the payment with subrogation took place.[69]

2. Limitations on the Extent of the Right Transferred.

Subrogation is not merely a transfer of rights; it is also an accessory benefit derived from the payment made of the debt of another. There lies a necessary limitation to the *transfer effect* of subrogation.

The second paragraph of **LSA-C.C. Art.1826-B** states, in part, "**An original obligee who has been paid only in part may exercise his right for the balance of the debt in preference to the new oblige . . ..**" It follows that subrogation takes place only up to the extent of the amount of the debt paid by the third person-subrogated solvens to the original obligee in order to discharge of the obligation of the obligor. The original obligee is given a preference over the newly subrogated obligee-solvens on the assets of the obligor for the payment of the balance due on the debt.[70] It is obvious, also, that should the debt owed by the obligor be indivisible, a subrogation could not turn it into a divisible obligation.

This same limitation applicable to conventional subrogation governs also subrogation by operation of law as stated in **LSA-C.C. Art. 1830: "When subrogation takes place by operation of law, the new obligee may recover from the obligor only to the extent of the performance rendered to the original obligee. The new obligee may not recover more by invoking conventional subrogation."**

Another limitation on the extent of the right of subrogation concerns those instances where an obligor, bound with others *in solido*, pays the whole debt to the obligee.

Whereas this original obligee had one single right of action he could have exercised against any one of his *in solido*, obligors thus bound together, the one co-obligor *in solido* who performed the whole obligation and, thereby, became subrogated to the original obligee[71] will have to divide his own subrogated claim between the remaining obligors. An illustration of this limitation to the extent of the right of subrogation is given by **LSA-C.C. Art. 1804**, which provides in its second paragraph, that "**[a] solidary obligor who has rendered the whole performance, though subrogated to the right of the obligee, may claim from the other**

---

[67] On Solidarity, see supra § 3.3.1.

[68] LSA-C.C. Art. 1893: see Appendix; on Compensation, see infra § 7.5.

[69] LSA-C.C. Art. 1900.

[70] This rule is an application of the principle: *Nemo censetur subrogare contra se*, meaning that no one is presumed to subrogate against one's own interest.

[71] LSA-C.C. Art. 1829(3): see Appendix.

obligors no more than the virile portion of each." However, in the third paragraph of the same article, one can read that if one of the co-obligors is the only one concerned in the performance of the obligation, if he is, in other words, the principal obligor, then the subrogated-third person solvens will be fully subrogated into the rights of the original obligee and will be entitled to claim payment of the whole debt from that principal obligor.[72] In the words of **LSA-C.C. Art. 1804:** " . . . **that obligor is liable for the whole to the other obligors who are then considered only as his sureties.**"

B.   Special Effects of Conventional Subrogation by the Creditor (Ex Parte Creditoris).

The second sentence of **LSA-C.C. Art. 1827** subjects this form of subrogation to the rules governing the assignment of rights.[73] The breadth of this statement is such that one is led to wonder whether a reasoning *a generali sensu* is appropriate under the circumstances. The issue is whether all the rules of an *assignment of rights* are applicable to a conventional subrogation by the obligee. In the Louisiana Civil Code, the assignment of rights is regulated by Articles 2642 to 2654 in *Chapter 15 of Title 7 Sale*[74] of Book Three. **Article 2642 provides that "[a]ll rights may be assigned, with the exception of those pertaining to obligations are strictly personal. The assignee is subrogated to the rights of the assignor against the debtor.**"

The *raison d'être* of an assignment of rights is the transfer (or sale) by an obligee to an assignee of the rights and claims the obligee holds against the obligor. In this respect, and broadly speaking, an assignment of rights and a payment with conventional subrogation are very much alike. Yet, unless this common foundation or purpose did not also serve to draw a distinction between these two institutions, there would be no need to preserve both of them. To mention subrogation *ex parte creditoris* in one code article, **Article 1827**, and to subject it fully to the rules of assignment of credits would serve no real purpose. Indeed, under **Article 2642**, "**the assignee is subrogated to the rights of the assignor against the debtor.**" So, there appears to be redundancy between the two institutions.

One must question, here, a far-reaching statement made in comment (d) to **LSA-C.C. Art. 1827:** "**Under this Article, the conventional subrogee is substituted to all of the rights of the original obligee. He is entitled to recover the full amount of the debt from the obligor, regardless of the amount actually paid by the subrogee to the original obligee. Prior decisions that, in cases of conventional subrogation, have limited the subrogee's recovery to the amount he actually paid the obligee are expressly overruled.**"[75]

It is important to point out that this statement was made in a *comment* to an article and that, at best, this comment may only have the force of a persuasive

---

[72] LSA-C.C. Art. 1804: see Appendix.

[73] LSA-C.C. Art. 1827: see Appendix. On Assignment of Rights, see LSA-C.C. Art. 2642 *et seq.*

[74] Emphasis ours.

[75] See the West ed. of the Civil Code, Art. 1827.

source of law, if that much. One must remember that only the code articles are considered as binding and authoritative sources of law on the interpreter. Thus, whenever it appears that the essence of two distinct concepts, such as conventional subrogation by the creditor and assignment of rights, differs, the rules applicable to one concept may or should vary, to a greater or to a lesser extent, from the rules applicable to the other. This is particularly true when no rule of public order is involved, as is the case here. To take the comment at face value would be to render totally useless the concept of conventional subrogation by the obligee and prevent parties from elaborating a distinction between an obligee's rights arising from a subrogation and those arising from an assignment of rights. There is no ambiguity in the code articles on "Subrogation" on the part of the creditor and those on "Assignment of Rights"; these articles should be applied, therefore, as sources of law of two distinguishable institutions. Indeed, the holder of a right, a patrimonial right, can "assign" his right without having received any payment meant to extinguish an obligation owed to him. Actually an assignment of a right can be done by means of a "donation" since a donor can "divest" himself of a thing in favor of another.[76] To assign, to divest . . . ? They are both modes of "Transfer of Obligations."[77] "Assignment of Rights" is out of place in Title 7 Sale of Book Three!

Former Civil Code Article 2162 of the Civil Code of 1870 stated that "[t]he subrogation . . . cannot injure the creditor, since, if he has been paid but in part, he may exercise his right for what remains due, in preference to him from whom he has received only a partial payment." This rule applied, then, to *the preceding articles*, which meant that both legal subrogation and conventional subrogation were controlled by that rule.

The letter of new **LSA-C.C. Art. 1830** limits its application to subrogation by operation of law: **"When subrogation takes place by operation of law, the new obligee may recover from the obligor only to the extent of the performance rendered to the original obligee. The new obligee may not recover more by invoking conventional subrogation."** We have, here, what appears to us a very strange, not to say contradictory application of the civil law rule according to *nemo censetur subrogare contra se.*[78] Indeed, who is the obligee who, under Article 1829 (1), or the purchaser under Article 1829 (2), or the obligor under Article 1829 (3) . . . would not pay the whole "extent of the performance" to the original obligee knowing that, if he did not pay the full extent, he would be subrogated only to the extent of the performance he rendered to the original obligee? What happens to the balance of the performance? What happens to the real rights of mortgage, privilege . . . meant to cover the full extent of the performance? How can comment (b) to this Article 1830 state that it "is the fairest solution" (fairest to whom one may ask?)? The third person-obligee could have entered into an assignment of right, paid the obligee-seller a lesser price than the full extent of the debt-performance and recovered from the obligor the full extent of that obligor's debt to the original obligee? In addition, an "assignment of a right includes its accessories

---

[76] See LSA-C.C. Art. 1468.

[77] See LSA-C.C. Art. 1821 *et seq.*

[78] No one is presumed to subrogate against his own interest.

such as security rights."[79] Is or isn't this assignment of a right the "fairest solution"?

The same **Article 1830** on subrogation by operation of law goes on to state that "the new obligee" who has rendered only a partial performance to the original obligee "**may not recover more by invoking conventional subrogation.**" How strange and odd is this last statement! Indeed, under **LSA-C.C. Art. 1826(B): "An original obligee who has been paid in part may exercise his right for the balance of the debt in preference to the new obligee . . . .**" So, even under this article a conventionally subrogated new obligee could not recover more from the obligor than his "part" of performance to the original obligee, because the latter "**may exercise his right for the balance of the debt in preference to the new obligee.**"

So, both under conventional subrogation and legal subrogation, a subrogated obligee would not recover more from the obligor than the amount he paid the original obligee either because the law says so under **LSA-C.C. Art. 1830** or because the original obligee can still exercise his right for the balance.

But what, then, of **Article 1827?**[80] We believe that it is an ill-disguised and ill-advised incorporation of the concept of assignment of rights into the law of subrogation and, for that reason, should be disregarded or, better, deleted. As mentioned previously, assignment of rights and subrogation are based on different justifications or policies. Indeed, the spirit of a subrogation differs from that inspiring an assignment of rights.

An assignment of rights can be, under the proper circumstances, tantamount to an act of speculation. It is, in many instances, an act of purchase made by an assignee who, for the assignment to him of a right belonging to another, the assignor, will pay a price which may be unrelated to the nominal value of the obligation which is bought. That price is often a discounted price reflecting the assignee's main motivation of gambling or speculating on the difference in value between the price he agrees to pay and the amount that he expects to collect from the obligor. There lies the very essence of some assignments of rights when they are actually couched in a contract of sale in which the buyer purchases a right, i.e. an "incorporeal thing,"[81] and expects to pay a lesser price than the full price with the consent and understanding of the seller.

Although a subrogation may be used also as a means of investing in the acquisition of a credit or a right, the motivation most likely to inspire the subrogated-obligee is elsewhere. It may consist merely in the desire to obtain reimbursement from the obligor for the price that the subrogated-obligee paid to the original obligee and to ensure that right of reimbursement through the sureties, which might be attached to the principal obligation. This is, after all, the

---

[79] LSA-C.C. Art. 2645: see Appendix.

[80] LSA-C.C. Art. 1827: see Appendix.

[81] See LSA-C.C. Art. 2448: " All things corporeal and incorporeal, susceptible of ownership, may be sold . . . "

true meaning of "sub rogare" or "to choose someone in place of another."[82] A subrogated obligee's principal cause or motive in a conventional subrogation can be one of altruism, one of extending some kind of help to another, be it the original obligee himself who needs his payment or the obligor who may not be in a position to make that payment. It is because of this altruistic intent that a subrogated obligee, as opposed to an assignee, enjoys the benefit of two rights of action against the obligor: he enjoys, first, his own personal action against the obligor for having paid his debt[83] and, second, he may resort to the very action which the original obligee himself had against the obligor, action which is at the heart of the concept of subrogation.

For these reasons, we believe that the statement made in the second sentence of Article 1827 is inappropriate and that the suggestion made in comment (d) to Article 1827 is not at all justified.[84] As explained above, no original obligee would consent to subrogate into his rights a third person-solvens new obligee unless that original obligee was either fully paid or could preserve his own rights of action against his obligor. If the original obligee is fully paid by the third person-solvens, the latter may then be subrogated into the obligee's right against the obligor for the payment he has made, that is to say the full amount. The obligor would then perform his own obligation *vis-à-vis* the third person-new subrogated obligee, again up to the full amount that he, the obligor, always owed.

In the instance where the original obligee would receive only a partial payment from the subrogated third person and new obligee, the latter could conceivably obtain from the original obligee that he would waive his right to claim the balance of the performance from his obligor. Only in that instance could the third person new obligee recover from the obligor the full amount of the performance and, thereby, make a profit. But, then, why would a third person want to obtain a subrogation when he would be as well off, if not better off, claiming an assignment of right? Such an assignment of right would automatically give the transferee the right to demand the full performance from the obligor. It would be so because, in general, the essence of an assignment is the acquisition of a right for a profit; it has a speculative purpose.

We believe that because **LSA-C.C. Art. 1827** eliminates any and all distinctions between a conventional subrogation by the obligee and an assignment of rights, it fails to take proper account of the difference in the philosophies of the two institutions and, in a sense, eliminates any room for the survival of an altruistic and non-speculative conventional subrogation by an obligee. It is much to be regretted.

---

[82] See "Subrogation" in *Dictionary of the Civil Code*, p. 537.

[83] LSA-C.C. Art. 1855: see Appendix.

[84] LSA-C.C. Art. 1827: see Appendix. Comment (d): " Under this Article, the conventional subrogee is substituted to all of the rights of the original obligee. He is entitled to recover the full amount of the debt from the obligor, regardless of the amount actually paid by the subrogee to the original obligee. Prior decisions that, in cases of conventional subrogation have limited the subrogee's recovery to the amount he actually paid the obligee are expressly overruled."

Chapter 6

PROOF OF OBLIGATIONS LSA-C.C. ART. 1831 TO 1853

Whenever a person claims to have a right or whenever a party argues that she has performed her obligation, she will be faced with the burden of proving her allegation.

"A party who demands performance of an obligation must prove the existence of the obligation.

A party who asserts that an obligation is null, or that it has been modified or extinguished, must prove the facts or acts giving rise to the nullity, modification, or extinction." (LSA-C.C. Art. 1831).

The burden of proof falling on a party will vary in its forms and its effects according to the source of the right one claims to have or the obligation one asserts has been extinguished. Broadly speaking, rights and obligations arise either from juridical acts or from juridical facts.

A juridical act is any manifestation of the will meant to be creative of juridical effects, which is to say that the effects of the manifestation of the will are sanctioned by law. As examples of juridical acts one can cite contracts that are meant to create obligations between the parties to it, or testaments which create rights and obligations on heirs, legatees.

A juridical fact consists either in a factual situation or an event (such as birth, death . . .) or an action (such as tort . . .) which, by its very happening, creates, modifies, alters or extinguishes rights and obligations. As an example, upon reaching the age of eighteen one becomes of age and capable of enjoying and exercising all rights.[1]

The principle of primacy of written proof suffers a few exceptions.

ARTICLE 1
THE PRINCIPLE OF WRITTEN PROOF

For centuries a written proof has been considered as the most reliable, the safest and most convincing means of proof, and the Louisiana Civil Code has followed in that tradition.

It is important to stress here that proving the *written* existence of a contract is not always the same thing as establishing the validity of that contract.

---

[1] LSA-C.C. Art. 29: see Appendix; see supra § 1.1.2 Juridical Acts and Juridical Facts as Sources of Obligations.

There are, indeed, many contracts which are perfectly valid under the law even though they are not couched in any written form. Such is the case, for example, of the contract of lease,[2] as well as of the contract of sale of movables,[3] which requires only "the thing, the price, and the consent of the parties . . . ."

On the other hand, there are some contracts which are not legally valid unless they are in writing. It follows that failure to meet this requirement will prevent the contract from having any existence to the extent that this contract could not be proved by any other means unless otherwise stated. In this respect, **LSA-C.C. Art. 1832** provides very clearly: "**When the law requires a contract to be in written form, the contract may not be proved by testimony or by presumption, unless the written instrument has been destroyed, lost, or stolen.**"

As illustrations of these formal or solemn contracts we can mention "**[t]he donation or the acceptance of a donation of an incorporeal movable of the kind that is evidenced by a certificate . . . or other writing . . . may be made by authentic act or by compliance with the requirements otherwise applicable to the transfer of that particular kind of incorporeal movable.**"[4] We can also mention a conventional mortgage[5] or, still, a transfer of immovable property, which "must be made by authentic act or by act under private signature. Nevertheless, an oral transfer is valid between the parties when the property has been actually delivered and the transferor recognizes the transfer when interrogated on oath." (**LSA-C.C. Art. 1839**). Furthermore "**[p]arol evidence is inadmissible to establish either a promise to pay the debt of a third person or a promise to pay a debt extinguished by prescription.**" (**LSA-C.C. Art. 1847**). In this particular instance of a promise to pay the debt of another, the formality of the writing is required to make sure that one will not be bound against his will to pay the debt of another and the writing will ensure, to some extent, that the promisor thought carefully about committing himself before putting it in writing.

The Civil Code distinguishes between two forms of written acts and allows for some exceptions to the strict requirement of a written proof.

§ 6.1.1. WRITTEN PROOF BY AUTHENTIC ACT.

The two recognized forms of written acts are the authentic act and the act under private signature. In some circumstances, an act invalid for want of form can be cured of its deficiency by means of confirmation or ratification.

---

[2] LSA-C.C. Art. 2668 *et seq.* See in particular Art. 2681: "A lease may be made orally or in writing . . . ."

[3] LSA-C.C. Art. 2439 *et seq.* as contrasted with LSA-C.C. Art. 2440 on the sale of immovables.

[4] See LSA-C.C. Art. 1550.

[5] LSA-C.C. Art. 3287.

A. Notion of Authentic Act.

An authentic act is defined as a writing executed before a notary public or an officer **"authorized to perform that function, in the presence of two witnesses and signed by each party who executed it, by each witness and by each notary public before whom it was executed."** (LSA-C.C. Art. 1833) The *Dictionary of the Civil Code* defines an authentic act as *"an act which, being executed or drawn by a competent public legal officer and according to the formalities required (on paper or electronically) is valid and is absolute proof by itself until it is challenged as a forgery."*[6]

Although it is not necessary that the same authentic act be executed in one particular place or at one single time, still it remains that it is necessary that the parties themselves execute the act before a notary who need not be the same for each party. The solemnity of the authentic act is further emphasized by the requirement that the signatures of all involved, parties, witnesses and notaries be executed on the act.

Although a notary is the most likely officer who will preside over the formalities of the act, other public officers are authorized to stand in the place of a notary to perform the latter's functions. As illustrations, the laws allows commissioned officers in the active service of the Armed Forces or the Coast Guard of the U.S.[7] as well as ambassadors, consuls[8] or recorders[9] to perform the functions of a notary.

B. Effects of an Authentic Act.

The importance of the role played by a notary in the formalism of the authentic act and the legal weight attached to his involvement in the performance of his duty are emphasized by **LSA-C.C. Art. 1834: "An act that fails to be authentic because of the lack of competence or capacity of the notary public, or because of a defect of form, may still be valid as an act under private signature."**

The weight of the proof attached to an authentic act and its binding force are transferred to accessory acts, which borrow from the nature of the principal act. Thus, a copy of an authentic act **"when certified by the notary public or other officer before whom the act was passed, constitutes proof of the contents of the original, unless the copy is proved to be incorrect."** (LSA-C.C. Art. 1840). Likewise **"[w]hen an authentic act or an acknowledged act under private signature has been filed for registry with a public officer, a copy of the act thus filed, when certified by that officer, constitutes proof of the contents of the original."** (LSA-C.C. Art. 1841).

The role played by the written instrument itself [*instrumentum*] in the prerequisites of a valid authentic act explains why the contents of such an act are given a binding force, which admits of few exceptions. Oral evidence, if freely

---

[6] *Dictionary of the Civil Code,* — word: authentique (2), p. 64.

[7] La. R.S. 35:7.

[8] La. R.S. 35:9.

[9] La. R.S. 44:101.

admitted, would so tamper with the contents of an authentic act as to deprive the latter of any value, at the same time it would seriously discredit the role and authority of notaries or other qualified public officers. This explains why LSA-C.C. Art. 1848 provides that "[t]estimonial or other evidence may not be admitted to negate or vary the contents of an authentic act or an act under private signature. Nevertheless, in the interest of justice, that evidence may be admitted to prove such circumstances as a vice of consent, or to prove that the written act was modified by a subsequent and valid oral agreement."

The exceptions listed above in **LSA-C.C. Art. 1848**, exceptions to the binding force of an authentic act, although not exclusive, do not detract from the legal nature of the authentic act but, rather, merge other important principles of law in a successful harmony with the particular nature of the authentic act. Indeed, what respect would an authentic act command if a party was not allowed to prove that the debt evidenced by the authentic act had been extinguished, by remission[10] for example? The paramount principle of good faith[11] justifies that oral evidence be admissible to establish that an authentic act was actually meant to be a simulated act or that the authentic act, if upheld, would violate rules of public order or good morals. The "**interest of justice**"[12] is the legitimate reason for these exceptions and others.

§ 6.1.2. WRITTEN PROOF BY ACT UNDER PRIVATE SIGNATURE.

In contrast with an authentic act, an act under private signature does not require any *extraordinary* formalism and, therefore, it can be understood why it does not carry as binding a force.

A. Notion of Act Under Private Signature.

An act under private signature is defined as an act "which need not be written by the parties, but must be signed by them." (**LSA-C.C. Arts. 1837**).[13]

The legal weight attached to such an act rests, as a consequence, upon the validity of the signatures of the parties, or party to it. It follows that a party against whom an act under private signature is asserted may attempt to deny his signature by any available means of proof. Conversely, any means of proof may be used to establish that the signature belongs to that party.[14]

An act under private signature may gain authority when it is duly acknowledged. "**An act under private signature may be acknowledged by a**

---

[10] On Remission, see infra § 7.4.1.

[11] LSA-C.C. Art. 1759: see Appendix.

[12] LSA-C.C. Art. 1848.

[13] *Dictionary of the Civil Code*, — word: acte sous seing privé, p. 19: written act (on paper or electronic medium) by the parties themselves under their signature alone (seing privé) without the involvement of any public legal officer.

[14] LSA-C.C. Art. 1838: see Appendix.

party to that act by recognizing the signature as his own before a court, or before a notary public, or other officer authorized to perform that function, in the presence of two witnesses. An act under private signature may be acknowledged also in any other manner authorized by law." (LSA-C.C. Art. 1836-2). Thus, an acknowledged act under private signature, although not equivalent to an authentic act, is vested with a greater weight of authority than a simple act under private signature.

The original legal nature of an acknowledged act under private signature is stressed in **LSA-C.C. Art. 1841**, which states, in part, that when "**an acknowledged act under private signature has been filed for registry with a public officer, a copy of the act thus filed, when certified by that officer, constitutes proof of the contents of the original.**"

B. Effects of Acts Under Private Signature.

An act under private signature facilitates the burden of proof of the party who claims its benefit even though the evidentiary weight of such an act is limited. The essential advantage for a plaintiff is to shift the burden of proof onto the defendant, who will have either to acknowledge or to deny his signature or, still, resort to other means of proof to establish the invalidity of the act.[15]

A party who asserts the validity of a contract embodied in an act under private signature bearing his signature need only show that the other party who failed to sign the contract has become a party to it by tacit acceptance or otherwise. In other words, despite the literal wording of **LSA-C.C. Art. 1837**,[16] it is accepted, in the jurisprudence at least, that an act under private signature is valid even though it has been signed by one party only.[17]

§ 6.1.3. CURABILITY OF DEFICIENCIES.

Whenever the validity of a juridical act depends on the fulfillment of some formalities, one question must always be asked: what becomes of the legal existence of that juridical act if one formality has not been carried out or if a defect exists in one of the required formalities? Should the answer be that the juridical act is null or nonexistent or should one attempt to repair the deficiency and cure the defect? The answer to these questions depends, in part, on whether the nullity of the juridical act can be confirmed or ratified.

A. Confirmation.

"**Confirmation is a declaration whereby a person cures the relative nullity of an obligation.**" (**LSA-C.C. Art. 1842**). Confirmation is, therefore, a unilateral juridical act, express or tacit, enabling a person to make *retroactively* valid a

---

[15] LSA-R.S.13:3720: "Instruments attested by witnesses and accompanied by affidavit; admissible in evidence."

[16] LSA-C.C. Art. 1837: see Appendix.

[17] Comment (b) to LSA-C.C. Art. 1837.

juridical act which was defective when first entered into.

The *raison d'être* of **LSA-C.C. Articles 1842** and **2031**[18] is to restrict the scope of application of confirmation to those juridical acts which are relatively null, that is to say to those acts which merely violate a **"rule intended for the protection of private parties."** (**LSA-C.C. Art. 2031**). Confirmation of a juridical act held to be absolutely null is, therefore, impossible, since such a nullity is meant to protect public order or public morality.[19]

1. Authentic Acts.

It would appear that the confirmation of an invalid authentic act ought to be allowed whenever the interest meant to be protected by the nullity is the very same interest that could confirm the act. An express act of confirmation containing or identifying the substance of the obligation and evidencing the party's intention to cure the act of its relative nullity would bring validity to the juridical act. Likewise, a tacit confirmation could result from a voluntary performance by the same party who could claim the benefit of the relative nullity.[20]

Whether an authentic act afflicted with a relative invalidity can be confirmed is questionable in light of **LSA-C.C. Art. 1845**. This article provides specifically for one instance of confirmation of an authentic act, a donation *inter vivos* that is null for lack of proper form: **"A donation *inter vivos* that is null for lack of proper form may be confirmed by the donor but the confirmation must be made in the form required for a donation.**

The universal successor of the donor may, after his death, expressly or tacitly confirm such a donation."

A cardinal rule of interpretation dictates that an exceptional statute must be read strictly [*exceptio est strictissimae interpretationis*]. When combined with an *a contrario* reasoning on **LSA-C.C. Art. 1845** [*qui dicit de uno de altero negat*] one should be led to conclude that only authentic acts of donation *inter vivos* null for lack of proper form may be confirmed. Moreover, **LSA-C.C. Art. 1834**[21] relegates some invalid authentic acts to the lower status of acts under private signature, holding them valid as such with apparently no possibility of confirmation to raise them back to the status of authentic acts.

This interpretation need not be so restrictive. To the extent that a party to an authentic act would be allowed to cure a defect in a requirement meant to protect that party's private interest, the nullity of the authentic act should be susceptible to confirmation. **LSA-C.C. Art. 1845** refers only to the violation of a rule of form in a donation *inter* vivos and, after declaring that this violation is sanctioned by a relative nullity, it goes on to allow this deficiency to be cured by confirmation. There exist other possible violations, such as capacity and consent, which are also sanctioned by a relative nullity of the juridical act involved and although they may

---

[18] LSA-C.C. Art. 1842: see Appendix; Art. 2031: see Appendix.

[19] LSA-C.C. Art. 2030.

[20] LSA-C.C. Art. 1842.

[21] See LSA-C.C. Art. 1834 in Appendix.

affect an authentic act they ought to be susceptible of confirmation for the same reason a defect of form may be confirmed.[22]

2. Acts Under Private Signature.

Acts under private signature are considered to be of lesser societal importance than authentic acts because, by nature, they are meant to protect only the private interests of the parties involved. It follows then that confirmation of these acts under private signature should be widely recognized as long as the juridical act of confirmation meets the legal requirements of **LSA-C.C. Art.1842**:

> **"Confirmation is a declaration whereby a person cures the relative nullity of an obligation.**
>
> **An express act of confirmation must contain or identify the substance of the obligation and evidence the intention to cure its relative nullity.**
>
> **Tacit confirmation may result from voluntary performance of the obligation."**

B. Ratification.

> **"Ratification is a declaration whereby a person gives his consent to an obligation incurred on his behalf by another without authority.**
>
> **An express act of ratification must evidence the intention to be bound by the ratified obligation.**
>
> **Tacit ratification results when a person, with knowledge of an obligation incurred on his behalf by another, accepts the benefit of that obligation." (LSA-C.C. Art. 1843).**

Ratification is, therefore, a unilateral juridical act, express or tacit, enabling a person to give her consent to a juridical act entered into on her behalf by another who had no authority to do so. In a sense, to ratify another person's juridical act is to vest power and authority in that person after the juridical act has been carried out [*ex post facto*] or retroactively in a sense.

The *represented* party, when ratifying, is thus willing to acquire the benefits and incur the burdens created by a juridical act by which she was not bound originally and to which she now becomes the principal party. Ratification will therefore have a retroactive effect[23] in the sense that a juridical act is fictitiously given the legal requirement that was missing for its validity and thereby made effective back to the date of its formation.

The difference between confirmation and ratification is, therefore, that confirmation erases a ground for nullity of a contract whereas ratification adds to a juridical act a necessary requirement for its validity.

---

[22] Reasoning *ubi eadem ratio idem lex*, or *a pari ratione* on LSA-C.C. Art. 1845.

[23] LSA-C.C. Art. 1844.

§ 6.1.4. EFFECTS OF CONFIRMATION AND RATIFICATION.

LSA-C.C. Art. 1844 lays down very clearly the governing principle of the retroactive effect of both confirmation and ratification: **"The effects of confirmation and ratification are retroactive to the date of the confirmed or ratified obligation. Neither confirmation nor ratification may impair the rights of the third persons."**

A juridical act which is confirmed or ratified is fictitiously considered to have been perfect, and therefore valid, as of the time it had been entered into [*ex tunc* or "as of then"], since it is cured retroactively of its defect. Although the parties to the juridical act are themselves considered to have been bound at the time the juridical act had been entered into, the retroactivity of the effects of that act ought not to impair the rights acquired, in the meantime, by good faith third parties.[24]

ARTICLE 2
WRITTEN PROOF: EXCEPTIONS

The principle still governing the law of formation of conventional obligations remains that of consensualism. By their mere consent parties may enter into a binding contract unless the law provides otherwise and requires a writing in addition to the exchange of wills.

In a sense, therefore, **LSA-C.C. Art. 1846** provides for the general situation where no writing is required by law:

> **"When a writing is not required by law, a contract not reduced to writing, for a price or, in the absence of a price, for a value not in excess of five hundred dollars may be proved by competent evidence.**
>
> **If the price or value is in excess of five hundred dollars, the contract must be proved by at least one witness and other corroborating circumstances."**

Whenever a written instrument is required, or where written proof is prescribed, an exception to these legal dispositions can be found in **LSA-C.C. Art. 1853** which provides for a judicial confession:

> **"A judicial confession is a declaration made by a party in a judicial proceeding. That confession constitutes full proof against the party who made it.**
>
> **A judicial confession is indivisible and it may be revoked only on the ground of error of fact."**

Such a confession made in a judicial proceeding can bear only on issues of fact because it is for the court to pass on the law applicable to the controversy. This division of the tasks between a party and the court explains why a judicial confession can be revoked only on the ground of error of fact. Actually, a party who agrees to abide by the judicial confession of his opponent is very much in the same

---

[24] See for example, LSA-C.C. Arts. 2021, 2035.

position as a party entering into a compromise[25] Both parties wish to prevent or put an end to a law suit and if a compromise cannot be rescinded on account of any error of law,[26] for the same reason a judicial confession cannot be rescinded on the ground of error of law.

Another exception to the legal requirement of written evidence can be found in **LSA-C.C. Art. 1832** where it is stated that when the required **"written instrument has been destroyed, lost or stolen"** then, and only then, can a contract be proved by testimony or by presumption.[27]

---

[25] LSA-C.C. Arts. 3071 *et seq.* in Appendix.

[26] LSA-C.C. Art. 3082: see Appendix.

[27] LSA-C.C. Art. 1832: see Appendix.

Chapter 7

EXTINCTION OF OBLIGATIONS LSA-C.C. ARTS. 1854 TO 1905

The mode of extinction of an obligation is as intimate a part of that obligation as is the mode of its creation; as much as the latter, the former must be contemplated, if at all possible, when an obligation is entered into. It is advisable for any party to an obligation, be it the obligee or the obligor, to keep in mind that there exists a great variety of modes of extinction of obligations. Some can be pre-arranged and others can be prompted by a variety of circumstances. A party to an obligation cannot be certain that the outcome, the end result, will be what had been contemplated at the outset when entering into an obligation. For that reason, it is recommended that one should think ahead and plan for the consequences of the different modes of extinction of obligations. To a great extent, the contents of an obligation should be dictated by the anticipated mode or modes of extinction of the obligation. This is where the distinctions and classifications made above between "obligations to give, to do and not to do," "obligations of result as distinguished from obligations of means," as well as the distinction between "personal and heritable obligations" will come into play and prove their usefulness.[1]

The variety of the modes of extinction of obligations is illustrated by the listing of concepts described in civil **LSA-C.C. Articles 1854 to 1905** which represent the normal and most common modes of extinction of obligations. This listing, however, is not exclusive of any other possible mode of extinction. Indeed, one should add prescription as well as specific performance and damages[2] as other legal devices or schemes whereby obligations can be extinguished.

In order to follow the structure of the code articles, only those modes of extinction of obligations which are "general" will be considered here, as they concern all sorts of obligations. In another Précis, special consideration will be given to conventional obligations or contracts and additional means of extinction of such obligations.[3]

ARTICLE 1
VOLUNTARY PERFORMANCE

Under this heading, we shall focus exclusively on the voluntary performance of his obligation by the obligor (to the exclusion of specific performance) and address

---

[1] See above Chapters 1 and 2.

[2] Such modes of extinction of obligations are mentioned in the law of Conventional Obligations or Contracts (LSA-C.C. Arts. 1906–2057) and will be presented in another Précis.

[3] See Précis: Louisiana Law of Conventional Obligations 2nd ed. 2015.

two alternative modes of performing an obligation either by way of imputation or by resorting to tender and deposit.

§ 7.1.1.   PERFORMANCE.

Performance of an obligation is the expected and normal mode of extinction of an obligation by an obligor. As **LSA-C.C. Art. 1854** states: "**Performance by the obligor extinguishes the obligation.**" Performance is, thus, the fulfillment of the juridical act or fact undertaken by the obligor with the intent to discharge his obligation *vis-à-vis* the obligee as is called for by the nature of their legal relationship.

A.   Parties to the Performance.

1.   Who May Perform?

LSA-C.C. Article 1855 states:

> "**Performance may be rendered by a third person, even against the will of the obligee, unless the obligor or the obligee has an interest in performance only by the obligor.**
>
> **Performance rendered by a third person effects subrogation only when so provided by law or by agreement.**"

Therefore, performance can, or should, always be rendered by the obligor [*solvens*] although, in proper circumstances, that same performance can be rendered by a representative of the obligor,[4] or a person concerned, such as a surety or a co-obligor,[5] or, even, a third person, a gestor, for example.[6]

As a matter of principle, the obligee-creditor may not refuse performance by someone other than the obligor except when the obligation was of an *intuitus personae* nature or when the obligee himself had a specific interest in the obligation being performed by the obligor. The performance of an obligation by a third person may extinguish the right that the obligee had to that performance against the obligor but it will not always extinguish that same obligation when looked at from the point of view of the obligor. Indeed, the "**performance rendered by a third person effects subrogation only when so provided by law or by agreement.**" (**LSA-C.C. Art. 1855**).[7]

A voluntary performance of his obligation by the obligor is a juridical act meant to extinguish that obligation; therefore, it is necessary that the obligor be capable of performing.[8] Furthermore, whenever the object of the performance is a thing which must be transferred from the obligor to the obligee, it is necessary that the

---

[4] LSA-C.C. Arts. 2985 *et seq.*

[5] LSA-C.C. Arts. 3035 *et seq.*

[6] LSA-C.C. Arts. 2292–2297.

[7] On Subrogation, see supra, § 5.2.1.

[8] LSA-C.C. Arts. 1918 *et seq.*

obligor be legally entitled to dispose of that thing. A valid transfer will then take place only if the obligor had the right to deliver the thing so as to extinguish his obligation.[9]

Likewise an obligor who would perform his obligation in violation of a writ of seizure[10] could not be said to have validly performed his obligation since the obligee could, in turn, be compelled to return the thing received from the obligor's unlawful performance.[11]

2. Who May Receive Performance?

In the words of **LSA-C.C. Art. 1857**:

> **"Performance must be rendered to the obligee or to a person authorized by him.**
>
> **However, a performance rendered to an unauthorized person is valid if the obligee ratifies it.**
>
> **In the absence of ratification, a performance rendered to an unauthorized person is valid if the obligee has derived a benefit from it, but only for the amount of the benefit."**

Therefore, a performance may be validly rendered to the obligee himself or to a third person empowered to receive the performance in the place and in the name of the obligee.[12]

Whenever the obligee himself has not received the benefit of the performance, that same obligee may still ratify the performance rendered by the obligor to a third person thereby extinguishing the obligation owed by the obligor.[13]

It may happen that a person, although an obligee, will receive a performance from an obligor other than his own obligor. Under these circumstances that obligee might be protected from the obligation to return the performance unduly received from an obligor other than his own original obligor. As a consequence, the party-obligor who performed, although not bound to, will have recourse against the true debtor-obligor who should have performed. This recourse or action is justified by the necessity to prevent the true debtor's enrichment at the expense of the person who performed in error.[14]

In the absence either of a mandate granted to a third person-obligee prior to the performance by the obligor or of a ratification executed by the original obligee subsequently to the performance to the third person-obligee, it is still possible that a performance received by an original obligee might amount to a partial extinction of the obligation involved. **LSA-C.C. Article 1857-3** provides "[i]n the absence of

---

[9] See LSA-C.C. Arts. 521, 522, 523.

[10] LSA-C.C.P. Arts. 2721 *et seq.*

[11] LSA-C.C. Art. 1859: see Appendix.

[12] See Representation, LSA-C.C. Arts. 2985–2988; see Mandate, LSA-C.C. Arts. 2989 *et seq.*

[13] On Ratification, see supra § 6.1.3(1).

[14] LSA-C.C. Arts. 2302 *et seq.*

ratification, a performance rendered to an unauthorized person is valid if the obligee has derived a benefit from it, but only for the amount of the benefit."

The importance of a voluntary performance as a mode of extinction of an obligation owed to an obligee is emphasized by the fact that the obligor cannot force his performance on an obligee who is not in a legal position to receive that performance. **LSA-C.C. Art. 1858** provides for this situation where it states: **"Performance rendered to an obligee without capacity to receive it is valid to the extent of the benefit he derived from it."** It is normal therefore that, under these circumstances, the obligor be charged with the duty of showing the extent to which the obligee, without the capacity to receive, has been enriched by the performance received.

B.   Object of the Performance.

The object of the obligor's performance must be the very same object of the obligation entered into. There must be identity between the object of the obligation and the object or item of the performance carried out to extinguish the obligation whether that object or item be a service to be performed or a thing to be delivered.

When the object of the obligation and, therefore, of the performance is **"a thing that is determined as to its kind only, the obligor need not give one of the best quality but he may not tender one of the worst."[15]** In those contracts that involve the delivery of things, which must be identified by reference to a sample, the actual object of the obligor's performance cannot be that very same thing but one of the same kind and with the same identifiable and special features. In these cases, the identity which must exist between the two objects is purely fictitious and achieved only by analogy or reference.

A fundamental principle that governs an obligor's performance is the principle of indivisibility of that performance. In a few specific instances this principle will suffer some exceptions.

1.   Principle of Indivisibility.

The indivisibility of an obligor's performance simply means that the obligor owes the entirety of the thing or item in one single performance. Unless the parties to a juridical act have provided otherwise, or unless the law states differently, an obligee-creditor cannot be compelled to receive a partial performance from his obligor. **LSA-C.C. Art. 1861** states this principle in very clear terms:

> **An obligee may refuse to accept a partial performance.**
>
> **Nevertheless, if the amount of an obligation to pay money is disputed in part and the obligor is willing to pay the undisputed part, the obligee may not refuse to accept that part. If the obligee is willing to accept the undisputed part, the obligor must pay it. In either case, the obligee preserves his right to claim the disputed part.**

---

[15] LSA-C.C. Art. 1860: see Appendix.

The indivisibility of the performance is controlling whether the object of that performance is indivisible by nature or susceptible of division.[16]

One must be very careful not to equate or analogize a partial performance accepted by an obligee with a partial remission of debt.[17] The fact that an obligee consents to receiving a partial performance should be considered, first and foremost, as evidence of his willingness to consent to a division of the object or item of the obligor's performance when the obligee would have been entitled to require that the performance be indivisible. It remains, therefore, that an obligee who receives a partial performance may demand performance of the balance of the object of the obligation or item of the performance.

A creditor-obligee who receives a partial performance from his obligor may, however, be inclined to terminate the legal relationship in existence by granting his obligor a partial remission of debt. Such a juridical act amounts to a new contractual relationship grafted upon a previously existing legal relationship. The purpose of that new contractual relationship is to terminate the previous one on grounds, or for a cause, other than those which had justified the creation of that original legal relationship. A contract that was originally negotiated as a sale may be turned into a partial donation of the price, if the vendor-obligee remits to his buyer partial payment of the price.

One reliable test to use in ascertaining the intent of the parties to such juridical acts is to remember that a remission of debt, although it can be tacit, must be accepted by the obligor who should indicate clearly that he is willing to enter into a new contractual relationship meant to extinguish a prior one by which he was bound to the obligee. Hence, in a case of partial performance of an obligation, one should not *presume* the existence of a remission of debt or a compromise when neither the *cause* nor the *consent* of the parties to that partial performance can be related to a contract of remission or a compromise.[18]

2. Exceptions to Indivisibility of Performance.

To all principles there are exceptions and such is the case of the principle of indivisibility.

In the event of the death of a single obligor, the obligation then surviving and passed on to his heirs will become divisible among them in its performance, if the division of the object or item of performance is legally and/or naturally possible. The heirs, or successors, will enjoy the benefit of division.[19]

The principle of indivisibility will suffer another exception whenever an obligor could avail himself of the benefit of compensation against his obligee-creditor.[20] In the event the obligor owes his obligee-creditor a lesser sum than the latter is

---

[16] LSA-C.C. Arts. 1815 and 1816; see Indivisibility supra § 4.4.2.

[17] LSA-C.C. Arts. 1888 *et seq.*; see Remission infra § 7.4.

[18] On Compromise see LSA-C.C. Arts. 3071–3083.

[19] LSA-C.C. Arts. 1416, 1817, 1819; on the latter two articles see Divisibility and Indivisibility of Obligations, supra § 4.4.2.

[20] LSA-C.C. Art. 1893: see Appendix; on Compensation, see infra § 7.5.

entitled to claim from the former, a partial compensation of debts may take place. This partial compensation will amount to a partial division of performance.

C. Additional Requirements Pertaining to the Performance.

The legality of a voluntary performance is conditional upon three additional requirements, which relate to the time, the place and the expenses of the performance.

1. Time of Performance.

Although there appears to be no specific code article dealing with the time of the performance under this particular title of the Civil Code on *Obligations In General*, it remains that performance on time is an essential requirement for the lawful extinction of an obligation. It is logical to refer here, by analogy, to **LSA-C.C. Art. 1777** which is concerned with the *term* for a performance:

> **"A term for the performance of an obligation may be express or it may be implied by the nature of the contract.**
>
> **Performance of an obligation not subject to a term is due immediately."**[21]

Thus, either an obligation is to be performed immediately, or else it is to be carried out at some express or implicit time. The importance of this requirement of a timely performance is stressed by the fact that an obligee could hold his obligor in default and demand the payment of moratory damages should the obligor fail to perform on time.[22]

2. Place of Performance.

Civil Code Article 1862 formulates a few specific rules on the matter of the place of performance of an obligation:

> **"Performance shall be rendered in the place either stipulated in the agreement or intended by the parties according to usage, the nature of the performance, or other circumstances.**
>
> **In the absence of agreement or other indication of the parties' intent, performance of an obligation to give an individually determined thing shall be rendered at the place the thing was when the obligation arose. If the obligation is of any other kind, the performance shall be rendered at the domicile of the obligor."**[23]

---

[21] On Term, see supra § 2.2-A.

[22] LSA-C.C. Arts. 1989 *et seq*; 1994 *et seq*. Moratory damages are defined by the *Dictionary of the Civil Code* in these terms: "Used to describe damages (i.e. moratory damages) which are intended to compensate for the harm resulting from the late performance of an obligation." See "moratoire," p. 383.

[23] As illustrations of this general Article one could cite the following codal provisions: LSA-C.C. Arts. 2484, 2550, 2937: see these articles in Appendix.

As illustrations of this general article one could cite the following specific LSA-C.C. Arts. **2484, 2550, 2937**, etc.

3. Expenses of the Performance.

LSA-C.C. Art. 1863 lays down a general rule to the effect that:

> **"Expenses that may be required to render performance shall be borne by the obligor."**

In a contract of sale, for example, the expenses or costs related to the seller's obligation to deliver the thing sold, or to be sold, are *chargeable to the seller* whereas those expenses related to the buyer's obligation to remove that same thing *are to be supported by the buyer*.[24]

§ 7.1.2. IMPUTATION OF PAYMENT.

When an obligor owes his obligee several obligations bearing on fungible things or when he owes several debts of money to the same obligee-creditor, it is important to determine which one of the many obligations or debts he owes, this obligor wishes to extinguish when making a payment. Such is the purpose of the codal provisions outlining the regime of imputation of payment.[25]

The mechanism of this mode of extinction of obligations is emphasized by the specificity of its rules as well as by the terminology used.

A. Terminology.

The tradition is to speak in terms of imputation of *payment* rather than of *performance*. **LSA-C.C. Art. 1864** preserves the expression *imputation of payment* in preference to *imputation of performance*. Payment is thus meant to refer to the performance of an obligation to pay money or to give fungible things. The *Dictionary of the Civil Code* defines "imputation" as follows: "Mode of calculation similar to a subtraction which consists in placing a value against another value, so as to deduct the first from the second in order to obtain, if it exists, a surplus to hand over . . . ."[26]

B. Rules Governing Imputation of Payment.

It was most important to enact suppletive rules of law on this matter because of the need to decide which of the interests involved, that of the obligee or that of the obligor, ought to prevail in the absence of agreement between the parties. If we assume, for example, that an obligor owes several debts of money to the same obligee and that one of these debts bears a higher interest rate than the others, it becomes critical to decide whether it is that debt or another one which will be extinguished first by the performance to be carried out. Likewise, if one of several

---

[24] LSA-C.C. Art. 2483.

[25] LSA-C.C. Arts. 1864–1868: see Appendix.

[26] *Dictionary of the Civil Code*, — word: imputation (1), p. 297.

debts is secured, guaranteed by some security, it becomes essential to ascertain whether the payment made will apply to the secured debt first or to the unsecured debts.

Voluntary performance or payment is a mode of extinction of obligations that will bind the parties; therefore, it is appropriate that the governing principle be that the intent of the parties must govern in this matter. In the absence of such an intent, it can be presumed, then, that the parties relied on the suppletive rules of law of imputation of payment to bring an end to their legal relationship.

1.   Principle: Imputation by the Parties.

The parties to an obligation may, by common agreement, decide which one of the debts owed by the obligor will be extinguished first when a payment is made. Unless the law raises an obstacle of public order to the goal pursued by the parties, a conventional imputation agreed upon by the parties should be fully enforceable.

When the parties involved have not specifically provided for this situation, preference of choice will then be given to the obligor since he is the party bearing the burden of the obligation. This preference is expressed in a principle stated in **LSA-C.C. Art. 1864**:

> **"An obligor who owes several debts to an obligee has the right to impute payment to the debt he intends to pay.**
>
> **The obligor's intent to pay a certain debt may be expressed at the time of payment or may be inferred from circumstances known to the obligee."**

There are limitations, however, to this principle:

(a) The first limitation is that an imputation of payment made by the obligor must extinguish the whole debt that he selected to pay first. In other words, an imputation cannot be used by an obligor to achieve a partial payment or performance in violation of the rules of indivisibility of performance.[27] However, the parties may provide otherwise since the rules on imputation of payment are not of public order.

(b) A second limitation imposed on the obligor is stated in **LSA-C.C. Art. 1865**: **"An obligor may not, without the obligee's consent, impute payment to a debt not yet due."** An illustration of this limitation can be found in a debt owed but which includes a term stipulated expressly, or presumed to be stipulated, in favor of the obligee. Such would be the case of a debt bearing payment of interest for the benefit of an obligee-lender; in this instance the obligor could not unilaterally impute payment to that interest bearing debt. The same limitation would apply to an obligor who would owe a debt carrying a term intended to benefit both parties.[28]

(c) A third limitation on the obligor's right to impute payment is expressed in **LSA-C.C. Art. 1866**: **"An obligor of a debt that bears interest may not, without**

---

[27]   On Indivisibility of Performance, see supra § 4.4.2.

[28]   On Term, see supra § 2.2-A.

the obligee's consent, impute a payment to principal when interest is due.

A payment made on principal and interest must be imputed first to interest."

(d) A fourth limitation to the right of imputation is of a general nature. It can be found in the good faith principle of Article 1759, as well as in the rules on the revocatory action.[29] This general limitation is justified on the ground that an obligor-debtor may not resort to an imputation of payment in favor of one particular obligee in order to deprive another obligee of his own rights.

In the event neither the above principle nor its limitations would apply and in the particular situation where the obligor has not exercised his own right to impute his payment on an existing debt, the obligee-creditor may, in turn, choose which debt he wishes to be extinguished first. That choice made by the obligee- creditor will be expressed in the receipt returned to the obligor. Actually, this type of imputation by the obligee-creditor is, in appearance only, left to the determination of the obligee. In fact, this imputation results from the bilateral consent of the obligee and the obligor since **LSA-C.C. Art. 1867** requires that the obligor accept the receipt on which the obligee recorded the imputation of payment: **"An obligor who has accepted a receipt that imputes payment to one of his debts may no longer demand imputation to another debt, unless the obligee has acted in bad faith."**

2. Suppletive Laws on Imputation of Payment.

In the event that neither the obligor nor the obligee have exercised their right to state which debt is to be discharged by imputation, the law lays down rules which supplement the wills of the parties by providing different ways in which that imputation of payment is to take place. These different ways are listed in **LSA-C.C. Art. 1868,** which attempts to clarify previously unsettled issues and to rank these suppletive modes of imputation so as to give the courts some guidelines:

> **"When the parties have made no imputation, payment must be imputed to the debt that is already due.**
>
> **If several debts are due, payment must be imputed to the debt that bears interest.**
>
> **If all, or none, of the debts that are due bear interest, payment must be imputed to the debt that is secured.**
>
> **If several unsecured debts bear interest, payment must be imputed to the debt that, because of the rate of interest, is most burdensome to the obligor.**
>
> **If several secured debts bear no interest, payment must be imputed to the debt that, because of the nature of the security, is most burdensome to the obligor.**
>
> **If the obligor had the same interest in paying all debts, payment must be imputed to the debt that became due first.**

---

[29] On the principle of good faith and LSA-C.C. Art. 1759. On the revocatory action, see LSA-C.C. Arts. 2036–2043.

If all debts are of the same nature and became due at the same time, payment must be proportionally imputed to all."

It is appropriate to point out here that the last paragraph of **Article 1868** suggests a solution which amounts to allowing a partial payment of the debts involved and, thus, their divisibility. One definite advantage of this solution is that it will benefit the obligee, who has apparently no reason to prefer the extinction of one debt over another, by suspending the liberative prescription on all the debts rather than a few selected at random.[30]

§ 7.1.3. TENDER AND DEPOSIT.

Although an obligor may be willing and ready to perform, it is still conceivable that his obligee might refuse to receive the performance offered. Whether the obligee's objections to the performance are valid or unreasonable, it remains that the obligor who is in a position to perform might suffer a prejudice should he have no alternative means of carrying through with his performance.

Taking into account the concerns and interests of both the obligee and the obligor, the law has devised the institution of *tender and deposit* as a means of providing a temporary solution to the conflicting rights of the two parties involved. The rationale of this particular mode of performance explains the existence of two forms of *tender and deposit*.[31]

A.   Notion and Rationale.

In order to amount to a performance of an obligation a *tender and deposit* must, to the extent possible, identify with that performance as it would have taken place had the obligee accepted to receive it.

It follows that, to achieve this goal, an obligor who can have recourse to a *tender and deposit* because of the nature of his obligation must do two things: he must, first, *tender* the object of his performance to the obligee and, upon refusal by the latter to accept that performance, the obligor must, second, *deposit* that object or item of performance in the care of a neutral and impartial party, the court, which may have to intervene in the dispute.

The very nature of such a *"tender and deposit"* necessarily limits its scope of application to the performance of obligations which have for their object something which can be delivered so that it can be deposited. In the first words of **LSA-C.C. Art. 2926**:

> **"A deposit is a contract by which a person, the depositor, delivers a movable thing to another person, the depositary, for safekeeping under the obligation of returning it to the depositor upon demand."**

---

[30] On Liberative Prescription, see LSA-C.C. Arts. 3445 *et seq.*

[31] On Tender and Deposit, see LSA-C.C. Arts. 1869–1872. On Deposit, see LSA-C.C. Arts. 2926–2940. See Appendix.

B. Forms of Tender and Deposit.

The Civil Code provides for two forms of *tender and deposit*. At the same time, it outlines the effects, both general and particular, of each one.

1. Offer to Tender and Deposit.

(a) Requirements.

In the event an obligee has, unequivocally and without apparent justification, refused to accept the performance offered by his obligor, the latter may, thereafter, make a *tender* followed by a *deposit* to the order of the court.

Such a juridical act of *tender and deposit* amounts to an act of disposition and requires, for its validity, that the obligor be legally capable of disposing of the thing to be deposited. Furthermore the thing deposited must be the very same thing the obligor had bound himself to give in the performance of his obligation.

(b) Effects.

A *tender and deposit* is meant to amount to the performance of the object or item of the obligation involved rather than be a substitute for it. The obligee must eventually receive exactly that which he had bargained for and his acceptance of the thing deposited, or the court's decision that the obligor has fully performed, will bring about the extinction of the obligation and the release of the obligor.

An ambiguity raised by a *tender and deposit* lies in the nature of the rights and duties of the parties between the time the obligor has tendered and deposited the thing and the moment when the obligee accepts the thing deposited.

Unquestionably, someone has to be the owner of the thing deposited and not yet accepted. The owner of that thing is still the obligor-depositor and, as such, he ought to have the right to withdraw the thing from the court's custody until it has been accepted by the obligee. As owner, should he also bear the risk of loss of the thing deposited?

If the obligor is considered as a depositor, in the sense of a true contact of deposit,[32] then he must also bear the risk of loss until acceptance of delivery by the obligee.[33] However, the unfairness of such an outcome leads one to advocate that the obligee, rather than the obligor, should be charged with the loss from the moment the *tender and deposit* has been validly made. Furthermore, if the thing deposited bears interest, the obligor ought to be released of the obligation to pay interest. In support of this view one could rely on **LSA-C.C. Art. 2939**[34] and, by an *a contrario* reasoning, hold the obligee liable for the risk of loss. Indeed, since the obligee is the party who, without proper justification, delayed the performance of the obligor by refusing to accept it, he should be considered as having breached his own obligation to accept the performance on time. From the moment the *tender and deposit* has

---

[32] LSA-C.C. Arts. 2926 *et seq.*

[33] LSA-C.C. Art. 2930.

[34] LSA-C.C. Art. 2939: see Appendix.

been made under the circumstances outlined in **Article 1869**, the burden of the risk of loss should shift to the obligee.[35]

An additional rationale for advocating the view that the risk of loss ought to fall on the obligee can be found, by analogy (*ubi eadem ratio idem lex*), in **LSA-C.C. Art. 2555**.[36] Whenever an obligor (such as a seller) has performed his obligation through a *tender and deposit*, he ought to be released from the degree of care required of a faithful administrator when it is the obligee (such as a buyer) who delays in obtaining possession. The justification behind **Article 2555** is the same as the justification which ought to be given in favor of an obligor who has had to resort to a *tender and deposit*.

It is most likely that a *tender and deposit* will be an onerous juridical act for the obligor. The latter will probably have to incur expenses for the preservation of the thing deposited, its storage or whatever else may be required. All these expenses must be borne by the obligee and reimbursed to the obligor after the former has accepted the deposit or subsequently to a court ruling the performance by the obligor lawful and valid:

> **"After the tender has been refused, the obligor may deposit the thing or the sum of money to the order of the court in a place designated by the court for that purpose, and may demand judgment declaring the performance valid.**
>
> **If the deposit is accepted by the obligee, or if the court declares the performance valid, all expenses of the deposit must be borne by the obligee."[37]**

It is possible that the thing tendered and deposited be a perishable product to be consumed or used within a relatively short period of time. A long storage might lead to the destruction of that thing despite all the diligence exercised by the obligor. To prevent such a useless outcome, **LSA-C.C. Art. 1872** offers the depositor, and the court, an alternative solution which will protect the interest the obligee has in the performance:

> **"If performance consists of the delivery of a perishable thing, or of a thing whose deposit and custody are excessively costly in proportion to its value, the court may order the sale of the thing under the conditions that it may direct, and the deposit of the proceeds."**

2.   Notice of Performance as Tender.

The second form of tender available to an obligor is outlined in **LSA-C.C. Article 1870**:

> **"If the obligor knows or has reason to know that the obligee will refuse the performance, or when the object of the performance is the delivery of a thing or a sum of money at a place other than the obligee's**

---

[35]   See LSA-C.C. Art. 1869 in Appendix.

[36]   LSA-C.C. Art. 2555: see Appendix.

[37]   LSA-C.C. Art. 1871.

domicile, a notice given to the obligee that the obligor is ready to perform has the same effect as a tender."

The importance of this rule of law is that it makes a mere notice of readiness to perform equivalent to a tender and vests in it the same legal effects. The factual circumstances giving rise to an application of this article are only slightly different from the circumstances governing the first form of tender. Essentially, **Article 1870** aims at covering the situation where the obligor is aware or has good reasons to believe that his performance will not be accepted by the obligee, as opposed to **Article 1869**, which applies to the case where the obligee has refused the obligor's performance.

It is obvious that under the circumstances outlined in **Article 1870**, the obligor is taking a great risk of having to perform a second time should he have failed to act in absolute good faith when he gave notice to his obligee. To free himself from that risk as much as possible, and to relieve himself from further obligations, the obligor ought to *deposit* the thing in the court's custody as he can under **Article 1869**.

A second set of circumstances that might give rise to an application of **Article 1870** concern the place of delivery of a thing or of a sum of money. According to **Article 1862**[38] there are several rules that govern the possible places of performance of an obligation. By agreement the parties may choose the domicile of either one of them as the place of performance although the general rule remains that performance is to be rendered at the domicile of the obligor. If one now considers **Article 1870** it states in part, as seen above, that **"when the object of the performance is the delivery of a thing or a sum of money at a place other than the obligee's domicile, a notice given to the obligee that the obligor is ready to perform has the same effect as a tender."** It is remarkable, as well as quite reasonable, that **Article 1870** singles out only the obligee's domicile under the circumstances described. For that very reason one would be justified in arguing that should performance have to take place at the obligor's domicile, a notice would have to be given by the obligor to the obligee for that notice to have the same effect as a tender. The rationale for this assertion is easy to understand. How else is the obligee to be apprised by the obligor that the latter is ready to perform at his *own* domicile? When performance is due at the obligee's domicile, there is no need for a notice for the simple reason that performance and notification take place simultaneously. If the obligee does not receive performance at his domicile, he is obviously and immediately aware that the obligor was not ready to perform.

ARTICLE 2
IMPOSSIBILITY OF PERFORMANCE

Whenever a legal relationship requires that a performance be undertaken in the future, be it a day, a month or a year, or when the performance itself spreads over a period of time, there always exists the danger that the expectations of the parties will be upset, betrayed or altered in one way or another. Events may occur which will interfere with the proper planning and anticipation of the parties. Sudden increases in the prices of commodities may endanger the existence of a corporation

---

[38] LSA-C.C. Art. 1862: see Appendix.

unable to make up for these unexpected and capricious fluctuations. The problem that is raised, then, is one of the revision of a contract and its rewriting in light of the new circumstances surrounding its execution in contrast with the circumstances which presided over its formation. Should the revision of a contract be allowed when the principle governing the law of contracts is that:

> **"Contracts have the effect of law for the parties and may be dissolved only through the consent of the parties or on grounds provided by law. Contracts must be performed in good faith." (LSA-C.C. Art. 1983)**[39]

The 1984–1985 revision of the law of obligations introduced a special title on *Impossibility of Performance* to address this problem, which had been at the heart of lengthy debates. The new articles define the notion of fortuitous event and detail some of the legal effects occurring under certain circumstances.

§ 7.2.1. NOTION OF FORTUITOUS EVENT.

From the point of view of legal terminology, the expressions *fortuitous event*, *force majeure* and *act of God* will be considered as synonymous and interchangeable. Furthermore, they will be taken as encompassing the same kinds of events although doctrinal writers may argue and disagree about the authentic meaning each expression should be given. As far as we are concerned, we shall not be involved here in these doctrinal debates.

A.   Definition of Fortuitous Event.

LSA-C.C. Article 1875 defines a fortuitous event in these terms:

> **"A fortuitous event is one that, at the time the contract was made, could not have been reasonably foreseen."**

The simplicity of this definition is misleading, in particular when one is asked to weigh the meaning of the requirement of *reasonableness*. It is important to remember that the Civil Code is largely built and shaped around the standard of the average reasonable man, the *bonus paterfamilias* of Roman law. "He" is the standard used to measure the validity of rights and obligations a capable person may derive from a legal transaction. There exists, in a sense, an <u>average objective standard</u> of the reasonableness of man against which individual parties are measured.

Is Article 1875 using an objective test of reasonableness or does it allow for a subjective one? Should a court ask itself the question whether the parties to a contract, because of their own personal and individual abilities and capacities, could not have foreseen the fortuitous event that disrupted their expectations and, therefore, whether these parties acted reasonably or not? Or should a court state that, because the parties have not lived up to the standard of the objective average reasonable man, they failed to act reasonably in not foreseeing the fortuitous event?

---

[39] LSA-C.C. Art. 1983. See Appendix.

Obviously, each one of the above two suggestions has merits and drawbacks. Because Article 1875 does not provide any hint of guidance in favor of one test or the other, one might be justified in suggesting that the courts should refer to an objective standard. On the other hand, one could very well argue that, because a contract is the law between the parties, the focus ought to be on the parties and, therefore, a subjective test of reasonableness should control.

The *Dictionary of the Civil Code* defines a fortuitous event or "force majeure" in these terms:

" a/ (classical trilogy). An unforeseeable and irresistible event, originating from an exterior cause, external to a debtor of an obligation or to the tortfeasor (force of nature[act of God], act of a third person, act of the Prince), which discharges him of his obligation or exonerate him from liability; a type of extraneous cause like the fortuitous event, different, though with the same effect, by the emphasis on the irresistible character of the event.

b/ (dominant interpretation). An event sufficiently characterized by its irresistibility and its exteriority, with the exception of cases where the foreseeability of the event combined with the possibility of avoiding it or neutralizing in advance its damaging effects by taking appropriate preventive measures excludes the exoneration of liability (involving an event which turns out to be inevitable, but which was neither unforeseeable nor unavoidable)."[40]

B. Criteria.

To ensure the stability of contracts, the security of business transactions and the reliability of the promises given, the courts should make use of certain criteria to test the reasonableness of the parties' failure to foresee a fortuitous event and plan their contractual obligations accordingly.

It is important, first of all, that the fortuitous event be just that, a fortuitous event outside the control of the parties or party. In addition, this event must be such as to render the performance of an obligation or obligations impossible or absolutely impracticable.

A second requirement ought to be that the occurrence of the fortuitous event was totally outside the realm of the contractual expectations of the parties and that, in a sense, the non-occurrence of that same event was a basic assumption taken into account by the parties.

A third criterion can be found in the principle of good faith, which is so fundamental to the law of obligations.[41] This principle that presides over the formation of a contract should also control the performances of the obligations flowing from it. If the whole economy of the contract is turned topsy-turvy, it would not be fully compatible with the good faith principle to require the forced execution of a contract, which has become one-sided or totally unbalanced. The principle of good faith justifies the preservation or re-establishment of an equilibrium between

---

[40] *Dictionary of the Civil Code*, — word: force majeure, p. 252.

[41] LSA-C.C. Art. 1759: see Appendix.

the performances seriously affected by the fortuitous event.

§ 7.2.2.   EFFECTS OF A FORTUITOUS EVENT.

The legal effects resulting from the occurrence of a fortuitous event that affects an obligor's performance will vary in extent with the time of that occurrence and its factual impact. In this respect, one can distinguish between an absolute impossibility for the obligor to perform and a partial impossibility to do so.

A.   Absolute Impossibility to Perform.

An obligor who, at the time the fortuitous event occurs, is not delinquent in the timing of his performance and not at all at fault in being placed in a position where he can no longer perform, will be exonerated from liability for failing to perform an obligation that has become absolutely impossible of performance.

LSA-C.C. Article 1873-1 formulates the general principle as follows:

> **"An obligor is not liable for his failure to perform when it is caused by a fortuitous event that makes performance impossible."**

The rationale, *ratio legis* or reason behind this principle can be extended, *a fortiori ratione*, to the situation where:

> **"An obligor who had been put in default when a fortuitous event made his performance impossible is not liable for his failure to perform if the fortuitous event would have likewise destroyed the object of the performance in the hands of the obligee had performance been timely rendered.**
>
> **That obligor is, however, liable for the damage caused by his delay."** (LSA-C.C. Article 1874).[42]

An illustration of this legal situation could be found in former **LSA-C.C. Art. 2470** which provided that "[i]f it is the seller who delays to deliver the thing, and it be destroyed, even by a fortuitous event, it is he who sustains the loss, unless it appears certain that the fortuitous event would equally have occasioned the destruction of the thing in the buyer's possession, after delivery."[43]

The legal consequence of this absolute impossibility to carry out an entire performance because of a fortuitous event is that **"the contract is dissolved"** and **"the other party may then recover any performance he has already rendered."** (LSA-C.C. Art.1876)[44]

Even though an impossibility to perform could be legally classified as absolute and therefore free the obligor of any liability, it remains that by the will of the parties, or because of the behavior of the obligor, the latter might not be totally exonerated from liability. Such would be the case where an obligor would be liable

---

[42] LSA-C.C. Art. 1874: see Appendix.

[43] Louisiana Civil Code of 1870.

[44] LSA-C.C. Art. 1876: see Appendix.

because of "his failure to perform when he has assumed the risk of such a fortuitous event." (LSA-C.C. Art.1873-2)[45] In addition, an "obligor is likewise liable when the fortuitous event that caused his failure to perform has been preceded by his fault, without which the failure would not have occurred."(LSA-C.C. Art.1873-4)[46]

B.   Partial Impossibility.

A fortuitous event may have a less drastic impact on an obligor's performance than to render that performance absolutely impossible. The fortuitous event may partially prevent a performance from being carried out in its entirety; it may also affect the scope of the performance while it is being carried out.

1.   Partial Impossibility Before Performing.

LSA-C.C. Article 1877 formulates an equitable rule in these terms:

> "When a fortuitous event has made a party's performance impossible in part, the court may reduce the other party's counterperformance proportionally, or, according to the circumstances, may declare the contract dissolved." (LSA-C.C. Art. 1877)[47]

A court will be given much discretion in deciding whether to preserve what may be salvaged of a contract or in ruling that, under the circumstances, what is left of the contract would be of no value to the parties and that, therefore, the contract ought to be dissolved. The intervention of the court will ensure that an equitable solution will be achieved and will prevent one party from taking advantage of the situation to either withdraw from the contract or to require that it be enforced regardless of the consequences for the other party.

2.   Partial Impossibility During Performance.

Former **LSA-C.C. Art 2293,**[48] on the quasi-contract of *negotiorum gestio*, present **LSA-C.C. Arts. 3006** and **3026**[49] on Mandate, and **Articles 2766** and **2767**[50] on lease, offer some instances of legal relationships that can be affected by a fortuitous event while the performances are being carried out.

These examples are illustrations of a general principle which has been embedded only in the year 1984 in **LSA-C.C. Art 1878:**

> "If a contract is dissolved because of a fortuitous event that occurred after an obligor has performed in part, the obligee is bound

---

[45] LSA-C.C. Art. 1873-2: see Appendix.

[46] LSA-C.C. Art. 1873-4: see Appendix.

[47] LSA-C.C. Art. 1877: see Appendix.

[48] Louisiana Civil Code of 1870.

[49] LSA-C.C. Arts. 3006 and 3026: see Appendix.

[50] LSA-C.C. Arts. 2766 and 2767: see Appendix.

but only to the extent that he was enriched by the obligor's partial performance."

The rationale for this new provision can be found in the necessity to prevent one party from being impoverished and the other from being unjustly enriched. This unexpected partial performance or somewhat different performance could, possibly, have led to a different consequence consisting in allowing the court to *rewrite* the contract in light of the unexpected changes brought about by the fortuitous event. With this article, the courts have been given some guidance in making use of the Civil Code articles on "Obligations Arising Without Agreement"[51] and "Enrichment Without Cause."[52]

ARTICLE 3

NOVATION-DELEGATION

In Roman law, novation was devised to by-pass the prohibition against the transfer of an obligation by one party to that obligation of a third person. Thus the "cession or transfer" of obligations was not possible. The only way to do so was to change the name of the creditor-obligee by creating a "new" contract with the name of a new obligee. Thus novation was conceived as a device meant to *extinguish* an existing obligation and, second, to *create* a new one. Today there does exist several legal devices to transfer obligations or to "apparently" extinguish an existing obligation and to create a new one somewhat different from the first one.[53] Furthermore, we do not frown as much upon third persons being bound to perform obligations to which they were not parties originally.

Novation is one of these legal devices meant, at the same time, to extinguish and to transfer an obligation. Although some forms of novation have lost much of their practical value to the benefit of other modes of transfer of obligations, it remains that novation is still recognized as an efficient way to substitute an essential component part of an obligation (person-object-cause . . .) with another so as to create a new obligation.

§ 7.3.1. DEFINITION AND CONCEPT.

The Louisiana Civil Code articles on novation do not offer a definition of the legal nature of this concept.[54] In the *Dictionary of the Civil Code*, we find the following definition: "Substitution to an obligation that is extinguished of a new obligation which is created ("novated" in relation to the old one which it is intended to replace), by changing the creditor, the debtor, the object (capital transformed into an annuity) or cause (a lease changed into hire-purchase)."[55]

---

[51] LSA-C.C. Arts 2292–2297; see Appendix.

[52] LSA-C.C. Arts 2298–2305: see Appendix.

[53] See supra Chapter 5 Transfer of Obligations.

[54] LSA-C.C. Arts. 1879–1887: see Appendix.

[55] *Dictionary of the Civil Code*, — word: novation, p. 398. Strangely enough, in the West Ed. of the Louisiana Civil Code, comment (a) to Article 1879 stresses that this very Article (based on former Article 2185 of the Code of 1870) is not meant to be a definition. It adds also that novation is not to be defined

Whether the LSA-C.C. gives a definition or not of novation, it is possible, in addition to the *Dictionary of the Civil Code*'s definition, to suggest a definition that would include all the types of agreements of novation. As a general rule, a novation is a juridical act, the creation of the wills of two parties at least, which brings about **"the extinguishment of an existing obligation by the substitution of a new one." (LSA-C.C. Art. 1879).**[56] It follows necessarily that a new obligation is substituted to a previously existing one through a change in one of the *essential* requirements constitutive of an obligation.[57] There takes place then a true legal metamorphosis of obligations.

A novation actually consists in the combination into one legal concept, the concept of novation, of two separate juridical acts: one juridical act extinguishes an existing obligation, while the other juridical act creates a new obligation. This dual effect of novation requires that some conditions be met for novation to take place, and it carries with it some important practical consequences.

§ 7.3.2.   CONDITIONS AND TYPES OF NOVATION.

Two fundamental conditions must be met for a novation to take place under whatever form it might appear.

A.   Conditions.

The first condition required is that of a succession of obligations and the second is that of the intent to novate (*animus novandi*).

1.   Succession of Two Obligations.

LSA-C.C. Article 1879 contemplates specifically this requirement of a succession of two obligations, or the substitution of a new one to an existing one, although it does not describe in precise legal terms the legal features of the obligations with which we ought to be concerned. Unquestionably, by agreement, parties to a legally binding obligation can extinguish it and change it into a new one. A legally binding obligation is one **"whereby a person, called the obligor, is bound to render a performance in favor of another, called the obligee. Performance may consist of giving, doing, or not doing something."(LSA-C.C. Art. 1756).**[58] This substitution of one binding or civil obligation to another one is the very reason why novation was originally devised.

The issue that has been raised in this matter is whether it is possible to novate either an obligation which is "null," or a "natural obligation" into a civil or legally binding obligation.

---

in terms of a contract. Still, and in an inconsistent statement, this same comment acknowledges that most novations are effected by an agreement.

[56] LSA-C.C. Art. 1879. This Art. describes more the effects of "novation" than it gives a definition.

[57] LSA-C.C. Art. 1915: See Appendix. The essential four requirements for all contracts are: capacity, consent, cause and object. See Précis "Louisiana Law of Conventional Obligations," LexisNexis 2015.

[58] LSA-C.C. Art. 1756: see Appendix.

As far as a "null obligation" is concerned it can be affected either by an absolute nullity or by a relative nullity. Considering that **"a contract that is absolutely null may not be confirmed"** and that **"an absolutely null contract . . . is deemed never to have existed,"**[59] an absolutely null obligation does not exist and it is, therefore, impossible to extinguish something that does not exist. Such an obligation, because it is deemed never to have existed, cannot be validated and, therefore, it cannot be cured of its nullity. Novation of an absolutely null obligation is an impossibility: **"Novation has no effect when the obligation it purports to extinguish does not exist or is absolutely null."**[60]

The same is not true, however, of an obligation which is only relatively null. A relatively null obligation is one which **"violates a rule intended for the protection of private parties . . . A contract that is only relatively null may be confirmed."**[61] **"Confirmation is a declaration whereby a person cures the relative nullity of an obligation."**[62] Since such a relatively null obligation can be confirmed, which means given full legal force, it should also be possible to novate it: **"If the obligation is only relatively null, the novation is valid, provided the obligor of the new one knew of the defect of the extinguished obligation."**[63]

The difference between *confirmation* of a relatively null obligation and *novation* is that confirmation results from the unilateral juridical act of declaration of will by the party wanting to cure the obligation of its nullity, which is meant to protect that party. On the other hand, *novation* would result from the bilateral juridical act of the two parties' agreement or exchange of wills. Although these two juridical acts would have the same effect of transforming a relatively null obligation into a binding one, confirmation would have the additional effect of making the new obligation valid retroactively to the time of the attempt to create the prior obligation.[64] A novated obligation, on the other hand, would have only a prospective effect beginning at the time the novation occurred. The uncertain past of the relatively null obligation could be said to have been extinguished, as is one of the two purposes of novation.[65]

As far as a *natural obligation* is concerned, it is defined as one in which the law implies a particular moral duty to render a performance.[66] The issue, then, is whether or not it is legally possible to *novate* a natural obligation into a *civil* or binding obligation, as one enforceable by legal action?

Comment (b) to Article 1879[67] states, in part, that *natural obligations may be novated*. This statement is too absolute in its formulation to be acceptable at face

---

[59] LSA-C.C. Arts. 2030 and 2033: see Appendix.

[60] LSA-C.C. Art. 1883: see Appendix.

[61] LSA-C.C. Art. 2031: see Appendix.

[62] LSA-C.C. Art. 1842: see Appendix.

[63] LSA-C.C. Art. 1883: see Appendix.

[64] See supra Confirmation § 6.1.3(1); see LSA-C.C. Art. 1844 in Appendix.

[65] Some legal scholars argue that any "null" obligation, whether relatively or absolutely null cannot be novated. One cannot novate that which does not exist.

[66] On Natural Obligations, see supra § 1.3.1; see LSA-C.C. Art. 1760 in Appendix.

[67] West Edition of the Louisiana Civil Code.

value. Indeed, one must recall here that the purposes of a novation are, first, to extinguish an existing obligation and, second, to substitute a new one in its place. A natural obligation is not one that can be extinguished, not even by prescription, as a civil binding obligation can, although the natural obligation can be transformed into a civil obligation.[68] How can one extinguish *a particular moral duty* by way of *compensation* for example?[69] Even if we looked upon novation as a form of confirmation, it is a fact that a natural obligation cannot be confirmed. Confirmation is defined as **"a declaration whereby a person cures the relative nullity of an obligation."**[70] A natural obligation is not an obligation affected with a relative nullity; it is merely an obligation "in which the law implies a particular moral duty to render a performance."[71] Therefore, if such a natural obligation cannot be confirmed, it cannot either be novated. What may be done with a natural obligation is merely to insert it into a contract as a component part of that contract, as its cause. **LSA-C.C. Art. 1761** states unequivocally that **"a contract made for the performance of a natural obligation is onerous."** In a sense, therefore, the natural obligation subsists (rather than being extinguished) as the cause for the civilly binding obligation of which it becomes a part. Only a "civil obligation" can be novated!

2.   Intent to Novate (Animus Novandi).

LSA-C.C. Art. 1880 states: **"The intention to extinguish the original obligation must be clear and unequivocal. Novation may not be presumed."** The intent to novate, or *"animus novandi"* must be specific in the sense that the parties must have meant both to extinguish an existing civil obligation and to change it into another civil obligation. It is in that special intent that, to a large extent, a novation finds its distinctive nature from other juridical acts, such as a delegation.[72] Furthermore the specific intent to novate will serve to distinguish a novation from a mere alteration, transformation or modification of an existing obligation. As **LSA-C.C. Art. 1881-3** states: **"Mere modification of an obligation, made without intention to extinguish it, does not effect a novation. The execution of a new writing, the issuance or renewal of a negotiable instrument, or the giving of new securities for the performance of an existing obligation are examples of such a modification."** Moreover, if the change intended is too drastic and meant, in reality, to abolish any connection between the new and the former obligations, then the intent of the parties may have been not to novate but to create an independent and unrelated obligation.

Since a novation is brought about, in large measure, by a specific intent, the *animus novandi*, it is obvious that the new obligation that is meant to be created would not be valid if a party lacked the proper legal capacity at the time of the attempted novation, or if some vice of consent can be established to have occurred at the time of the attempted novation, since novation is an agreement.

---

[68] See supra Natural Obligations § 1.3.1.

[69] See Compensation infra § 7.5; see LSA-C.C. Art. 1893 in Appendix.

[70] LSA-C.C. Art. 1842; see supra Confirmation § 6.1.3(1).

[71] LSA-C.C. Art. 1760.

[72] LSA-C.C. Art 1886; see Delegation infra § 7.3.4.

B.   Forms of Novation.

A novation is the outcome of a change in an *essential* component part of an obligation (parties, cause, object) or in the substitution of a modality, which affects the very existence of an obligation.

1.   Novation Resulting from a Change in an Essential Element of an Existing Obligation.

Such a change may be described as either objective or subjective.

(a) Objective Novation.

An objective "[n]ovation takes place when, by agreement of the parties, a new performance is substituted for that previously owed, or a new cause is substituted for that of the original obligation. If any substantial part of the original performance is still owed, there is no novation.

Novation takes place also when the parties expressly declare their intention to novate an obligation." (LSA-C.C. Art.1881).[73]

There are, therefore, three kinds of objective novation: novation resulting from a new performance, from a new cause or from an express intention.

A novation resulting from a new performance is one bearing on the *object* or *item of the performance*. Where, for example, the parties had agreed that the obligor would perform some services for the benefit of the obligee, the same parties can decide to novate that obligation by agreeing that the obligor will now pay a sum of money. From an obligation to do something the parties have switched to an obligation to give something.

A novation may also occur as a result of a change in the *cause* of the original obligation. The *cause*[74] is the reason for entering into a contractual relationship; thus, the parties may change the nature of their contractual relationship by substituting a new cause to the cause that led to the creation of the original obligation. For example, it is possible for the parties to enter into a contract of lease requiring the lessee to pay a monthly rent. The same parties may novate that contract of lease into a contract of sale by the substitution of a new cause. Whereas the lease maintained the ownership of the premises in the lessor's hands, the sale transfers that ownership to the buyer (former lessee).

The parties may also change the cause of an obligation so as to transform it in its very nature. For example, where a loan had been extended to the borrower, the parties may agree that a donation will be substituted, novating an onerous cause into a gratuitous one.

LSA-C.C. Art. 1881 introduces, in its second *paragraph*, a rather unusual third kind of objective novation: "**Novation takes place also when the parties expressly**

---

[73] LSA-C.C. Art. 1881-1 and 2: see Appendix.

[74] On Cause, see LSA-C.C. Arts.1966–1970. See also Précis on Louisiana Law of Conventional Obligations.

declare their intention to novate an obligation."

Comment (d) to this article posits that "even if a new performance or a new cause is not substituted, a novation takes place if there is an express declaration of the parties to that effect."[75] One wonders how such a novation could occur. Unless the parties mean to extinguish "**an existing obligation by the substitution of a new one,**"[76] consent by itself is powerless unless it bears on an essential component part which can turn an existing obligation into a new one.

(b) Subjective Novation.

LSA-C.C. Art. 1882 provides expressly for one form of subjective novation by substitution of an obligor to another. When the same article remains silent as to the possibility of a subjective novation of an obligee to another, one must wonder, *a contrario sensu*, whether such a form of novation is expressly prohibited (*inclusio unius, exclusio alterius*) or whether it ought to be allowed for the same reasons that justify the existence of a novation of obligors (*ubi eadem ratio, idem lex*).

(i) Novation of obligors. **LSA-C.C. Art. 1882** states that a novation of obligors **"takes place when a new obligor is substituted for a prior obligor who is discharged by the obligee. In that case, the novation is accomplished even without the consent of the prior obligor, unless he had an interest in performing the obligation himself."** For such a novation to occur it is essential, first of all, that the obligee and the new obligor do intend to extinguish the prior obligation involving the original obligor and, second, that the same two parties do mean to create a new obligation. We can observe in this form of novation an illustration of the principle which states that an obligation may be discharged by a third person unless the obligor had an interest in performing himself.[77]

The novation, once accomplished, creates a new obligation and a new contractual relationship between the obligee and his new obligor. As a result, the original obligor is released of all performance *vis-à-vis* the obligee who has discharged him. It follows that the obligee may not subrogate the new obligor to his rights against the original obligor[78] since a subrogation would defeat the whole essence of the institution of novation which is the substitution of a new obligation to a prior one. In addition we are far removed from the concept of stipulation for the benefit of another since, in that last instance, the original obligor would not be released of his obligation.[79] Lastly, a novation of obligors does not amount to an assumption of obligations since, under the latter institution the original obligor would not be released by the assuming obligor who becomes also liable.[80]

The particular effects of novation are well illustrated in the situation where two or more obligors are solidarily bound *vis-à-vis* the obligee. A consequence of the combination of the effects of novation and solidarity is that:

---

[75] West Ed. Louisiana Civil Code.

[76] LSA-C.C. Art. 1879, emphasis ours. See Art. 1879 in Appendix.

[77] LSA-C.C. Arts. 1822 and 1855: see supra Performance § 7.1.

[78] LSA-C.C. Art. 1827; on Subrogation, see supra § 5.2.

[79] LSA-C.C. Arts. 1978 to 1982.

[80] LSA-C.C. Arts. 1821 to 1824; see Assumption of Obligations, supra § 5.1.

"A novation made by the obligee and one of the obligors of a solidary obligation releases the other solidary obligors.

In that case, the security given for the performance of the extinguished obligation may be retained by the obligee only on property of that obligor with whom the novation has been made.

If the obligee requires that the other co-obligors remain solidarily bound, there is no novation unless the co-obligors consent to the new obligation."[81]

A novation having for its purpose the extinction of an existing obligation and, simultaneously, the creation of a new one, it follows logically that the solidary obligors who did not expressly consent to the novation cannot be bound by the new obligation entered into by one of them. In addition, and unless otherwise clearly indicated, it cannot be said that the solidary obligor who agreed to the novation had been given a mandate by his co-solidary obligors to enter into a new obligation. On this particular issue the last paragraph of Civil Code Article 1885 is very clear.

(ii) Novation of obligees. **LSA-C.C. Art. 1882** does not mention this form of subjective novation as a possibility open to parties to an obligation. However one can find in comment (d)[82] to that article a statement that explains briefly why a novation of obligees was not mentioned in Article 1882. The comment states: "*subjective novation by substitution of a new obligee is not provided for because the effects of such a novation are readily achieved through an assignment of credit.*" Not only is this statement far too broad to be accurate and, thus, convincing, but it also fails to take into consideration both the *raison d'être* of a novation of obligees and the *raison d'être* of an assignment of credit, as well as some of the fundamental differences between these two institutions.

For example, an assignment of credit (or assignment of right)[83] is a transfer that takes place between the obligee-assignor and the third party assignee without the involvement of the obligor, the latter receiving merely a notice of the transfer. In a novation of obligees the existing obligor must consent to the novation contemplated by his obligee so as to create a new obligation and a right of action for the benefit of the new obligee against him. Furthermore, an assignment of credit does not alter the nature of the obligation that is transferred; the same obligation that existed before the transfer or assignment remains in existence after the transfer. It means, therefore, that the obligor can raise against the assignee the same exceptions and defenses he could have raised against the original obligee-assignor. In a novation of obligees, on the other hand, because a new obligation results from the substitution of a new obligee to the original one, the obligor who has consented to the novation may not raise against the new obligee the defenses he had available against the original obligee. Lastly, an assignment of credit transfers an obligation with all its accessory rights of security that guarantee the performance of that obligation. In a novation of obligees, the obligation that is created is a new one and none of the

---

[81] LSA-C.C. Art. 1885: see Appendix.

[82] West Ed. Louisiana Civil Code.

[83] LSA-C.C. Arts. 2642 to 2654, Sale of a Right or Assignment of a Right; see *Louisiana Law of Sale and Lease, a Précis*, § 2.3.5.

accessory rights attached to the former obligation are transferred to the new obligee. In addition, because the obligation is new, it will be subject to its own (and new) prescriptive period.

It appears, therefore, that the conceptualistic differences between an assignment of credit and a novation of obligees lead to important differences in the legal effects of the two institutions. Although a novation of obligees can be a dangerous operation for the new obligee, it remains that it need not be as formal as an assignment of rights[84] and that it might be more beneficial to an obligor who, under the new bond of law, might be better able to perform *vis-à-vis* his new obligee.

2. Novation of an Obligation by Substitution of a Modality.

We have previously described a *condition* as an event which, in the course of time, may or may not occur and to which is tied the existence or the extinction of a bond of law.[85] To add a suspensive condition to a pure and simple obligation it is to *novate* that obligation. By this addition the very existence of that obligation has been altered; from an existing and enforceable bond of law it has now become a conditional bond of law, that is to say one whose existence may or may not happen in the future. The same is true of the addition of a resolutory condition to a pure and simple obligation since the occurrence of the resolutory condition would retroactively annihilate the existence of the obligation it affects. The reverse process of deleting or removing a condition from an obligation thereby made conditional would carry with it a novation of that obligation since it would become pure and simple.

A term, on the other hand, affects merely the execution or performance of an obligation and not its existence.[86] Therefore the addition of a term, the extension of an existing term or the repeal of a term would have an impact merely on the timing of the performance of his obligation by the obligor bound under the existing obligation. Adding a term to an existing obligation or deleting a term from such an obligation does not "*novate*" the obligation.

§ 7.3.3. EFFECTS OF NOVATION.

The immediate effects of novation are essentially two: 1) extinction of an existing obligation and 2) its replacement by a new one.

A. Extinction of an Obligation.

LSA-C.C. Art. 1879 states unequivocally that "[n]ovation **is the extinguishment of an existing obligation by the substitution of a new one.**" It follows that, from the moment of the creation of a <u>new</u> obligation, all the accessory rights that ensured the performance of the original primary obligation are also extinguished as is suggested, specifically, by **LSA-C.C. Art. 1884: "Security given**

---

[84] See in particular LSA-C.C. Arts. 2642 and 2643.

[85] See Condition, supra § 2.2-B.

[86] See Term, supra § 2.2-A.

for the performance of the extinguished obligation may not be transferred to the new obligation without agreement of the parties who gave the security."[87]

Thus, where a new obligor is substituted to the original obligor, the security provided by the original obligor cannot be transferred to guarantee the new obligation unless the new obligor and the original obligor so agree. A creditor-obligee may, indeed, make a novation conditional upon retaining his former securities, which can be done with the consent of all the parties involved.

"If the new obligor has assumed the obligation and acquired the thing given as security, the discharge of any prior obligor by the obligee does not affect the security or its rank."(LSA-C.C. Art.1887) [88]

Although the original obligor has been discharged, it remains that because the security guaranteeing the performance of the new obligation is the same as that which guaranteed the original obligor's obligation, the ranking that was then assigned to the security remains unaffected. This is a somewhat unusual consequence since, in this instance, an accessory right (the security) has a controlling impact on a principal right (the obligation itself). We are encountering here a rule of law which is the opposite of the well known principle, *accessorium sequitur principale* (the accessory follows the principal).[89] This rule can easily be explained by the fact that all parties involved have to consent to the preservation of the security and, in addition, it is meant to encourage novations of obligations since the obligee will not lose any of his previously acquired rights.

The first effect of a novation, to wit the extinction of an obligation, can be emphasized from another point of view. When a novation takes place it brings about the extinction of an obligation and creates in its place a new obligation. But what should happen if the "new" obligation is null or is annulled, therefore does not exist or cannot exist? One could make the argument that since the parties meant to put an end to an existing obligation by creating a new one, if they fail to create a new obligation, the failure to agree on a new obligation should be the end of the parties' relationship. However, it is also possible to make the argument that if a novation fails, since its purpose was to create a new obligation, the failure to novate means obviously that the creation of a "new" obligation was not successful and that, therefore, the prior-original obligation should still be in existence. In a sense, the past could not be erased and should still govern the relationship between the parties to the original obligation.

B.   Creation of a New Obligation.

The new obligation which emerges from the juridical act of novation is free of all the rights of action and exceptions which were attached to the former and original obligation. The new obligation takes on its particular legal features and a legal existence of its own.[90]

---

[87]   LSA-C.C. Art. 1884 in Appendix.

[88]   LSA-C.C. Art. 1887 in Appendix.

[89]   See *Dictionary of the Civil Code*, Index of Legal Adages, p.659.

[90]   See however LSA-C.C. 1887 above.

In conclusion, it appears that a novation is a rather complex juridical act in addition to being fraught with dangers for the obligee. It may explain why a novation of obligations is not a very common legal transaction, all the more so since most of its effects can be realized through other juridical acts, such as delegation, assumption of debt, assignment of credit, stipulation for the benefit of another, etc. Still it should be considered as an available mode of extinguishing an obligation and creating a new one, should all the parties involved intend to do so.

§ 7.3.4. DELEGATION.

A. Notion of Delegation.

LSA-C.C. Art. 1886 states:

> **"A delegation of performance by an obligor to a third person is effective when that person binds himself to perform.**
>
> **A delegation effects a novation only when the obligee expressly discharges the original obligor."**

One should notice that the first paragraph of **Article 1886** refers to the "performance" of an obligation and not to the obligation itself. Indeed, a delegation is a juridical act whereby the debtor-obligor instructs another, the third person or delegated debtor, to become a debtor and perform an obligation for the benefit of the obligee. A "delegation" is, therefore a *"triangular operation wherein on the order of a person, the délégant-delegator, another person, the délégué-delegated, undertakes an obligation towards a third person, the délégataire-delegatee, who accepts the latter as debtor."*[91]

Under these circumstances, the consent of the obligee is not necessary as his right of action against his original obligor is preserved. Actually the obligee receives the additional benefit of a second obligor for the same obligation owed by his original obligor. However, whenever the performance owed under the obligation is one that calls upon the personal services of the original obligor, the delegation could not bind the delegated obligor unless the obligee himself has consented to it. Indeed, a personal obligation on the part of the obligor cannot be delegated as long as the obligee has not agreed to make that same obligation personal on the part of the delegated obligor.

In most instances, a delegation will take place between at least three parties who are already bound in some way by a prior juridical act. For example, it is not uncommon for an obligor-debtor who, himself, holds a claim against his own debtor, to turn to the latter and request that he agree to become a delegated debtor *vis-à-vis* the obligee. Such a delegation, if it is perfected and carried out, will result in the extinction of two obligations by one single payment: the delegated-debtor, by paying directly the obligee, extinguished both his own obligation *vis-à-vis* the obligor-debtor (his own obligee) and the latter's obligation *vis-à-vis* the original obligee.

---

[91] *Dictionary of the Civil Code,* — word: délégation (2), p. 160.

B.   Effects of Delegation.

1.   Effects of Delegation in the Relationship Between the Obligee and the Delegated Obligor.

On the order or request of the original obligor, the delegated obligor binds himself *vis-à-vis* the obligee and, thereby, creates an obligation that is totally independent and distinct from the obligation still binding the original obligor towards the obligee. It follows that the delegated obligor cannot oppose to the original obligee the exceptions and defenses which he could have raised against his own obligee, who is the original obligor. Such an effect of delegation is based on the premise that the obligee who receives the performance due to him from the delegated obligor is unaware of the *cause* of the obligation binding his own, the original, obligor and the delegated obligor. The latter could not raise the defense of *error* resulting from his contractual relationship with the original obligor nor even that of nullity of that same relationship. It appears, therefore, that these effects of delegation are in sharp contrast with those of an assumption of obligations resulting from an agreement between an obligor and a third person as stated in **LSA-C.C. Art. 1822.**[92] In addition, in contrast with an assumption of obligations, a delegation does not have to be in writing to be valid, although it would certainly be advisable to enter into a written agreement to secure the proof of the promise made by the delegated obligor to pay the debt of another, the original obligor.[93] Furthermore, a delegation does not create a bond of solidarity between the original obligor and the delegated obligor as an assumption of obligations would create between an obligor and a third person.[94]

2.   Effects of Delegation in the Relationship Between the Obligee and the Original Obligor.

The legal nature of these effects will vary with the kind of delegation involved. Indeed, a delegation can be perfect or imperfect.

A perfect delegation amounts to a novation when the obligee expressly discharges the original obligor.[95] "Perfect delegation" is the *"name given to the delegation in which the délégatairee-delegatee, as creditor of the délégant-delegator, becomes creditor of the délégué-delegated and expressly discharges the delegator, so that the delegation effects a novation by change of debtor."*[96] In this particular type of delegation, the obligee must expressly consent to the delegation-novation so as to extinguish the debt owed by his original obligor. There are, therefore, two steps necessary for a perfect delegation to occur: there must exist, first of all, a delegation between the original obligor and the delegated obligor; second, the obligee must consent to that delegation and expressly intend to novate by agreeing to fully

---

[92] See Assumption of Obligations supra § 5.1. See LSA-C.C. Art. 1822 in Appendix.

[93] LSA-C.C. Art. 1847: see Appendix.

[94] LSA-C.C. Art. 1821: see Appendix; see Assumption of Obligations supra § 5.1.

[95] LSA-C.C. Art. 1886: see Appendix.

[96] *Dictionary of the Civil Code,* — word: délégation parfaite, p. 160.

discharge the original obligor of his obligation.

An imperfect delegation does not amount to a novation because the obligee does not wish to discharge the original obligor. By means of such a delegation *"the délégataire-delegatee receives the promise of the délégué-delegated without, however, discharging the délégant-delegator so that the delegation gives him a second debtor."*[97] The obligee is then entitled to call upon either one of two obligors. These two obligors ought not to be bound solidarily since solidarity is an exception to the law of obligations with multiple persons and is not to be presumed but, rather, must arise either from a clear expression of the parties intent or from the letter of the law.[98] What is stated elsewhere specifically about solidarity and assumption of obligations[99] does not include by implication delegation and, therefore, solidarity ought not control the relationship of two obligors bound only by an imperfect delegation.

ARTICLE 4
REMISSION OF DEBT

A remission of debt is a conventional mode of extinction of an obligation. It is an *"act (extinctive of an obligation) by which a creditor voluntarily renounces receiving payment (although occasionally with self-interested motives; ex. arrangement with creditors), and releases the debtor (who accepts: hence it is a contract) of his obligation."*[100] A remission may achieve different purposes according to the legal nature it may take on.

§ 7.4.1. DEFINITION AND CONCEPTS.

A. Definition.

A remission of debt can be defined as a bilateral juridical act or contract, gratuitous or onerous, whereby an obligee gives up the right to demand the performance of an obligation owed by his obligor. **LSA-C.C. Article 1888** states **"[a] remission of debt by an obligee extinguishes the obligation. That remission may be express or tacit."**

The rules of formation of contracts will apply to a remission of debt. One rule which is explicitly referred to concerns the requirement of consent. A remission of debt is not a unilateral juridical act[101] in the sense that, if it were, the sole will of the obligee would be sufficient to bring about a remission. In other words, if a remission were classified as a unilateral juridical act the obligee could impose his will on his obligor. That is not the case as regards a remission of debt. For a remission of debt to be valid two wills must coexist: the obligor, in particular, must agree to the remission offered to him by his obligee. **LSA-C.C. Art. 1890** states, in

---

[97] *Dictionary of the Civil Code*, — word: délégation imparfaite, p. 160.

[98] See Solidarity supra § 3.3.1.

[99] LSA-C.C. Art. 1821.

[100] *Dictionary of the Civil Code*, — word: remise de dette, p.489–490.

[101] On "Juridical Acts", see supra § 1.1.2.

part, "[a]cceptance of a remission is always presumed, unless the obligor rejects the remission within a reasonable time."[102] Consent is presumed merely because a remission consists usually in a benefit being given to the obligor. Any reasonable person is presumed to want to accept a benefit and not give anything in return. However, like a donation, which is not binding until accepted by the donee, a remission is not a remission until it has been presumably or expressly accepted by the obligor. An obligor who would want to reject a remission of his debt would have to expressly manifest his opposition or rejection. One cannot be forced to accept a "gift," a "gratuity," which is often the case of a remission of debt. In a sense, the obligee "forgives" the debt owed by his obligor with, at least, the "presumed" of that obligor.

B.   Concepts of Remission.

1.   Remission as a Gratuitous Juridical Act.

When remitting a debt, expressly, tacitly, or by presumption, an obligee might be motivated by a purely gratuitous intent: the intent to donate. Through the extinction of his obligor's obligation by means of remission, the obligee is actually making to his obligor a donation of the performance owed; the obligor is relieved of the burden of doing or giving something he was bound to perform. Such a gratuitous juridical act must then be subjected to the substantive rules governing the validity of donations. For example, the capacity required of an obligee willing to gratuitously remit a debt must be the same capacity that is required of a donor making a donation. It will follow that an emancipated minor may not be allowed to consent to a remission of debt if the "authentic act" which granted him "limited emancipation" does not confer on him the right to enter into this "kind of juridical act."[103] Until the year 1991, the same incapacity or limited capacity was provided with respect to a "doctor of physic or surgeon who might be indebted to a patient."[104] Should the patient have died of his sickness while attended by the doctor or surgeon, the latter could not receive "any benefit from donation *inter vivos* or *mortis causa* made in [his] favor by the sick person during that sickness." A remission of debt that would have been granted by a patient to his medical doctor could have become such a donation and would have been prohibited.

In addition to the rules on capacity, one ought to be concerned also with the applicability of the rules on collation,[105] reduction of excessive donations and revocation of donations.[106] Thus, a remission of debt cannot be used as a device to by-pass the fundamental rules on the validity of parallel legal institutions.

In contrast with the substantive rules above described, the requirements of form pertaining to the formation of gratuitous acts are not applicable. To the extent that a remission of debt takes place between living persons (as opposed to a remission

---

[102] LSA-C.C. Art. 1890: see Appendix.

[103] LSA-C.C. Art. 368.

[104] Former LSA-C.C. Art. 1489.

[105] LSA-C.C. Arts. 1227 *et seq.*

[106] LSA-C.C. Arts. 1503 *et seq.*; Arts. 1556 *et seq.*

of debt by way of a disposition in a testament), it will not be subjected to any particular form, except where the rules governing the proof of obligations would be applicable.

2.   Remission of Debt as an Onerous Juridical Act.

In a few instances a remission of debt may have an onerous cause. Such can be the case when it is grafted upon another juridical act of which it becomes a part. For example, a voluntary respite and a remission can be combined in a juridical act whereby "**all the creditors consent to the proposal, which the debtor makes, to pay in a limited time the whole or part of his debt.**"[107] In this instance there could occur a partial remission of debt.

§ 7.4.2.   PROOF OF REMISSION OF DEBT.

A remission of debt, as any juridical act, is subjected to the rules of *Proof of Obligations*.

The effectiveness of a remission of debt, its binding effect and its proof are contingent upon the obligor receiving the communication of the obligee's intent. As **LSA-C.C. Art. 1890** states: "**A remission of debt is effective when the obligor receives the communication from the obligee. Acceptance of a remission is always presumed unless the obligor rejects the remission within a reasonable time.**" The selection of the *receipt theory*, as the time of effectiveness of the remission, is quite reasonable since it assumes that the obligor will accept the benefit of the remission of debt. Few are, indeed, the obligors who would not want to be discharged of their obligations. The obligor needs to prove only the time at which he received communication of the obligee's intent.

Besides this tacit acceptance by the obligor, the law has provided for instances of presumption of remission of debt. One such example is referred to in **LSA-C.C. Art. 1889** in these terms: "**An obligee's voluntary surrender to the obligor of the instrument evidencing the obligation gives rise to a presumption that the obligee intended to remit the debt.**" Thus the voluntary delivery by the obligee to his obligor of the instrument evidencing the obligation creates a rebuttable presumption that the obligee intended to remit the debt. This intent can be defeated or, on the contrary, established by one party or the other to the presumed remission. In other words, an obligee may surrender an instrument to his obligor for other reasons than wanting to remit a debt.

It is important to recall, at this point, **LSA-C.C. Art. 1803-2** which provides that "**[s]urrender to one solidary obligor of the instrument evidencing the obligation gives rise to a presumption that the remission of debt was intended for the benefit of all the solidary obligors.**" The wording, intent and reasons for these two articles complement each other very well.

---

[107] On Respite, see LSA-C.C. Arts. 3084 to 3098.

§ 7.4.3. EFFECTS OF REMISSION OF DEBT.

A distinction must be drawn between the discharge of one single obligor, the discharge of one of multiple obligors, as well as the discharge of a surety.

A. Discharge of a Single Obligor.

Once an obligor has had his obligation remitted, he is discharged of any future performance. The extinction of the primary obligation will carry with it the discharge of any accessory obligation by virtue of the principle *accessorium sequitur principale*. Thus, if the obligor had given anything in pledge or provided a security of some kind, that accessory obligation meant to guarantee the performance of the primary obligation will be automatically extinguished with the remission of the principal debt. The thing given in pledge or as a security will have to be returned to the obligor.

On the other hand, "**[r]elease of a real security given for performance of the obligation does not give rise to a presumption of remission of debt.**" (LSA-C.C. Art. 1891). The fact that an obligee would consent to allow his obligor to recover a thing given in pledge or to cancel a mortgage is not equivalent to a remission of the principal obligation. The discharge of an accessory obligation does not affect the existence of the principal obligation. The latter can survive without the support of the former.

B. Remission of Debt and Multiple Obligors.

When obligors are joint obligors[108] each one owes a share of the whole performance. It follows that a remission of debt to one of them does not discharge the others of their own performance, since each one is actually bound separately. The remission of debt benefits only the joint obligor who was offered, and who accepted, the discharge granted to him.

Should multiple obligors be bound solidarily or indivisibly, then each one of them can be called upon to perform the whole obligation.[109] One logical and reverse consequential effect could then be that a remission granted to one solidary obligor would discharge all the solidary obligors since, under the law, performance by one of them would have amounted to performance by all. Such is not, however, the solution dictated by the law here. Departing from the law of solidarity as it existed before 1984, the new code articles have opted for a rational principle by providing that "**[r]emission of debt by the obligee in favor of one obligor, or a transaction or compromise between the obligee and one obligor, benefits the other solidary obligors in the amount of the portion of that obligor.**" (LSA-C.C. Art. 1803-1). The solidary obligors who were not offered the remission of their personal share of the debt will, therefore, benefit from the remission granted to one of them, only up to the amount of the share for which the discharged solidary obligor was liable.

---

[108] On Joint Obligors see supra § 3.2; see LSA-C.C. Art. 1788 in Appendix.

[109] On Solidarity and Indivisibility, see supra § 4.4.2. See LSA-C.C. Arts. 1789, 1794, 1795 in Appendix.

C. Remission of Debt and Sureties.

Whenever the principal obligation is guaranteed by the accessory obligations of sureties, a variety of rules may become applicable as illustrated in **LSA-C.C. Art. 1892.**[110]

In its first paragraph, this article states: "**remission of debt granted to the principal obligor releases the sureties.**" This rule is but an application of the principle that the accessory follows the fate of the principal (*accessorium sequitur principale*).[111]

However, a "**remission of debt granted to the sureties does not release the principal obligor.**" (**LSA-C.C. Art. 1892-2**). This rule follows the long established principle which states that, since a primary obligation has an existence of its own independent from that of its accessory obligations, a discharge of an accessory obligation owed by a surety has no impact on the preservation of the primary obligation.

The third paragraph of **LSA-C.C. Art. 1892** states: "**Remission of debt granted to one surety releases the other sureties only to the extent of the contribution the other sureties might have recovered from the surety to whom the remission was granted.**" If multiple sureties are bound together, as joint obligors would be, that is to say that each one of them owes only a share of the principal obligation, a remission granted to one surety will not discharge the other sureties who remain bound for their own share as they had always been.

However, where a surety would have had a right of contribution from another surety or sureties, as in the case of solidary sureties, then the same rule that applies to solidary obligors will control the relationship between the solidary sureties. The remission of debt granted to a solidary surety will benefit the other(s) solidary surety (sureties) up to the amount of the contribution that should have been made by the discharged surety.[112]

Lastly "**[i]f the obligee grants a remission of debt to a surety in return for an advantage, that advantage will be imputed to the debt, unless the surety and the obligee agree otherwise.**" (**LSA-C.C. Art. 1892-4**). This fourth paragraph of Article 1892 introduces a new rule in the law of obligations. It states that whenever a surety performs his accessory obligation, this performance will count towards the performance of the primary obligation, as owed by the principal obligor.[113] Such is the function of a surety. However, by agreement the surety who performs and the obligee who receives that performance may stipulate that the surety's performance is merely carried out to release the surety of his contingent and accessory obligation and should not be counted towards the performance of the principal obligation. In other words, although the surety has undertaken to perform his accessory obligation, that same surety is also advising the obligee that

---

[110] LSA-C.C. Art. 1892: see Appendix.

[111] See *Dictionary of the Civil Code*, Index of Legal Adages, p. 659.

[112] LSA-C.C. Arts. 3045, 3055 *et seq.*

[113] On Imputation, see supra § 7.1.2.

the latter must still call upon the principal obligor to obtain performance of the principal obligation, which is in no way to be reduced by the surety's performance. The surety is not wiling, yet, to take the risk of having to claim reimbursement from the principal obligor.

ARTICLE 5
COMPENSATION

Compensation is a somewhat unique mode of extinction of obligations limited in its application to a particular type of obligation. Compensation is the *"total or partial extinction of two reciprocal obligations, between the same persons involving a sum of money or a certain quantity of **fongibles**-fungible things of the same species."*[114]

Compensation is unique in the sense that it achieves two simultaneous goals not pre-planned by the parties involved. An extinction of obligations by compensation achieves, as its first goal, a simplification of the reciprocal performances of two obligations by either extinguishing both of them completely before they are carried out or by limiting them to a reduced performance of the lesser of the two obligations in existence. The second goal achieved by a compensation of obligations is to provide a kind of legal guarantee or privilege of payment to a creditor *vis-à-vis* the other creditors of the same debtor. In this respect, the usefulness of compensation is that a creditor receives this guarantee in the course of time even though he had not pre-arranged any security to guarantee the payment of the obligation his debtor owes him.

The uniqueness of this form of extinction of obligations is emphasized by its limited domain of application. Compensation is basically restricted to reciprocal or correlative obligations to give,[115] since its essence consists in assigning a part of an obligor's patrimony or assets to the performance of the obligation he owes.

Compensation may occur in one of three different ways: 1) by operation of law; 2) by contractual agreement between the parties; 3) by judicial declaration.

§ 7.5.1.   COMPENSATION BY OPERATION OF LAW.

A.   Concept and Conditions.

LSA-C.C. Art. 1893 describes compensation by operation of law in these terms: **"Compensation takes place by operation of law when two persons owe to each other sums of money or quantities of fungible things identical in kind, and these sums or quantities are liquidated and presently due.**

In such a case, compensation extinguishes both obligations to the extent of the lesser amount.

Delays of grace do not prevent compensation."

---

[114] *Dictionary of the Civil Code*, entry "Compensation" 1. p. 118.

[115] LSA-C.C. Arts. 1908–1909: see Appendix; on Obligations to Give, see supra § 1.2.1.

This type of compensation will take "**place regardless of the sources of the obligations.**" (**LSA-C.C. Art. 1894-1**). It follows that an obligation owed by one party as a result of a tort he committed may be compensated with a contractual obligation owed the tortfeasor by the other party. As long as each party is indebted to the other, it is not necessary that the two reciprocal obligations find their sources in one and the same juridical act or fact.

Compensation by operation of law is circumscribed, however, by a series of conditions which limit its scope of application. There are four conditions:

1. Reciprocity of Obligations.

The first condition is that the two persons must be indebted to each other in the same capacity as principal obligors and entitled to claim a performance from each other in the same capacity as principal obligees. Thus each party must be, at the same time, principal obligor and principal obligee. This condition explains why "**compensation between obligee and surety does not extinguish the obligation of the principal obligor.**" (**LSA-C.C. Art. 1897-2**).[116] A simple surety is not on the same level as the principal obligor; he does not owe directly and immediately to the obligee and his obligation is only secondary to or contingent upon the existence of an obligation owed by the principal obligor.

An additional consequence of this requirement is that "**compensation between obligee and principal obligor extinguishes the obligation of a surety.**" (**LSA-C.C. Art. 1897-1**). A simple surety may therefore oppose to a creditor the defense of compensation by operation of law when it has taken place between the creditor-obligee and the obligor. Once compensation has occurred by operation of law there is no longer any principal obligation for a surety to guarantee and, therefore, the surety's secondary obligation is also extinguished.

The rationale of the legal relationship between two solidary obligors justifies that the benefit of the defense of compensation by operation of law be subjected to a rule different from the one governing simple sureties. **LSA-C.C. Art. 1898-1** provides that: "**Compensation between the obligee and one solidary obligor extinguishes the obligation of the other solidary obligors only for the portion of that obligor.**"[117] When compensation by operation of law takes place between the obligee and a solidary obligor, compensation extinguishes only that part of the obligation that would normally be owed by the solidary obligor who claims the benefit of compensation. As a result, the remaining solidary obligors are released only of the amount of that share or part. Under these circumstances the benefit of compensation is both personal and common. It is personal in the sense that only the solidary obligor who claimed that benefit is fully released by this fictitious method of payment, and it is common in the sense that the remaining solidary obligors may all argue that compensation has occurred up to a certain amount thanks to the right of one of them to claim that benefit.

---

[116] LSA-C.C. Art. 1897: see Appendix.

[117] LSA-C.C. Art. 1898: see Appendix.

In the event a solidary obligor is also, and at the same time, the principal obligor because he is the only one concerned,[118] should he be sued by the obligee, compensation by operation of law will then amount to a full payment of the principal obligation and release the other solidary obligors of their obligation *vis-à-vis* the obligee. The reason for this rule is that the other solidary obligors have become simple sureties of the principal obligor when compensation by operation of law occurred. To that extent, and under these specific circumstances, compensation by operation of law is a defense common to all the remaining solidary obligors.

It is most important to point out here a specific exception of public policy to the above rules. Indeed, according to **LSA-C.C. Art. 1898-3: "The compensation provided in this Article does not operate in favor of a liability insurer."** This exception must be interpreted strictly (*exceptio est strictissimae interpretationis*; an exception must be interpreted restrictively) and ought not to apply to conventional guarantors.

Solidarity can also exist between obligees and **LSA-C.C. Art. 1898-2** addresses this particular situation: **"Compensation between one solidary obligee and the obligor extinguishes the obligation only for the portion of that obligee."** Since this rule is fundamentally the same as the rule governing solidary obligors, it suffices here to *transplant* the above discussion to the situation covered under **Article 1898-2.**[119]

2.   Fungibility of Objects.

Compensation by operation of law may occur only between obligations of sums of money or between obligations bearing on things which are fungible and of the same kind.[120] This form of compensation by operation of law is, therefore, circumscribed to obligations to give things that are fungible. Excluded from the domain of compensation by operation of law are those obligations described as *to do* something. Indeed, the fact that an obligor would not have to perform an obligation to do cannot be said to be the same thing as receiving the benefit of an actual performance from the other party. Therefore, if compensation by operation of law were possible, it would not amount to a dual reciprocal performance.

3.   Liquidated and Presently Due.

A debt is liquidated when it is certain and its amount determined. A debt which is contested, as when it is being litigated, is not liquidated and, in addition, its amount is not fixed or determined.

An obligation is due whenever it is demandable so that the creditor can obtain its immediate performance. Therefore, an obligation under a suspensive condition cannot be compensated because it is not presently due and may actually never be due. The same is true of an obligation under a suspensive term since such a legal device delays the time of performance of the obligation; it is not due yet! However,

---

[118]   LSA-C.C. Art. 1804-3: see Art. 1804 in Appendix; see Solidarity supra § 3.3.1.

[119]   Reasoning *"ubi eadem ratio idem lex."*

[120]   LSA-C.C. Art. 1893: see Appendix.

"delays of grace do not prevent compensation."[121] This particular type of term or delay is granted to an obligor either by a court or by a contract and is tantamount to a favor extended to the obligor. Such a favor becomes unjustified as soon as the obligor is in a position to perform *vis-à-vis* his obligee, performance which is automatically achieved by way of compensation.

In the particular case of a natural obligation, the obligee may not demand that the obligor perform because the obligee does not have a right to a judicial action. If we assume that an obligee, who is entitled only to the performance of a natural obligation, subsequently becomes an obligor of his own *natural* obligor, the question could be raised whether compensation by operation of law could take place between the legal obligation and the natural obligation. The answer ought to be in the negative. The reason why no compensation by operation of law could take place is simply that the obligee (creditor of the natural obligation) cannot *impose or compel* payment of his natural obligation by his obligor. To allow compensation would amount to granting the obligee a legal action against the obligor in such a way that the obligee would, both, be exempted of his own performance and, fictitiously, receive a forced performance of the natural obligation which is an impossibility.

B. Obstacles and Exceptions to Compensation by Operation of Law.

1. Obstacles.

LSA-C.C. Art. 1894-2 states, in part: **"Compensation does not take place, however, if one of the obligations is to return a thing of which the owner has been unjustly dispossessed, or is to return a thing given in deposit or loan for use, or if the object of one of the obligations is exempt from seizure."**[122] The first and second exclusions under this article will be discussed below under *exceptions* and only the third one will be analyzed here.

This last obstacle to legal compensation is justified by rules of public policy meant to protect a debtor and assure him of a minimum standard of living. As an illustration of this policy, one could refer to a statutory provision, which exempts from seizure a part of the income, or some property, of a debtor.[123] Since some things cannot be seized, legal compensation cannot occur because it would amount to a forced performance bearing on those things.

Another general obstacle to compensation by operation of law is mentioned in **LSA-C.C. Art. 1899: "Compensation can neither take place nor may it be renounced to the prejudice of rights previously acquired by third parties."** An illustration of this rule can be found in another code article, which states that an **"assuming obligor . . . may not invoke compensation based on an obligation owed by the obligee to the original obligor." (LSA-C.C. Art. 1824-4).**[124]

---

[121]　LSA-C.C. Art. 1893 3: see Appendix.

[122]　LSA-C.C. Art. 1894: see Appendix.

[123]　LSA-R.S. 13:3881.

[124]　On Assumption of Obligations, see supra § 5.1.

The same is true of an assignment of credit, where the transferee would suffer a prejudice if the debtor was allowed to raise the defense of compensation that could have occurred between himself and the transferor before the transfer or assignment took place.[125]

Under **LSA-C.C. Art. 1899**, should an obligor who held a secured claim against his own obligee fail to claim the benefit of compensation when it occurred and then proceed with the performance of his own obligation *vis-à-vis* his obligee, that obligor would automatically lose the securities which guaranteed his own claim against the obligee. He will become an unsecured creditor. His failure to claim compensation will be held against him and benefit both the sureties on whom he could have counted for payment of his claim and who will be released, as well as the third persons or other creditors of the same obligee. In the same line of thought *"he who being a debtor, has become creditor since the attachment made by a third person in his hands, can not, in prejudice to the person seizing, oppose compensation."*[126]

2. Exceptions.

As mentioned above, **LSA-C.C. Art. 1894-2** lists three important exceptions to compensation by operation of law: **"Compensation does not take place, however, if one of the obligations is to return a thing of which the owner has been unjustly dispossessed, or is to return a thing given in deposit or loan for use, or if the object of one of the obligations is exempt from seizure."**

If we assume that an owner has been unjustly disposed of a thing, now in the possession of another, should the owner become subsequently indebted to the wrongful possessor, the latter will not be entitled to claim the benefit of compensation by operation of law. The same is true of a depositary or a borrower who is under a legal obligation to return to its rightful owner the thing entrusted to him. Considerations of equity justify that compensation be denied to a wrongful possessor or a depositary as there should be no obstacle to the owner's right to claim back a thing he owns and has owned without any restriction. As regards the third exception, it illustrates a matter of public policy which cannot allow that an "object" essential to the livelihood of a person, or to his/her professional life be taken away from that person who, otherwise, might become a ward of the state.

C. Effects of Compensation by Operation of Law.

Although compensation does occur by operation of law, it is not of public order and may, therefore, be renounced.

1. Occurrence by Operation of Law.

Occurrence by operation of law means simply that compensation takes place automatically even unbeknownst to the parties. As soon as the requirements for compensation by operation of law are met, the two obligations involved are

---

[125] LSA-C.C. Arts. 2642 to 2654.

[126] Former article 2215 (in part) of the Civil Code of 1870.

extinguished either entirely or *pro tanto*; "**Compensation extinguishes both obligations to the extent of the lesser amount.**" (**LSA-C.C. Art. 1893-2**). If one of the two reciprocally indebted obligors owes payments to the other on more than one account, then the rules on imputation of payment will apply.[127]

The automaticity of compensation by operation of law is such that it occurs even though the obligations are not to be performed at the same place. In that case, however, "**allowance must be made . . . for the expenses of remittance.**" (**LSA-C.C. Art. 1895**)

2. Compensation by Operation of Law Must Be Demanded.

There exists this paradox that, although compensation takes place by operation of law, it must, however, be demanded, claimed or pleaded. Under **LSA-C.C. Art. 1900,**

> "**An obligor who has consented to an assignment of the credit by the obligee to a third party may not claim against the latter any compensation that otherwise he could have claimed against the former.**
>
> > **An obligor who has been given notice of an assignment to which he did not consent may not claim compensation against the assignee for an obligation of the assignor arising after that notice.**"

It follows from this article that, in the event of an assignment of credit, the obligor is denied the right to claim compensation when he has consented to the assignment. It is obvious, then, that the automaticity of the compensation, its occurrence by mere operation of law, is a fiction since it is not available to the obligor despite the fact that it should have taken place unbeknownst to the obligor and the transferor. What does happen actually is that, as soon as the conditions for compensation by operation of law are met, there will occur, at the moment compensation is claimed, a retroactivity of that compensation to the time when its conditions were met. Thus, when a court is faced with a claim of compensation by operation of law, the court will only have to ascertain that, some time ago, compensation did indeed take place and that, retroactively, the obligations were extinguished as of that time. Properly speaking, the court does not "declare" compensation by law, it merely "acknowledges or recognizes" that it took place and expresses it. This form of compensation is not of public order, it is a right that the parties may or may not claim and the court should not substitute its will to that of the obligors involved.

If we keep in mind that compensation is actually a form of payment or a type of performance of an obligation, in order for compensation to interrupt the prescription of an obligation it must be claimed just as a payment must be made or demanded. Not to claim compensation would be to renounce it and would have the same effect as a failure to demand performance of an obligation on time.

---

[127] On Imputation of Payment, see supra § 7.1.2; LSA-C.C. Art. 1896: see Appendix.

3. Compensation by Operation of Law May Be Renounced.

Once compensation has occurred as a result of all its conditions being met, the parties, or a party, may renounce it. A creditor who subsequently becomes a debtor of his own debtor may well want the actual performance of the obligation owed to him and prefer to renounce the compensation that took place in his favor. Compensation by operation of law is, therefore, only a quick and simple mode of extinction of obligations but it is not of public order and the parties might prefer to resort to the longer process of a reciprocal performance of their respective obligations.

An example of a tacit renunciation to compensation is given in the first paragraph of **LSA-C.C. Art. 1900,** which provides that a debtor may consent to an assignment of credit by his obligee and that, thereafter, that debtor loses the right to claim any compensation that, otherwise, he could have claimed against his obligee. By consenting to the assignment, the debtor waived his right to claim the benefit of compensation.

It is obvious that a renunciation by an obligor to his right to legal compensation might cause a prejudice to third parties, such as the obligor's sureties. When compensation does occur upon fulfillment of all the required conditions and when it is claimed, we have performance or payment of reciprocal obligations; they are extinguished at least up to the amount of the lesser one. Should that payment, and extinction, of obligations by operation of law automatically and immediately benefit the debtor's sureties or should their fate be left to the debtor's decision to claim or to renounce the benefit of compensation? In answer to this question **LSA-C.C. Art. 1899** states: "**Compensation can neither take place nor may it be renounced to the prejudice of rights previously acquired by third parties.**" The guarantees attached to a principal obligation affect the rights of third parties, such as surety, mortgagor. Since compensation itself cannot take place to the prejudice of the rights of third parties, *a fortiori ratione* a renunciation to compensation may not occur to the detriment of third parties whose rights to the extinction of their own accessory obligation were acquired upon occurrence of the compensation of the principal obligation. Third parties are released of their obligations at the time compensation could have been claimed by the principal obligor. Analogies can be drawn here with the impact of novation on a security given for an extinguished obligation, as well as with a remission of debt granted to the principal obligor which releases the sureties.[128] The rationale or reasons justifying these rules are the same: whenever the principal obligation is extinguished or ought to be extinguished, the sureties are necessarily and automatically also extinguished since there is no longer any support for their own existence.

§ 7.5.2. CONVENTIONAL COMPENSATION.

LSA-C.C. Art. 1901 lays down a very reasonable rule which is but an illustration of the general principle of freedom of contracts: "**Compensation of obligations may take place also by agreement of the parties even though the requirements**

---

[128] See LSA-C.C. Arts. 1884 and 1892-1 in Appendix.

for compensation by operation of law are not met."[129]

Whenever a debt is not liquidated or not yet demandable, or where the objects of the two reciprocal obligations are not fungible, the parties to these obligations may still enter into an agreement to bring about compensation between their obligations. For example, a creditor may renounce the benefit of a term stipulated in his favor and bring about a conventional compensation between the obligation he owes and that which is owed to him. Moreover, if parties to reciprocal obligations, consisting one in a sum of money and the other in the delivery of a corporeal movable, wish to compensate their obligations they may do so even though the requirements for compensation by operation of law are not met. The will of the parties is sufficient to extinguish their obligations as they see fit.

There exists, nevertheless, an important difference between compensation by operation of law and conventional compensation. Whereas the former has a retroactive effect, the second has only a prospective effect. A conventional compensation is effective only from the time it is entered into; it can have no retroactive effect because it is the intent of the parties that brings about the compensation. It is tantamount to the performance of reciprocal obligations at the time the parties choose to perform. On the contrary, it is a series of events or requirements operating beyond the control of the parties that triggers compensation by operation of law.

§ 7.5.3. COMPENSATION BY JUDICIAL DECLARATION.

The third form of compensation is the judicial compensation.

A court may allow compensation to take place despite the nonexistence of all the conditions required for compensation by operation of law. "**Although the obligation claimed in compensation is unliquidated, the court can declare compensation as to that part of the obligation that is susceptible of prompt and easy liquidation.**" (**LSA-C.C. Art. 1902**)[130]

A judicial compensation requires that a defendant appear before a court and demand that his own right of action against the plaintiff be recognized. Such a judicial compensation is the normal outcome of a reconventional demand under Articles 1061 and 1062 of the Code of Civil Procedure.

ARTICLE 5
CONFUSION

§ 7.6.1. CONCEPT OF CONFUSION.

Confusion is the merging in the same person of the qualities of obligee and principal obligor with respect to the same obligation. As **LSA-C.C. Article 1903** states: "**When the qualities of obligee and obligor are united in the same**

---

[129] LSA-C.C. Art. 1901: see Appendix.

[130] LSA-C.C. Art. 1902: see Appendix.

person, the obligation is extinguished by confusion."[131] The *Dictionary of the Civil Code* defines confusion as follows: "The union, in the same person, of the qualities of obligor/debtor and obligee/creditor, which leads to the extinction of the obligation (and results from the fact that the obligee inherits from the debtor or vice-versa)."[132]

For confusion to occur one must assume the existence of an obligation and a party who is, at the same time, obligee and obligor of that obligation. A typical example of confusion would occur in matters of succession, where an obligee could inherit from his obligor.[133] To prevent the confusion in his own person of the qualities of obligor of the succession and obligee-owner of the inheritance, an heir would have to accept the succession under some conditions or renounce the succession.[134]

Likewise, an obligor could become the beneficiary of an assignment of the credit held against him by his obligee. As a result of this assignment, the obligor would become his own obligee, so that confusion will occur.

It appears from these examples that confusion consists more in an impossibility to perform an obligation against oneself than in a true extinction of that obligation. One could say that as a result of the confusion the obligation is frozen or paralyzed. Confusion thus creates an obstacle to a legal action by the party involved against himself.[135]

§ 7.6.2.   EFFECTS OF CONFUSION.

LSA-C.C. Art. 1904-1 provides another illustration of the principle according to which the fate of an accessory obligation is determined by the fate of the principal obligation: "**Confusion of the qualities of obligee and obligor in the person of the principal obligor extinguishes the obligation of the surety.**"[136] When the principal obligation is extinguished by confusion, the accessory obligation will also disappear.

It is important to point out here that confusion extinguishes an obligation only when the qualities of obligee and obligor are combined, mixed, in the same principal party. If, on the other hand, an obligee should become also his own surety, no confusion would take place because the surety is merely an accessory obligor and his disappearance in the person of the obligee would not affect the existence of the principal obligation. The same rule would apply, *a fortiori ratione*, whenever the principal obligor becomes also a surety. **LSA-C.C. Art. 1904-2** expresses this rule in the following terms: "**Confusion of the qualities of obligee and obligor in the**

---

[131] LSA-C.C. Art. 1903: see Appendix.

[132] *Dictionary of the Civil Code*, — word: confusion, p. 127.

[133] LSA-C.C. Arts. 935 *et seq.*

[134] LSA-C.C. Arts. 947 *et seq.*

[135] See an application of this concept in "Sale with a right of redemption" in Louisiana Law of Sale and Lease, a Précis, § 3.2.1 *et seq.*

[136] LSA-C.C. Art. 1904: see Appendix.

person of the surety does not extinguish the obligation of the principal obligor."

A confusion may only be partial when some part or portion of an obligation is not susceptible of performance. Such could be the case in the event an obligation involves solidary obligors or solidary obligees. **LSA-C.C. Art. 1905** states that:

"If a solidary obligor becomes an obligee, confusion extinguishes the obligation only for the portion of that obligor.

If a solidary obligee becomes an obligor, confusion extinguishes the obligation only for the portion of that obligee."

If we assume that four obligors are solidarily bound to one obligee and that one of the solidary obligors thereafter inherits from his obligee, there will occur confusion up to one fourth of the obligation, the three remaining solidary obligors being still bound for three fourths of the obligation. Such would be the rule unless **"the circumstances giving rise to the solidary obligation concern only one of the obligors, that obligor is liable for the whole to the other obligors who are then considered only as his sureties."** (**LSA-C.C. Art. 1804-3**). Under these circumstances, if the solidary obligor, who is also the only one concerned by the obligation, should become his own obligee, confusion will occur and extinguish the whole obligation.

The unusual legal nature of confusion is illustrated by the fact that, because it is not truly an extinction of obligations, it is possible for an obligation to survive for some purposes despite the occurrence of confusion. For example, in the event an heir was a debtor of a succession, should that heir inherit that same succession, confusion would take place but the credit or right the succession held against the heir will have to be subjected to collation and be evaluated to determine the proper amount of the legitime or forced portion, if it is the case, or the disposable portion.[137]

The same limitation to the effects of confusion would occur under the circumstances described in **LSA-C.C. Art. 1829-2**. The purchaser of a mortgaged immovable **"who uses the purchase money to pay creditors holding any privilege, pledge, mortgage, or security interest"** becomes legally subrogated to them and thus acquires a mortgage on his own property. In this instance, confusion did not even extinguish the accessory obligation of mortgage, which survives for the benefit of the purchaser, obligor but also obligee.

---

[137] LSA-C.C. Arts. 1493 *et seq.*; Arts. 1237 *et seq.*

Appendix I

LOUISIANA CIVIL CODE 2015

Art. 1   Sources of law

The sources of law are legislation and custom.

Art. 2   Legislation

Legislation is a solemn expression of legislative will.

Art. 3   Custom

Custom results from practice repeated for a long time and generally accepted as having acquired the force of law. Custom may not abrogate legislation.

Art. 4   Absence of legislation or custom

When no rule for a particular situation can be derived from legislation or custom, the court is bound to proceed according to equity. To decide equitably, resort is made to justice, reason, and prevailing usages.

Art. 7   Laws for the preservation of the public interest

Persons may not by their juridical acts derogate from laws enacted for the protection of the public interest. Any act in derogation of such laws is an absolute nullity.

Art. 29   Age of majority

Majority is attained upon reaching the age of eighteen years.

Art. 96   Civil effects of absolutely null marriage; putative marriage

An absolutely null marriage nevertheless produces civil effects in favor of a party who contracted it in good faith for as long as that party remains in good faith.

When the cause of the nullity is one party's prior undissolved marriage, the civil effects continue in favor of the other party, regardless of whether the latter remains in good faith, until the marriage is pronounced null or the latter party contracts a valid marriage.

A marriage contracted by a party in good faith produces civil effects in favor of a child of the parties.

A purported marriage between parties of the same sex does not produce any civil effects.

Art. 196   Formal acknowledgment; presumption

A man may, by authentic act or by signing the birth certificate, acknowledge a child not filiated to another man. The acknowledgment creates a presumption that the man who acknowledges the child is the father. The presumption can be invoked only on behalf of the child. Except in those cases handled by the Department of Social Services, the acknowledgment does not create a presumption in favor of the man who acknowledges the child. In those support and visitation cases handled by the Department of Social Services, the acknowledgment is deemed to be a legal finding of paternity and is sufficient to establish an obligation to support the child and to establish visitation without the necessity of obtaining a judgment of paternity.

Art. 215   Filial honor and respect

A child, whatever be his age, owes honor and respect to his father and mother.

Art. 227   Parental support and education of children

Fathers and mothers, by the very act of marrying, contract together the obligation of supporting, maintaining, and educating their children.

Art. 477   Ownership; content

A. Ownership is the right that confers on a person direct, immediate, and exclusive authority over a thing. The owner of a thing may use, enjoy, and dispose of it within the limits and under the conditions established by law.

Art. 485   Fruits produced by a third person; reimbursement

When fruits that belong to the owner of a thing by accession are produced by the work of another person, or from seeds sown by him, the owner may retain them on reimbursing such person his expenses.

Art. 486   Possessor's right to fruits

A possessor in good faith acquires the ownership of fruits he has gathered. If he is evicted by the owner, he is entitled to reimbursement of expenses for fruits he was unable to gather.

A possessor in bad faith is bound to restore to the owner the fruits he has gathered, or their value, subject to his claim for reimbursement of expenses.

Art. 496   Constructions by possessor in good faith

When constructions, plantings, or works are made by a possessor in good faith, the owner of the immovable may not demand their demolition and removal. He is bound to keep them and at his option to pay to the possessor either the cost of the materials and of the workmanship, or their current value, or the enhanced value of the immovable.

Art. 497   Constructions by bad faith possessor

When constructions, plantings, or works are made by a bad faith possessor, the owner of the immovable may keep them or he may demand their demolition and removal at the expense of the possessor, and, in addition, damages for the injury that he may have sustained. If he does not demand demolition and removal, he is bound to pay at his option either the current value of the materials and of the workmanship of the separable improvements that he has kept or the enhanced value of the immovable.

Art. 535   Usufruct

Usufruct is a real right of limited duration on the property of another. The features of the right vary with the nature of the things subject to it as consumables or nonconsumables.

Art. 576   Standard of care

The usufructuary is answerable for losses resulting from his fraud, default, or neglect.

Art. 641   Persons having the servitude

A right of use may be established in favor of a natural person or a legal entity.

Art. 646   Predial servitude; definition

A predial servitude is a charge on a servient estate for the benefit of a dominant estate.

The two estates must belong to different owners.

Art. 697   Right to establish predial servitudes; limitations

Predial servitudes may be established by an owner on his estate or acquired for its benefit.

The use and extent of such servitudes are regulated by the title by which they are created, and, in the absence of such regulation, by the following rules.

Art. 705   Servitude of passage

The servitude of passage is the right for the benefit of the dominant estate whereby persons, animals, or vehicles are permitted to pass through the servient estate. Unless the title provides otherwise, the extent of the right and the mode of its exercise shall be suitable for the kind of traffic necessary for the reasonable use of the dominant estate.

Art. 762   Use by co-owner

If the dominant estate is owned in indivision, the use that a co-owner makes of the servitude prevents the running of prescription as to all.

If the dominant estate is partitioned, the use of the servitude by each owner preserves it for his estate only.

Art. 770   Abandonment of servient estate

A predial servitude is extinguished by the abandonment of the servient estate, or of the part on which the servitude is exercised. It must be evidenced by a written act. The owner of the dominant estate is bound to accept it and confusion takes place.

Art. 935   Acquisition of ownership; seizin

Immediately at the death of the decedent, universal successors acquire ownership of the estate and particular successors acquire ownership of the things bequeathed to them.

Prior to the qualification of a succession representative only a universal successor may represent the decedent with respect to the heritable rights and obligations of the decedent.

Art. 1416 Liability of universal successors to creditors

A. Universal successors are liable to creditors for the payment of the estate debts in proportion to the part which each has in the succession, but each is liable only to the extent of the value of the property received by him, valued as of the time of receipt.

B. A creditor has no action for payment of an estate debt against a universal successor who has not received property of the estate.

Art. 1420 Regulation of payment of debts by testament or by agreement among successors

The provisions of this Section pertaining to responsibility of the successors among themselves for estate debts do not prevent that responsibility from being otherwise regulated by the testament or by agreement of the successors. Nevertheless, the rights of creditors of the estate cannot be impaired by the testament or by agreement among the successors.

Art. 1468 Donations inter vivos; definition

A donation inter vivos is a contract by which a person, called the donor, gratuitously divests himself, at present and irrevocably, of the thing given in favor of another, called the donee, who accepts it.

Art. 1505 Calculation of disposable portion on mass of succession

A. To determine the reduction to which the donations, either inter vivos or mortis causa, are subject, an aggregate is formed of all property belonging to the donor or testator at the time of his death; to that is fictitiously added the property disposed of by donation inter vivos within three years of the date of the donor's death, according to its value at the time of the donation.

B. The sums due by the estate are deducted from this aggregate amount, and the disposable quantum is calculated on the balance, taking into consideration the number of forced heirs.

C. Neither the premiums paid for insurance on the life of the donor nor the proceeds paid pursuant to such coverage shall be included in the above calculation. Moreover, the value of such proceeds at the donor's death payable to a forced heir, or for his benefit, shall be deemed applied and credited in satisfaction of his forced share.

D. Employer and employee contributions under any plan of deferred compensation adopted by any public or governmental employer or any plan qualified under Sections 401 or 408 of the Internal Revenue Code, and any benefits payable by reason of death, disability, retirement, or termination of employment under any such plans, shall not be included in the above calculation, nor shall any of such contributions or benefits be subject to the claims of forced heirs. However, the value of such benefits paid or payable to a forced heir, or for the benefit of a forced heir, shall be deemed applied and credited in satisfaction of his forced share.

Former Art. 1534 (Civil Code of 2008)

The donor may stipulate the right of return of the objects given, either in case of his surviving the donee alone, or in case of his surviving the donee and his descendants.

That right can be stipulated for the advantage of the donor alone.

Former Art. 1535 (Civil Code of 2008)

The effect of the right of return is, that it cancels all alienations of the property given that may have been made by the donee or his descendants, and causes the property to return to the donor, free and clear of all incumbrances and mortgages.

Art. 1556   Causes for revocation or dissolution

A donation inter vivos may be revoked because of ingratitude of the donee or dissolved for the nonfulfillment of a suspensive condition or the occurrence of a resolutory condition. A donation may also be dissolved for the nonperformance of other conditions or charges.

Art. 1560   Revocation for ingratitude, restoration

In case of revocation for ingratitude, the donee shall return the thing given. If he is not able to return the thing itself, then the donee shall restore the value of the thing donated, measured as of the time the action to revoke is filed.

Art. 1562   Dissolution for nonfulfillment of suspensive condition or for occurrence of resolutory condition

If a donation is subject to a suspensive condition, the donation is dissolved of right when the condition can no longer be fulfilled.

If a donation is subject to a resolutory condition, the occurrence of the condition does not of right operate a dissolution of the donation. It may be dissolved only by consent of the parties or by judicial decree.

Art. 1575   Olographic testament

A. An olographic testament is one entirely written, dated, and signed in the handwriting of the testator. Although the date may appear anywhere in the testament, the testator must sign the testament at the end of the testament. If anything is written by the testator after his signature, the testament shall not be invalid and such writing may be considered by the court, in its discretion, as part of the testament. The olographic testament is subject to no other requirement as to form. The date is sufficiently indicated if the day, month, and year are reasonably ascertainable from information in the testament, as clarified by extrinsic evidence, if necessary.

B. Additions and deletions on the testament may be given effect only if made by the hand of the testator.

Art. 1586   General legacy

A general legacy is a disposition by which the testator bequeaths a fraction or a certain proportion of the estate, or a fraction or certain proportion of the balance of the estate that remains after particular legacies. In addition, a disposition of property expressly described by the testator as all, or a fraction or a certain proportion of one of the following categories of property, is also a general legacy: separate or community property, movable or immovable property, or corporeal or incorporeal property. This list of categories is exclusive.

Art. 1614   Interpretation as to after-acquired property

Absent a clear expression of a contrary intention, testamentary dispositions shall be interpreted to refer to the property that the testator owns at his death.

Art. 1756   Obligations; definition

An obligation is a legal relationship whereby a person, called the obligor, is bound to render a performance in favor of another, called the obligee. Performance may consist of giving, doing, or not doing something.

Art. 1758   General effects

A. An obligation may give the obligee the right to:

(1) Enforce the performance that the obligor is bound to render;

(2) Enforce performance by causing it to be rendered by another at the obligor's expense;

(3) Recover damages for the obligor's failure to perform, or his defective or delayed performance.

B. An obligation may give the obligor the right to:

(1) Obtain the proper discharge when he has performed in full;

(2) Contest the obligee's actions when the obligation has been extinguished or modified by a legal cause.

Art. 1759   Good faith

Good faith shall govern the conduct of the obligor and the obligee in whatever pertains to the obligation.

Art. 1760   Moral duties that may give rise to a natural obligation

A natural obligation arises from circumstances in which the law implies a particular moral duty to render a performance.

Art. 1761   Effects of a natural obligation

A natural obligation is not enforceable by judicial action. Nevertheless, whatever has been freely performed in compliance with a natural obligation may not be reclaimed.

A contract made for the performance of a natural obligation is onerous.

Art. 1762 Examples of circumstances giving rise to a natural obligation

Examples of circumstances giving rise to a natural obligation are:

(1) When a civil obligation has been extinguished by prescription or discharged in bankruptcy.

(2) When an obligation has been incurred by a person who, although endowed with discernment, lacks legal capacity.

(3) When the universal successors are not bound by a civil obligation to execute the donations and other dispositions made by a deceased person that are null for want of form.

Art. 1764 Effects of real obligation

A real obligation is transferred to the universal or particular successor who acquires the movable or immovable thing to which the obligation is attached, without a special provision to that effect.

But a particular successor is not personally bound, unless he assumes the personal obligations of his transferor with respect to the thing, and he may liberate himself of the real obligation by abandoning the thing.

Art. 1766 Strictly personal obligation

An obligation is strictly personal when its performance can be enforced only by the obligee, or only against the obligor.

When the performance requires the special skill or qualification of the obligor, the obligation is presumed to be strictly personal on the part of the obligor. All obligations to perform personal services are presumed to be strictly personal on the part of the obligor.

When the performance is intended for the benefit of the obligee exclusively, the obligation is strictly personal on the part of that obligee.

Art. 1767 Suspensive and resolutory condition

A conditional obligation is one dependent on an uncertain event.

If the obligation may not be enforced until the uncertain event occurs, the condition is suspensive.

If the obligation may be immediately enforced but will come to an end when the uncertain event occurs, the condition is resolutory.

Art. 1768 Expressed and implied conditions

Conditions may be either expressed in a stipulation or implied by the law, the nature of the contract, or the intent of the parties.

Art. 1769 Unlawful or impossible condition

A suspensive condition that is unlawful or impossible makes the obligation null.

Art. 1770   Condition that depends on the
whim or the will of the obligor

A suspensive condition that depends solely on the whim of the obligor makes the obligation null.

A resolutory condition that depends solely on the will of the obligor must be fulfilled in good faith.

Art. 1771   Obligee's right pending condition

The obligee of a conditional obligation, pending fulfillment of the condition, may take all lawful measures to preserve his right.

Art. 1772   Fault of a party

A condition is regarded as fulfilled when it is not fulfilled because of the fault of a party with an interest contrary to the fulfillment.

Art. 1773   Time for fulfillment of condition that an event shall occur

If the condition is that an event shall occur within a fixed time and that time elapses without the occurrence of the event, the condition is considered to have failed.

If no time has been fixed for the occurrence of the event, the condition may be fulfilled within a reasonable time.

Whether or not a time has been fixed, the condition is considered to have failed once it is certain that the event will not occur.

Art. 1774   Time for fulfillment of condition
that an event shall not occur

If the condition is that an event shall not occur within a fixed time, it is considered as fulfilled once that time has elapsed without the event having occurred.

The condition is regarded as fulfilled whenever it is certain that the event will not occur, whether or not a time has been fixed.

Art. 1775   Effects retroactive

Fulfillment of a condition has effects that are retroactive to the inception of the obligation. Nevertheless, that fulfillment does not impair the validity of acts of administration duly performed by a party, nor affect the ownership of fruits produced while the condition was pending. Likewise, fulfillment of the condition does not impair the right acquired by third persons while the condition was pending.

Art. 1776   Contract for continuous or periodic performance

In a contract for continuous or periodic performance, fulfillment of a resolutory condition does not affect the validity of acts of performance rendered before fulfillment of the condition.

Art. 1777   Express or implied term

A term for the performance of an obligation may be express or it may be implied by the nature of the contract.

Performance of an obligation not subject to a term is due immediately.

Art. 1778   Term for performance

A term for the performance of an obligation is a period of time either certain or uncertain. It is certain when it is fixed. It is uncertain when it is not fixed but is determinable either by the intent of the parties or by the occurrence of a future and certain event. It is also uncertain when it is not determinable, in which case the obligation must be performed within a reasonable time.

Art. 1779   Term presumed to benefit the obligor

A term is presumed to benefit the obligor unless the agreement or the circumstances show that it was intended to benefit the obligee or both parties.

Art. 1780   Renunciation of a term

The party for whose exclusive benefit a term has been established may renounce it.

Art. 1781   Performance before end of term

Although performance cannot be demanded before the term ends, an obligor who has performed voluntarily before the term ends may not recover the performance.

Art. 1782   If the obligor is insolvent

When the obligation is such that its performance requires the solvency of the obligor, the term is regarded as nonexistent if the obligor is found to be insolvent.

Art. 1783   Impairment or failure of security

When the obligation is subject to a term and the obligor fails to furnish the promised security, or the security furnished becomes insufficient, the obligee may require that the obligor, at his option, either perform the obligation immediately or furnish sufficient security. The obligee may take all lawful measures to preserve his right.

Art. 1784   Term for performance not fixed

When the term for performance of an obligation is not marked by a specific date but is rather a period of time, the term begins to run on the day after the contract is made, or on the day after the occurrence of the event that marks the beginning of the term, and it includes the last day of the period.

Art. 1785   Performance on term

Performance on term must be in accordance with the intent of the parties, or with established usage when the intent cannot be ascertained.

Art. 1786   Several, joint, and solidary obligations

When an obligation binds more than one obligor to one obligee, or binds one obligor to more than one obligee, or binds more than one obligor to more than one obligee, the obligation may be several, joint, or solidary.

Art. 1787   Several obligations; effects

When each of different obligors owes a separate performance to one obligee, the obligation is several for the obligors.

When one obligor owes a separate performance to each of different obligees, the obligation is several for the obligees.

A several obligation produces the same effects as a separate obligation owed to each obligee by an obligor or by each obligor to an obligee.

Art. 1788   Joint obligations for obligors or obligees

When different obligors owe together just one performance to one obligee, but neither is bound for the whole, the obligation is joint for the obligors.

When one obligor owes just one performance intended for the common benefit of different obligees, neither of whom is entitled to the whole performance, the obligation is joint for the obligees.

Art. 1789   Divisible and indivisible joint obligation

When a joint obligation is divisible, each joint obligor is bound to perform, and each joint obligee is entitled to receive, only his portion.

When a joint obligation is indivisible, joint obligors or obligees are subject to the rules governing solidary obligors or solidary obligees.

Art. 1790   Solidary obligations for obligees

An obligation is solidary for the obligees when it gives each obligee the right to demand the whole performance from the common obligor.

Art. 1791   Extinction of obligation by performance

Before a solidary obligee brings action for performance, the obligor may extinguish the obligation by rendering performance to any of the solidary obligees.

Art. 1792   Remission by one obligee

Remission of debt by one solidary obligee releases the obligor but only for the portion of that obligee.

Art. 1793   Interruption of prescription

Any act that interrupts prescription for one of the solidary obligees benefits all the others.

Art. 1794 Solidary obligation for obligors

An obligation is solidary for the obligors when each obligor is liable for the whole performance. A performance rendered by one of the solidary obligors relieves the others of liability toward the obligee.

Art. 1795 Solidary obligor may not request division; action against one obligor after action against another

An obligee, at his choice, may demand the whole performance from any of his solidary obligors. A solidary obligor may not request division of the debt.

Unless the obligation is extinguished, an obligee may institute action against any of his solidary obligors even after institution of action against another solidary obligor.

Art. 1796 Solidarity not presumed

Solidarity of obligation shall not be presumed. A solidary obligation arises from a clear expression of the parties' intent or from the law.

Art. 1797 Solidary obligation arising from different sources

An obligation may be solidary though it derives from a different source for each obligor.

Art. 1798 Obligation subject to condition or term

An obligation may be solidary though for one of the obligors it is subject to a condition or term.

Art. 1799 Interruption of prescription

The interruption of prescription against one solidary obligor is effective against all solidary obligors and their heirs.

Art. 1800 Solidary liability for damages

A failure to perform a solidary obligation through the fault of one obligor renders all the obligors solidarily liable for the resulting damages. In that case, the obligors not at fault have their remedy against the obligor at fault.

Art. 1801 Defenses that solidary obligor may raise

A solidary obligor may raise against the obligee defenses that arise from the nature of the obligation, or that are personal to him, or that are common to all the solidary obligors. He may not raise a defense that is personal to another solidary obligor.

Art. 1802 Renunciation of solidarity

Renunciation of solidarity by the obligee in favor of one or more of his obligors must be express. An obligee who receives a partial performance from an obligor separately preserves the solidary obligation against all his obligors after deduction of that partial performance.

Art. 1803   Remission of debt to or transaction or compromise with one obligor

Remission of debt by the obligee in favor of one obligor, or a transaction or compromise between the obligee and one obligor, benefits the other solidary obligors in the amount of the portion of that obligor.

Surrender to one solidary obligor of the instrument evidencing the obligation gives rise to a presumption that the remission of debt was intended for the benefit of all the solidary obligors.

Art. 1804   Liability of solidary obligors between themselves

Among solidary obligors, each is liable for his virile portion. If the obligation arises from a contract or quasi-contract, virile portions are equal in the absence of agreement or judgment to the contrary. If the obligation arises from an offense or quasi-offense, a virile portion is proportionate to the fault of each obligor.

A solidary obligor who has rendered the whole performance, though subrogated to the right of the obligee, may claim from the other obligors no more than the virile portion of each.

If the circumstances giving rise to the solidary obligation concern only one of the obligors, that obligor is liable for the whole to the other obligors who are then considered only as his sureties.

Art. 1805   Enforcement of contribution

A party sued on an obligation that would be solidary if it exists may seek to enforce contribution against any solidary co-obligor by making him a third party defendant according to the rules of procedure, whether or not that third party has been initially sued, and whether the party seeking to enforce contribution admits or denies liability on the obligation alleged by plaintiff.

Art. 1807   Conjunctive obligation

An obligation is conjunctive when it binds the obligor to multiple items of performance that may be separately rendered or enforced. In that case, each item is regarded as the object of a separate obligation.

The parties may provide that the failure of the obligor to perform one or more items shall allow the obligee to demand the immediate performance of all the remaining items.

Art. 1808   Alternative obligation

An obligation is alternative when an obligor is bound to render only one of two or more items of performance.

Art. 1809   Choice belongs to the obligor

When an obligation is alternative, the choice of the item of performance belongs to the obligor unless it has been expressly or impliedly granted to the obligee.

Art. 1810   Delay in exercising choice

When the party who has the choice does not exercise it after a demand to do so, the other party may choose the item of performance.

Art. 1811   Obligor may not choose part of one item

An obligor may not perform an alternative obligation by rendering as performance a part of one item and a part of another.

Art. 1812   Impossibility or unlawfulness of one item of performance

When the choice belongs to the obligor and one of the items of performance contemplated in the alternative obligation becomes impossible or unlawful, regardless of the fault of the obligor, he must render one of those that remain.

When the choice belongs to the obligee and one of the items of performance becomes impossible or unlawful without the fault of the obligor, the obligee must choose one of the items that remain. If the impossibility or unlawfulness is due to the fault of the obligor, the obligee may choose either one of those that remain, or damages for the item of performance that became impossible or unlawful.

Art. 1813   Impossibility or unlawfulness of all items of performance

If all of the items of performance contemplated in the alternative obligation become impossible or unlawful without the obligor's fault, the obligation is extinguished.

Art. 1814   Obligor's liability for damages

When the choice belongs to the obligor, if all the items of performance contemplated in the alternative obligation have become impossible and the impossibility of one or more is due to the fault of the obligor, he is liable for the damages resulting from his failure to render the last item that became impossible.

If the impossibility of one or more items is due to the fault of the obligee, the obligor is not bound to deliver any of the items that remain.

Art. 1815   Divisible and indivisible obligation

An obligation is divisible when the object of the performance is susceptible of division.

An obligation is indivisible when the object of the performance, because of its nature or because of the intent of the parties, is not susceptible of division.

Art. 1816   Effect of divisible obligation
between single obligor and obligee

When there is only one obligor and only one obligee, a divisible obligation must be performed as if it were indivisible.

Art. 1817   Effects of divisible obligation among successors

A divisible obligation must be divided among successors of the obligor or of the obligee.

Each successor of the obligor is liable only for his share of a divisible obligation.

Each successor of the obligee is entitled only to his share of a divisible obligation.

Art. 1818   Effects of indivisible obligations between more than one obligor or obligee

An indivisible obligation with more than one obligor or obligee is subject to the rules governing solidary obligations.

Art. 1819   Effect of indivisible obligation among successors

An indivisible obligation may not be divided among the successors of the obligor or of the obligee, who are thus subject to the rules governing solidary obligors or solidary obligees.

Art. 1820   Solidarity is not indivisibility

A stipulation of solidarity does not make an obligation indivisible.

Art. 1821   Assumption by agreement between obligor and third person

An obligor and a third person may agree to an assumption by the latter of an obligation of the former. To be enforceable by the obligee against the third person, the agreement must be made in writing.

The obligee's consent to the agreement does not effect a release of the obligor.

The unreleased obligor remains solidarily bound with the third person.

Art. 1822   Third person bound for amount assumed

A person who, by agreement with the obligor, assumes the obligation of the latter is bound only to the extent of his assumption.

The assuming obligor may raise any defense based on the contract by which the assumption was made.

Art. 1823   Assumption by agreement between obligee and third person

An obligee and a third person may agree on an assumption by the latter of an obligation owed by another to the former. That agreement must be made in writing. That agreement does not effect a release of the original obligor.

Art. 1824   Defenses

A person who, by agreement with the obligee, has assumed another's obligation may not raise against the obligee any defense based on the relationship between the assuming obligor and the original obligor.

The assuming obligor may raise any defense based on the relationship between the original obligor and obligee. He may not invoke compensation based on an obligation owed by the obligee to the original obligor.

Art. 1825   Definition

Subrogation is the substitution of one person to the rights of another. It may be conventional or legal.

Art. 1827   Conventional subrogation by the obligee

An obligee who receives performance from a third person may subrogate that person to the rights of the obligee, even without the obligor's consent. That subrogation is subject to the rules governing the assignment of rights.

Art. 1828   Conventional subrogation by the obligor

An obligor who pays a debt with money or other fungible things borrowed for that purpose may subrogate the lender to the rights of the obligee, even without the obligee's consent.

The agreement for subrogation must be made in writing expressing that the purpose of the loan is to pay the debt.

Art. 1829   Subrogation by operation of law

Subrogation takes place by operation of law:

(1) In favor of an obligee who pays another obligee whose right is preferred to his because of a privilege, pledge, mortgage, or security interest;

(2) In favor of a purchaser of movable or immovable property who uses the purchase money to pay creditors holding any privilege, pledge, mortgage, or security interest on the property;

(3) In favor of an obligor who pays a debt he owes with others or for others and who has recourse against those others as a result of the payment;

(4) In favor of a successor who pays estate debts with his own funds; and

(5) In the other cases provided by law.

Art. 1830   Effects of legal subrogation

When subrogation takes place by operation of law, the new obligee may recover from the obligor only to the extent of the performance rendered to the original obligee. The new obligee may not recover more by invoking conventional subrogation.

Art. 1832   Written form required by law

When the law requires a contract to be in written form, the contract may not be proved by testimony or by presumption, unless the written instrument has been destroyed, lost, or stolen.

Art. 1833   Authentic act

A. An authentic act is a writing executed before a notary public or other officer authorized to perform that function, in the presence of two witnesses, and signed by each party who executed it, by each witness, and by each notary public before whom it was executed. The typed or hand-printed name of each person shall be placed in a legible form immediately beneath the signature of each person signing the act.

B. To be an authentic act, the writing need not be executed at one time or place, or before the same notary public or in the presence of the same witnesses, provided that each party who executes it does so before a notary public or other officer authorized to perform that function, and in the presence of two witnesses and each party, each witness, and each notary public signs it. The failure to include the typed or hand-printed name of each person signing the act shall not affect the validity or authenticity of the act.

C. If a party is unable or does not know how to sign his name, the notary public must cause him to affix his mark to the writing.

Art. 1837   Act under private signature

An act under private signature need not be written by the parties, but must be signed by them.

Art. 1838   Party must acknowledge or deny signature

A party against whom an act under private signature is asserted must acknowledge his signature or deny that it is his.

In case of denial, any means of proof may be used to establish that the signature belongs to that party.

Art. 1842   Confirmation

Confirmation is a declaration whereby a person cures the relative nullity of an obligation.

An express act of confirmation must contain or identify the substance of the obligation and evidence the intention to cure its relative nullity.

Tacit confirmation may result from voluntary performance of the obligation.

Art. 1844   Effects of confirmation and ratification

The effects of confirmation and ratification are retroactive to the date of the confirmed or ratified obligation. Neither confirmation nor ratification may impair the rights of third persons.

Art. 1847   Debt of a third person and debt extinguished by prescription

Parol evidence is inadmissible to establish either a promise to pay the debt of a third person or a promise to pay a debt extinguished by prescription.

Art. 1854   Extinction by performance

Performance by the obligor extinguishes the obligation.

Art. 1855   Performance by a third person

Performance may be rendered by a third person, even against the will of the obligee, unless the obligor or the obligee has an interest in performance only by the obligor.

Performance rendered by a third person effects subrogation only when so provided by law or by agreement.

Art. 1859   Performance in violation of seizure

A performance rendered to an obligee in violation of a seizure is not valid against the seizing creditor who, according to his right, may force the obligor to perform again.

In that case, the obligor may recover the first performance from the obligee.

Art. 1860   Quality of thing to be given

When the performance consists of giving a thing that is determined as to its kind only, the obligor need not give one of the best quality but he may not tender one of the worst.

Art. 1862   Place of performance

Performance shall be rendered in the place either stipulated in the agreement or intended by the parties according to usage, the nature of the performance, or other circumstances.

In the absence of agreement or other indication of the parties' intent, performance of an obligation to give an individually determined thing shall be rendered at the place the thing was when the obligation arose. If the obligation is of any other kind, the performance shall be rendered at the domicile of the obligor.

Art. 1864   Imputation by obligor

An obligor who owes several debts to an obligee has the right to impute payment to the debt he intends to pay.

The obligor's intent to pay a certain debt may be expressed at the time of payment or may be inferred from circumstances known to the obligee.

Art. 1865   Imputation to debt not yet due

An obligor may not, without the obligee's consent, impute payment to a debt not yet due.

Art. 1866   Payment imputed to interest

An obligor of a debt that bears interest may not, without the obligee's consent, impute a payment to principal when interest is due.

A payment made on principal and interest must be imputed first to interest.

Art. 1867   Imputation by obligee

An obligor who has accepted a receipt that imputes payment to one of his debts may no longer demand imputation to another debt, unless the obligee has acted in bad faith.

Art. 1868   Imputation not made by the parties

When the parties have made no imputation, payment must be imputed to the debt that is already due.

If several debts are due, payment must be imputed to the debt that bears interest.

If all, or none, of the debts that are due bear interest, payment must be imputed to the debt that is secured.

If several unsecured debts bear interest, payment must be imputed to the debt that, because of the rate of interest, is most burdensome to the obligor.

If several secured debts bear no interest, payment must be imputed to the debt that, because of the nature of the security, is most burdensome to the obligor.

If the obligor had the same interest in paying all debts, payment must be imputed to the debt that became due first.

If all debts are of the same nature and became due at the same time, payment must be proportionally imputed to all.

Art. 1869   Offer to perform and deposit by obligor

When the object of the performance is the delivery of a thing or a sum of money and the obligee, without justification, fails to accept the performance tendered by the obligor, the tender, followed by deposit to the order of the court, produces all the effects of a performance from the time the tender was made if declared valid by the court.

A valid tender is an offer to perform according to the nature of the obligation.

Art. 1873   Obligor not liable when failure caused by fortuitous event

An obligor is not liable for his failure to perform when it is caused by a fortuitous event that makes performance impossible.

An obligor is, however, liable for his failure to perform when he has assumed the risk of such a fortuitous event.

An obligor is liable also when the fortuitous event occurred after he has been put in default.

An obligor is likewise liable when the fortuitous event that caused his failure to perform has been preceded by his fault, without which the failure would not have occurred.

Art. 1874   Fortuitous event that would have destroyed object in hands of obligee

An obligor who had been put in default when a fortuitous event made his performance impossible is not liable for his failure to perform if the fortuitous event would have likewise destroyed the object of the performance in the hands of the obligee had performance been timely rendered.

That obligor is, however, liable for the damage caused by his delay.

Art. 1876   Contract dissolved when performance becomes impossible

When the entire performance owed by one party has become impossible because of a fortuitous event, the contract is dissolved.

The other party may then recover any performance he has already rendered.

Art. 1879   Extinguishment of existing obligation

Novation is the extinguishment of an existing obligation by the substitution of a new one.

Art. 1880   Novation not presumed

The intention to extinguish the original obligation must be clear and unequivocal. Novation may not be presumed.

Art. 1881   Objective novation

Novation takes place when, by agreement of the parties, a new performance is substituted for that previously owed, or a new cause is substituted for that of the original obligation. If any substantial part of the original performance is still owed, there is no novation.

Novation takes place also when the parties expressly declare their intention to novate an obligation.

Mere modification of an obligation, made without intention to extinguish it, does not effect a novation. The execution of a new writing, the issuance or renewal of a negotiable instrument, or the giving of new securities for the performance of an existing obligation are examples of such a modification.

Art. 1882   Subjective novation

Novation takes place when a new obligor is substituted for a prior obligor who is discharged by the obligee. In that case, the novation is accomplished even without the consent of the prior obligor, unless he had an interest in performing the obligation himself.

Art. 1883   No effect when obligation is invalid

Novation has no effect when the obligation it purports to extinguish does not exist or is absolutely null.

If the obligation is only relatively null, the novation is valid, provided the obligor of the new one knew of the defect of the extinguished obligation.

Art. 1884   Security for extinguished obligation

Security given for the performance of the extinguished obligation may not be transferred to the new obligation without agreement of the parties who gave the security.

Art. 1885   Novation of solidary obligation

A novation made by the obligee and one of the obligors of a solidary obligation releases the other solidary obligors.

In that case, the security given for the performance of the extinguished obligation may be retained by the obligee only on property of that obligor with whom the novation has been made.

If the obligee requires that the other co-obligors remain solidarily bound, there is no novation unless the co-obligors consent to the new obligation.

Art. 1886   Delegation of performance

A delegation of performance by an obligor to a third person is effective when that person binds himself to perform.

A delegation effects a novation only when the obligee expressly discharges the original obligor.

Art. 1887   Discharge of any prior obligor does not affect security

If the new obligor has assumed the obligation and acquired the thing given as security, the discharge of any prior obligor by the obligee does not affect the security or its rank.

Art. 1888   Express or tacit remission

A remission of debt by an obligee extinguishes the obligation. That remission may be express or tacit.

Art. 1890   Remission effective when
communication is received by the obligor

A remission of debt is effective when the obligor receives the communication from the obligee. Acceptance of a remission is always presumed unless the obligor rejects the remission within a reasonable time.

Art. 1892   Remission granted to sureties

Remission of debt granted to the principal obligor releases the sureties.

Remission of debt granted to the sureties does not release the principal obligor.

Remission of debt granted to one surety releases the other sureties only to the extent of the contribution the other sureties might have recovered from the surety to whom the remission was granted.

If the obligee grants a remission of debt to a surety in return for an advantage, that advantage will be imputed to the debt, unless the surety and the obligee agree otherwise.

Art. 1893 Compensation extinguishes obligations

Compensation takes place by operation of law when two persons owe to each other sums of money or quantities of fungible things identical in kind, and these sums or quantities are liquidated and presently due.

In such a case, compensation extinguishes both obligations to the extent of the lesser amount.

Delays of grace do not prevent compensation.

Art. 1894 Obligation not subject to compensation

Compensation takes place regardless of the sources of the obligations.

Compensation does not take place, however, if one of the obligations is to return a thing of which the owner has been unjustly dispossessed, or is to return a thing given in deposit or loan for use, or if the object of one of the obligations is exempt from seizure.

Art. 1896 Rules of imputation of payment

If an obligor owes more than one obligation subject to compensation, the rules of imputation of payment must be applied.

Art. 1897 Compensation extinguishes obligation of surety

Compensation between obligee and principal obligor extinguishes the obligation of a surety.

Compensation between obligee and surety does not extinguish the obligation of the principal obligor.

Art. 1898 Compensation between obligee and solidary obligor

Compensation between the obligee and one solidary obligor extinguishes the obligation of the other solidary obligors only for the portion of that obligor.

Compensation between one solidary obligee and the obligor extinguishes the obligation only for the portion of that obligee.

The compensation provided in this Article does not operate in favor of a liability insurer.

Art. 1901 Compensation by agreement

Compensation of obligations may take place also by agreement of the parties even though the requirements for compensation by operation of law are not met.

Art. 1902 Compensation by judicial declaration

Although the obligation claimed in compensation is unliquidated, the court can declare compensation as to that part of the obligation that is susceptible of prompt and easy liquidation.

Art. 1903 Union of qualities of obligee and obligor

When the qualities of obligee and obligor are united in the same person, the obligation is extinguished by confusion.

Art. 1904 Obligation of the surety

Confusion of the qualities of obligee and obligor in the person of the principal obligor extinguishes the obligation of the surety.

Confusion of the qualities of obligee and obligor in the person of the surety does not extinguish the obligation of the principal obligor.

Art. 1905 Solidary obligations

If a solidary obligor becomes an obligee, confusion extinguishes the obligation only for the portion of that obligor.

If a solidary obligee becomes an obligor, confusion extinguishes the obligation only for the portion of that obligee.

Art. 1907 Unilateral contracts

A contract is unilateral when the party who accepts the obligation of the other does not assume a reciprocal obligation.

Art. 1908 Bilateral or synallagmatic contracts

A contract is bilateral, or synallagmatic, when the parties obligate themselves reciprocally, so that the obligation of each party is correlative to the obligation of the other.

Art. 1909 Onerous contracts

A contract is onerous when each of the parties obtains an advantage in exchange for his obligation.

Art. 1915 Rules applicable to all contracts

All contracts, nominate and innominate, are subject to the rules of this title.

Art. 1948 Vitiated consent

Consent may be vitiated by error, fraud, or duress.

Art. 1966 No obligation without cause

An obligation cannot exist without a lawful cause.

Art. 1967 Cause defined; detrimental reliance

Cause is the reason why a party obligates himself.

A party may be obligated by a promise when he knew or should have known that the promise would induce the other party to rely on it to his detriment and the other party was reasonable in so relying. Recovery may be limited to the expenses incurred or the damages suffered as a result of the promisee's reliance on the promise. Reliance on a gratuitous promise made without required formalities is not reasonable.

Art. 1968   Unlawful cause

The cause of an obligation is unlawful when the enforcement of the obligation would produce a result prohibited by law or against public policy.

Art. 1969   Cause not expressed

An obligation may be valid even though its cause is not expressed.

Art. 1970   Untrue expression of cause

When the expression of a cause in a contractual obligation is untrue, the obligation is still effective if a valid cause can be shown.

Art. 1977   Obligation or performance by a third person

The object of a contract may be that a third person will incur an obligation or render a performance.

The party who promised that obligation or performance is liable for damages if the third person does not bind himself or does not perform.

Art. 1978   Stipulation for a third party

A contracting party may stipulate a benefit for a third person called a third party beneficiary.

Once the third party has manifested his intention to avail himself of the benefit, the parties may not dissolve the contract by mutual consent without the beneficiary's agreement.

Art. 1983   Law for the parties; performance in good faith

Contracts have the effect of law for the parties and may be dissolved only through the consent of the parties or on grounds provided by law. Contracts must be performed in good faith.

Art. 1985   Effects for third parties

Contracts may produce effects for third parties only when provided by law.

Art. 1986   Right of the obligee

Upon an obligor's failure to perform an obligation to deliver a thing, or not to do an act, or to execute an instrument, the court shall grant specific performance plus damages for delay if the obligee so demands. If specific performance is impracticable, the court may allow damages to the obligee.

Upon a failure to perform an obligation that has another object, such as an obligation to do, the granting of specific performance is at the discretion of the court.

Art. 1987   Right to restrain obligor

The obligor may be restrained from doing anything in violation of an obligation not to do.

Art. 1989   Damages for delay

Damages for delay in the performance of an obligation are owed from the time the obligor is put in default.

Other damages are owed from the time the obligor has failed to perform.

Art. 1990   Obligor put in default by arrival of term

When a term for the performance of an obligation is either fixed, or is clearly determinable by the circumstances, the obligor is put in default by the mere arrival of that term. In other cases, the obligor must be put in default by the obligee, but not before performance is due.

Art. 1991   Manners of putting in default

An obligee may put the obligor in default by a written request of performance, or by an oral request of performance made before two witnesses, or by filing suit for performance, or by a specific provision of the contract.

Art. 1992   Risk devolves upon the obligor

If an obligee bears the risk of the thing that is the object of the performance, the risk devolves upon the obligor who has been put in default for failure to deliver that thing.

Art. 1993   Reciprocal obligations

In case of reciprocal obligations, the obligor of one may not be put in default unless the obligor of the other has performed or is ready to perform his own obligation.

Art. 1994   Obligor liable for failure to perform

An obligor is liable for the damages caused by his failure to perform a conventional obligation.

A failure to perform results from nonperformance, defective performance, or delay in performance.

Art. 1995   Measure of damages

Damages are measured by the loss sustained by the obligee and the profit of which he has been deprived.

Art. 2002   Reasonable efforts to mitigate damages

An obligee must make reasonable efforts to mitigate the damage caused by the obligor's failure to perform. When an obligee fails to make these efforts, the obligor may demand that the damages be accordingly reduced.

Art. 2029   Nullity of contracts

A contract is null when the requirements for its formation have not been met.

Art. 2030 Absolute nullity of contracts

A contract is absolutely null when it violates a rule of public order, as when the object of a contract is illicit or immoral. A contract that is absolutely null may not be confirmed.

Absolute nullity may be invoked by any person or may be declared by the court on its own initiative.

Art. 2031 Relative nullity of contracts

A contract is relatively null when it violates a rule intended for the protection of private parties, as when a party lacked capacity or did not give free consent at the time the contract was made. A contract that is only relatively null may be confirmed.

Relative nullity may be invoked only by those persons for whose interest the ground for nullity was established, and may not be declared by the court on its own initiative.

Art. 2033 Effects

An absolutely null contract, or a relatively null contract that has been declared null by the court, is deemed never to have existed. The parties must be restored to the situation that existed before the contract was made. If it is impossible or impracticable to make restoration in kind, it may be made through an award of damages.

Nevertheless, a performance rendered under a contract that is absolutely null because its object or its cause is illicit or immoral may not be recovered by a party who knew or should have known of the defect that makes the contract null. The performance may be recovered, however, when that party invokes the nullity to withdraw from the contract before its purpose is achieved and also in exceptional situations when, in the discretion of the court, that recovery would further the interest of justice.

Absolute nullity may be raised as a defense even by a party who, at the time the contract was made, knew or should have known of the defect that makes the contract null.

Art. 2036 Act of the obligor that causes or increases his insolvency

An obligee has a right to annul an act of the obligor, or the result of a failure to act of the obligor, made or effected after the right of the obligee arose, that causes or increases the obligor's insolvency.

Art. 2044 Insolvency by failure to exercise right

If an obligor causes or increases his insolvency by failing to exercise a right, the obligee may exercise it himself, unless the right is strictly personal to the obligor.

For that purpose, the obligee must join in the suit his obligor and the third person against whom that right is asserted.

Art. 2292   Management of affairs; definition

There is a management of affairs when a person, the manager, acts without authority to protect the interests of another, the owner, in the reasonable belief that the owner would approve of the action if made aware of the circumstances.

Art. 2293   Application of rules governing mandate

A management of affairs is subject to the rules of mandate to the extent those rules are compatible with management of affairs.

Art. 2294   Duties of the manager; notice to the owner

The manager is bound, when the circumstances so warrant, to give notice to the owner that he has undertaken the management and to wait for the directions of the owner, unless there is immediate danger.

Art. 2295   Duties of the manager; liability for loss

The manager must exercise the care of a prudent administrator and is answerable for any loss that results from his failure to do so. The court, considering the circumstances, may reduce the amount due the owner on account of the manager's failure to act as a prudent administrator.

Art. 2296   Capacity

An incompetent person or a person of limited legal capacity may be the owner of an affair, but he may not be a manager. When such a person manages the affairs of another, the rights and duties of the parties are governed by the law of enrichment without cause or the law of delictual obligations.

Art. 2297   Obligations of the owner

The owner whose affair has been managed is bound to fulfill the obligations that the manager has undertaken as a prudent administrator and to reimburse the manager for all necessary and useful expenses.

Art. 2298   Enrichment without cause; compensation

A person who has been enriched without cause at the expense of another person is bound to compensate that person. The term "without cause" is used in this context to exclude cases in which the enrichment results from a valid juridical act or the law. The remedy declared here is subsidiary and shall not be available if the law provides another remedy for the impoverishment or declares a contrary rule.

The amount of compensation due is measured by the extent to which one has been enriched or the other has been impoverished, whichever is less.

The extent of the enrichment or impoverishment is measured as of the time the suit is brought or, according to the circumstances, as of the time the judgment is rendered.

Art. 2299   Obligation to restore

A person who has received a payment or a thing not owed to him is bound to restore it to the person from whom he received it.

Art. 2300   Obligation that does not exist

A thing is not owed when it is paid or delivered for the discharge of an obligation that does not exist.

Art. 2301   Obligation under suspensive condition

A thing is not owed when it is paid or delivered for discharge of an obligation that is subject to a suspensive condition.

Art. 2302   Payment of the debt of another person

A person who paid the debt of another person in the erroneous belief that he was himself the obligor may reclaim the payment from the obligee. The payment may not be reclaimed to the extent that the obligee, because of the payment, disposed of the instrument or released the securities relating to the claim. In such a case, the person who made the payment has a recourse against the true obligor.

Art. 2303   Liability of the person receiving payment

A person who in bad faith received a payment or a thing not owed to him is bound to restore it with its fruits and products.

Art. 2304   Restoration of a thing or its value

When the thing not owed is an immovable or a corporeal movable, the person who received it is bound to restore the thing itself, if it exists.

If the thing has been destroyed, damaged, or cannot be returned, a person who received the thing in good faith is bound to restore its value if the loss was caused by his fault. A person who received the thing in bad faith is bound to restore its value even if the loss was not caused by his fault.

Art. 2305   Liability when the thing is alienated

A person who in good faith alienated a thing not owed to him is only bound to restore whatever he obtained from the alienation. If he received the thing in bad faith, he owes, in addition, damages to the person to whom restoration is due.

Art. 2315   Liability for acts causing damages

A. Every act whatever of man that causes damage to another obliges him by whose fault it happened to repair it.

B. Damages may include loss of consortium, service, and society, and shall be recoverable by the same respective categories of persons who would have had a cause of action for wrongful death of an injured person. Damages do not include costs for future medical treatment, services, surveillance, or procedures of any kind unless such treatment, services, surveillance, or procedures are directly related to a manifest physical or mental injury or disease. Damages shall include any sales taxes paid by the owner on the repair or replacement of the property damaged.

Art. 2316   Negligence, imprudence or want of skill

Every person is responsible for the damage he occasions not merely by his act, but by his negligence, his imprudence, or his want of skill.

Art. 2323-A   Comparative fault

A. In any action for damages where a person suffers injury, death, or loss, the degree or percentage of fault of all persons causing or contributing to the injury, death, or loss shall be determined, regardless of whether the person is a party to the action or a nonparty, and regardless of the person's insolvency, ability to pay, immunity by statute, including but not limited to the provisions of R.S. 23:1032, or that the other person's identity is not known or reasonably ascertainable. If a person suffers injury, death, or loss as the result partly of his own negligence and partly as a result of the fault of another person or persons, the amount of damages recoverable shall be reduced in proportion to the degree or percentage of negligence attributable to the person suffering the injury, death, or loss.

Art. 2324.1   Damages; discretion of judge or jury

In the assessment of damages in cases of offenses, quasi offenses, and quasi contracts, much discretion must be left to the judge or jury.

Art. 2439   Definition

Sale is a contract whereby a person transfers ownership of a thing to another for a price in money.

The thing, the price, and the consent of the parties are requirements for the perfection of a sale.

Art. 2456   Transfer of ownership

Ownership is transferred between the parties as soon as there is agreement on the thing and the price is fixed, even though the thing sold is not yet delivered nor the price paid.

Art. 2460   Sale on view or trial

When the buyer has reserved the view or trial of the thing, ownership is not transferred from the seller to the buyer until the latter gives his approval of the thing.

Art. 2467   Transfer of risk

The risk of loss of the thing sold owing to a fortuitous event is transferred from the seller to the buyer at the time of delivery.

That risk is so transferred even when the seller has delivered a nonconforming thing, unless the buyer acts in the manner required to dissolve the contract.

Art. 2477   Methods of making delivery

Delivery of an immovable is deemed to take place upon execution of the writing that transfers its ownership.

Delivery of a movable takes place by handing it over to the buyer. If the parties so intend delivery may take place in another manner, such as by the seller's handing over to the buyer the key to the place where the thing is stored, or by negotiating to him a document of title to the thing, or even by the mere consent of the parties if the thing sold cannot be transported at the time of the sale or if the buyer already has the thing at that time.

Art. 2481 Incorporeals, method of making delivery

Delivery of incorporeal movable things incorporated into an instrument, such as stocks and bonds, takes place by negotiating such instrument to the buyer. Delivery of other incorporeal movables, such as credit rights, takes place upon the transfer of those movables.

Art. 2484 Place of delivery

Delivery must be made at the place agreed upon by the parties or intended by them. In the absence of such agreement or intent, delivery must be made at the place where the thing is located at the time of the sale.

Art. 2489 Condition of thing at time of delivery

The seller must deliver the thing sold in the condition that, at the time of the sale, the parties expected, or should have expected, the thing to be in at the time of delivery, according to its nature.

Art. 2550 Time and place of payment of price

Payment of the price is due at the time and place stipulated in the contract, or at the time and place of delivery if the contract contains no such stipulation.

Art. 2555 Liability of the buyer who fails to take delivery

A buyer who fails to take delivery of the thing after a tender of such delivery, or who fails to pay the price, is liable for expenses incurred by the seller in preservation of the thing and for other damages sustained by the seller.

Art. 2567 Right of redemption, definition

The parties to a contract of sale may agree that the seller shall have the right of redemption, which is the right to take back the thing from the buyer.

Art. 2571 Application of time limit against all persons including minors

The period for redemption is peremptive and runs against all persons including minors. It may not be extended by the court.

Art. 2572 Redemption against second purchaser

When the thing is immovable, the right of redemption is effective against third persons only from the time the instrument that contains it is filed for registry in the parish where the immovable is located.

When the thing is movable, the right of redemption is effective against third persons who, at the time of purchase, had actual knowledge of the existence of that right.

Art. 2575 Ownership of fruits and products pending redemption

The fruits and products of a thing sold with right of redemption belong to the buyer.

Art. 2588 Encumbrances created by buyer

The seller who exercises the right of redemption is entitled to recover the thing free of any encumbrances placed upon it by the buyer. Nevertheless, when the thing is an immovable, the interests of third persons are governed by the laws of registry.

Art. 2589 Rescission for lesion beyond moiety

The sale of an immovable may be rescinded for lesion when the price is less than one half of the fair market value of the immovable. Lesion can be claimed only by the seller and only in sales of corporeal immovables. It cannot be alleged in a sale made by order of the court.

The seller may invoke lesion even if he has renounced the right to claim it.

Art. 2591 Option of buyer to supplement price

When a sale is subject to rescission for lesion the buyer may elect either to return the immovable to the seller, or to keep the immovable by giving to the seller a supplement equal to the difference between the price paid by the buyer and the fair market value of the immovable determined according to the preceding Article.

Art. 2623 Bilateral promise of sale; contract to sell

An agreement whereby one party promises to sell and the other promises to buy a thing at a later time, or upon the happening of a condition, or upon performance of some obligation by either party, is a bilateral promise of sale or contract to sell. Such an agreement gives either party the right to demand specific performance.

A contract to sell must set forth the thing and the price, and meet the formal requirements of the sale it contemplates.

Art. 2624 Deposit, earnest money

A sum given by the buyer to the seller in connection with a contract to sell is regarded to be a deposit on account of the price, unless the parties have expressly provided otherwise.

If the parties stipulate that a sum given by the buyer to the seller is earnest money, either party may recede from the contract, but the buyer who chooses to recede must forfeit the earnest money, and the seller who so chooses must return the earnest money plus an equal amount.

When earnest money has been given and a party fails to perform for reasons other than a fortuitous event, that party will be regarded as receding from the contract.

Art. 2642 Assignability of rights

All rights may be assigned, with the exception of those pertaining to obligations that are strictly personal. The assignee is subrogated to the rights of the assignor against the debtor.

Art. 2643   Assignment effective from the time of knowledge or notice

The assignment of a right is effective against the debtor and third persons only from the time the debtor has actual knowledge, or has been given notice of the assignment.

If a partial assignment unreasonably increases the burden of the debtor he may recover from either the assignor or the assignee a reasonable amount for the increased burden.

Art. 2645   Accessories included in assignment of right

The assignment of a right includes its accessories such as security rights.

Art. 2655   Giving in payment, definition

Giving in payment is a contract whereby an obligor gives a thing to the obligee, who accepts it in payment of a debt.

Art. 2683   The lessee's principal obligations

The lessee is bound:

(1) To pay the rent in accordance with the agreed terms;

(2) To use the thing as a prudent administrator and in accordance with the purpose for which it was leased; and

(3) To return the thing at the end of the lease in a condition that is the same as it was when the thing was delivered to him, except for normal wear and tear or as otherwise provided hereafter.

Art. 2684   Obligations to deliver the thing at the agreed time and in good condition

The lessor is bound to deliver the thing at the agreed time and in good condition suitable for the purpose for which it was leased.

Art. 2720   Termination of lease with a fixed term

A lease with a fixed term terminates upon the expiration of that term, without need of notice, unless the lease is reconducted or extended as provided in the following Articles.

Art. 2746   Limited duration of contract

A man can only hire out his services for a certain limited time, or for the performance of a certain enterprise.

Art. 2754   Liability for loss or damage

Carriers and waterman [watermen] are liable for the loss or damage of the things intrusted to their care, unless they can prove that such loss or damage has been occasioned by accidental and uncontrollable events.

Art. 2756   Building by plot and work by job, definitions

To build by a plot, or to work by the job, is to undertake a building or a work for a certain stipulated price.

Art. 2762   Liability of contractor for damages due to badness of workmanship

If a building, which an architect or other workman has undertaken to make by the job, should fall to ruin either in whole or in part, on account of the badness of the workmanship, the architect or undertaker shall bear the loss if the building falls to ruin in the course of ten years, if it be a stone or brick building, and of five years if it be built in wood or with frames filled with bricks.

Art. 2766   Termination of contract by death of workman

Contracts for hiring out work are canceled by the death of the workman, architect or undertaker, unless the proprietor should consent that the work should be continued by the heir or heirs of the architect, or by workmen employed for that purpose by the heirs.

Art. 2767   Payment to heirs of contractor for work or materials completed

The proprietor is only bound, in the former case, to pay to the heirs of the undertaker the value of the work that has already been done and that of the materials already prepared, proportionably to the price agreed on, in case such work and materials may be useful to him.

Art. 2769   Contractor's liability for non-compliance with contract

If an undertaker fails to do the work he has contracted to do, or if he does not execute it in the manner and at the time he has agreed to do it, he shall be liable in damages for the losses that may ensue from his non-compliance with his contract.

Art. 2817   Partnership debts; liability

A partnership as principal obligor is primarily liable for its debts. A partner is bound for his virile share of the debts of the partnership but may plead discussion of the assets of the partnership.

Art. 2891   Loan for use; definition

The loan for use is a gratuitous contract by which a person, the lender, delivers a nonconsumable thing to another, the borrower, for him to use and return.

Art. 2894   Preservation and limited use

The borrower is bound to keep, preserve, and use the thing lent as a prudent administrator. He may use it only according to its nature or as provided in the contract.

Art. 2904   Loan for consumption; definition

The loan for consumption is a contract by which a person, the lender, delivers consumable things to another, the borrower, who binds himself to return to the lender an equal amount of things of the same kind and quality.

Art. 2905   Ownership and risk of loss of the thing lent

The borrower in a loan for consumption becomes owner of the thing lent and bears the risk of loss of the thing.

Art. 2906   Loan of nonfungible things

A loan of a nonfungible thing, in the absence of contrary agreement, is not a loan for consumption, but is a loan for use.

Art. 2907   Loan of money or commodities

When the loan is of money, the borrower is bound to repay the same numerical amount in legal tender of the country whose money was lent regardless of fluctuation in the value of the currency.

When commodities are lent, the borrower is bound to return the same quantity and quality regardless of any increase or diminution of value.

Art. 2908   Lender's liability for damage caused by defects in the thing

The lender is liable to the borrower when defects in the thing lent for consumption cause damage or loss sustained by the borrower, if the lender knew or should have known of the defects and failed to inform the borrower.

Art. 2909   Inability to demand performance until expiration of term

The lender may not demand from the borrower the performance of his obligation to return an equal amount of things of the same kind and quality before expiration of the term. In the absence of a certain term or of an agreement that performance will be exigible at will, a reasonable term is implied.

Art. 2910   Substance and place of performance

The borrower is bound to render performance at the place agreed upon. When the place for performance is not fixed in the contract, performance shall be rendered at the place where the loan is contracted.

Art. 2911   Payment of value when restitution is impossible

When it is impossible for the borrower to return to the lender things of the same quantity and quality as those lent, the borrower is bound to pay the value of the things lent, taking into account the time and place they should have been returned according to the contract.

When the time and place are not fixed in the contract, the borrower owes the value of the things at the time the demand for performance is made and at the place where the loan is contracted.

Art. 2912　Payment of interest in case of default

When the borrower does not return the things lent or their value at the time when due, he is bound to pay legal interest from the date of written demand.

Art. 2930　Diligence and prudence required

When the deposit is onerous, the depositary is bound to fulfill his obligations with diligence and prudence.

When the deposit is gratuitous, the depositary is bound to fulfill his obligations with the same diligence and prudence in caring for the thing deposited that he uses for his own property.

Whether the deposit is gratuitous or onerous, the depositary is liable for the loss that the depositor sustains as a result of the depositary's failure to perform such obligations.

Art. 2933　Return of the thing deposited

The depositary is bound to return the precise thing that he received in deposit.

Art. 2937　Place and expense of return

When the contract of deposit specifies the place of return, the thing deposited is to be returned there and the depositor bears the expense of transportation. If the contract of deposit does not specify the place of return, the thing deposited is to be returned at the place where the deposit was made.

Art. 2939　Retention of the deposit

The depositary may retain the thing deposited until his claims arising from the contract of deposit are paid. He may not retain the thing until payment of a claim unrelated to the contract of deposit or by way of setoff.

Art. 2985　Representation

A person may represent another person in legal relations as provided by law or by juridical act. This is called representation.

Art. 2986　The authority of the representative

The authority of the representative may be conferred by law, by contract, such as mandate or partnership, or by the unilateral juridical act of procuration.

Art. 2989　Mandate defined

A mandate is a contract by which a person, the principal, confers authority on another person, the mandatary, to transact one or more affairs for the principal.

Art. 3001　Mandatary's duty of performance; standard of care

The mandatary is bound to fulfill with prudence and diligence the mandate he has accepted. He is responsible to the principal for the loss that the principal sustains as a result of the mandatary's failure to perform.

Art. 3002 Gratuitous mandate; liability of a mandatary

When the mandate is gratuitous, the court may reduce the amount of loss for which the mandatary is liable.

Art. 3006 Fulfillment of the mandate by the mandatary

In the absence of contrary agreement, the mandatary is bound to fulfill the mandate himself.

Nevertheless, if the interests of the principal so require, when unforeseen circumstances prevent the mandatary from performing his duties and he is unable to communicate with the principal, the mandatary may appoint a substitute.

Art. 3010 Performance of obligations contracted by the mandatary

The principal is bound to the mandatary to perform the obligations that the mandatary contracted within the limits of his authority. The principal is also bound to the mandatary for obligations contracted by the mandatary after the termination of the mandate if at the time of contracting the mandatary did not know that the mandate had terminated.

The principal is not bound to the mandatary to perform the obligations that the mandatary contracted which exceed the limits of the mandatary's authority unless the principal ratifies those acts.

Art. 3014 Interest on sums expended by the mandatary

The principal owes interest from the date of the expenditure on sums expended by the mandatary in performance of the mandate.

Art. 3015 Liability of several principals

Multiple principals for an affair common to them are solidarily bound to their mandatary.

Art. 3026 Incapacity of the principal

In the absence of contrary agreement, neither the contract nor the authority of the mandatary is terminated by the principal's incapacity, disability, or other condition that makes an express revocation of the mandate impossible or impractical.

Art. 3030 Acts of the mandatary after principal's death

The mandatary is bound to complete an undertaking he had commenced at the time of the principal's death if delay would cause injury.

Art. 3035 Definition of suretyship

Suretyship is an accessory contract by which a person binds himself to a creditor to fulfill the obligation of another upon the failure of the latter to do so.

Art. 3037   Surety ostensibly bound as a principal with another; effect of knowledge of the creditor

One who ostensibly binds himself as a principal obligor to satisfy the present or future obligations of another is nonetheless considered a surety if the principal cause of the contract with the creditor is to guarantee performance of such obligations.

A creditor in whose favor a surety and principal obligor are bound together as principal obligors in solido may presume they are equally concerned in the matter until he clearly knows of their true relationship.

Art. 3045   Liability of sureties to creditor; division and discussion abolished

A surety, or each surety when there is more than one, is liable to the creditor in accordance with the provisions of this Chapter, for the full performance of the obligation of the principal obligor, without benefit of division or discussion, even in the absence of an express agreement of solidarity.

Art. 3047   Rights of the surety

A surety has the right of subrogation, the right of reimbursement, and the right to require security from the principal obligor.

Art. 3048   Surety's right of subrogation

The surety who pays the principal obligation is subrogated by operation of law to the rights of the creditor.

Art. 3071   Compromise; definition

A compromise is a contract whereby the parties, through concessions made by one or more of them, settle a dispute or an uncertainty concerning an obligation or other legal relationship.

Art. 3078   After-acquired rights

A compromise does not affect rights subsequently acquired by a party, unless those rights are expressly included in the agreement.

Art. 3141   Pledge, defined

Pledge is a real right established by contract over property of the kind described in Article 3142 to secure performance of an obligation.

Art. 3142   Property susceptible of pledge

The only things that may be pledged are the following:

(1) A movable that is not susceptible of encumbrance by security interest.

(2) The lessor's rights in the lease of an immovable and its rents.

(3) Things made susceptible of pledge by law.

Art. 3143 Pledge of property susceptible of encumbrance by security interest

A contract by which a person purports to pledge a thing that is susceptible of encumbrance by security interest does not create a pledge under this Title but may be effective to create a security interest in the thing.

Art. 3144 Accessory nature of pledge

Pledge is accessory to the obligation that it secures and may be enforced by the pledgee only to the extent that he may enforce the secured obligation.

Art. 3145 Preference afforded by pledge

Pledge gives the pledgee the right to be satisfied from the thing pledged and its fruits in preference to unsecured creditors of the pledgor and to other persons whose rights become effective against the pledgee after the pledge has become effective as to them.

Art. 3146 Obligations for which pledge may be given

A pledge may be given to secure the performance of any lawful obligation, including obligations that arise in the future. As to all obligations, present and future, secured by the pledge, notwithstanding the nature of the obligations or the date they arise, the pledge has effect between the parties from the time that the requirements for formation of the contract of pledge are satisfied and has effect as to third persons from the time that the applicable requirements of Articles 3153 through 3155 are satisfied.

Art. 3147 Pledge securing obligation that is not for the payment of money

A pledge that secures an obligation other than one for the payment of money, such as an obligation for the performance of an act, secures the claim of the pledgee for the damages he may suffer from the breach of the obligation.

Art. 3148 Pledge securing an obligation of another person

A person may pledge his property to secure an obligation of another person. In such a case, the pledgor may assert against the pledgee any defense that the obligor could assert except lack of capacity or discharge in bankruptcy of the obligor. The pledgor may also assert any other defenses available to a surety.

Art. 3149 Formal requirements of contract of pledge

The pledge of a corporeal movable is effective between the parties only if the thing pledged has been delivered to the pledgee or a third person who has agreed to hold the thing for the benefit of the pledgee. The pledge of other things is effective between the parties only if established by written contract, but delivery is not required.

Art. 3150 Acceptance

A written contract of pledge need not be signed by the pledgee, whose consent is presumed and whose acceptance may be tacit.

Art. 3151 Power to pledge

A contract of pledge may be established only by a person having the power to alienate the thing pledged.

Art. 3152 Pledge of a thing not owned

A pledge given over a thing that the pledgor does not own is established when the thing is acquired by the pledgor and the other requirements for the establishment of the pledge have been satisfied.

Art. 3153 General requirements for effectiveness of pledge against third persons

A pledge is without effect as to third persons unless it has become effective between the parties and is established by written contract.

Art. 3179 Ownership of property pledged; rights of creditor upon default of debtor

The creditor does not become owner of the pledged immovable by failure of payment at the stated time; any clause to the contrary is null, and in this case it is only lawful for him to sue his debtor before the court in order to obtain a sentence against him, and to cause the objects which have been put in his hands in pledge to be seized and sold.

Art. 3183 Debtor's property common pledge of creditors; exceptions to pro rata distribution

The property of the debtor is the common pledge of his creditors, and the proceeds of its sale must be distributed among them ratably, unless there exist among the creditors some lawful causes of preference.

Art. 3278 Mortgage defined

Mortgage is a nonpossessory right created over property to secure the performance of an obligation.

Art. 3279 Rights created by mortgage

Mortgage gives the mortgagee, upon failure of the obligor to perform the obligation that the mortgage secures, the right to cause the property to be seized and sold in the manner provided by law and to have the proceeds applied toward the satisfaction of the obligation in preference to claims of others.

Art. 3280 Mortgage is an indivisible real right

Mortgage is an indivisible real right that burdens the entirety of the mortgaged property and that follows the property into whatever hands the property may pass.

Art. 3281 Mortgage established only in authorized cases

Mortgage may be established only as authorized by legislation.

Art. 3282   Accessory nature

Mortgage is accessory to the obligation that it secures. Consequently, except as provided by law, the mortgagee may enforce the mortgage only to the extent that he may enforce any obligation it secures.

Art. 3283   Kinds of mortgages

Mortgage is conventional, legal, or judicial, and with respect to the manner in which it burdens property, it is general or special.

Art. 3285   General and special mortgages distinguished

A general mortgage burdens all present and future property of the mortgagor.

A special mortgage burdens only certain specified property of the mortgagor.

Art. 3286   Property susceptible of mortgage

The only things susceptible of mortgage are:

(1) A corporeal immovable with its component parts.

(2) A usufruct of a corporeal immovable.

(3) A servitude of right of use with the rights that the holder of the servitude may have in the buildings and other constructions on the land.

(4) The lessee's rights in a lease of an immovable with his rights in the buildings and other constructions on the immovable.

(5) Property made susceptible of conventional mortgage by special law.

Art. 3293   Obligations for which mortgage may be established

A conventional mortgage may be established to secure performance of any lawful obligation, even one for the performance of an act. The obligation may have a term and be subject to a condition.

Art. 3337   Cancellation of mortgages and privileges from the records

The recorder shall cancel a mortgage or privilege from his records in the manner prescribed by law.

Art. 3448   Prescription of nonuse

Prescription of nonuse is a mode of extinction of a real right other than ownership as a result of failure to exercise the right for a period of time.

Art. 3477   Precarious possessor; inability to prescribe

Acquisitive prescription does not run in favor of a precarious possessor or his universal successor.

Art. 3492   Delictual actions

Delictual actions are subject to a liberative prescription of one year. This prescription commences to run from the day injury or damage is sustained. It does not run against minors or interdicts in actions involving permanent disability and brought pursuant to the Louisiana Products Liability Act or state law governing product liability actions in effect at the time of the injury or damage.

Art. 3503   Solidary obligors

When prescription is interrupted against a solidary obligor, the interruption is effective against all solidary obligors and their successors.

When prescription is interrupted against a successor of a solidary obligor, the interruption is effective against other successors if the obligation is indivisible. If the obligation is divisible, the interruption is effective against other successors only for the portions for which they are bound.

Art. 3506   General definitions of terms

Whenever the terms of law, employed in this Code, have not been particularly defined therein, they shall be understood as follows:

1. The masculine gender comprehends the two sexes, whenever the provision is not one, which is evidently made for one of them only:

Thus, the word man or men includes women; the word son or sons includes daughters; the words he, his and such like, are applicable to both males and females.

2. The singular is often employed to designate several persons or things: the heir, for example, means the heirs, where there are more than one.

28. Successor. — Successor is, generally speaking, the person who takes the place of another.

There are in law two sorts of successors: the universal successor, such as the heir, the universal legatee, and the general legatee; and the successor by particular title, such as the buyer, donee or legatee of particular things, the transferee.

The universal successor represents the person of the deceased, and succeeds to all his rights and charges.

The particular successor succeeds only to the rights appertaining to the thing which is sold, ceded or bequeathed to him.

32. Third Persons. — With respect to a contract or judgment, third persons are all who are not parties to it. In case of failure, third persons are, particularly, those creditors of the debtor who contracted with him without knowledge of the rights which he had transferred to another.

Appendix II

LOUISIANA CODE OF CIVIL PROCEDURE

C.C.P. Art. 423   Implied right to enforce obligation; prematurity

An obligation implies a right to enforce it which may or may not accrue immediately upon the creation of the obligation. When the obligation allows a term for its performance, the right to enforce it does not accrue until the term has elapsed. If the obligation depends upon a suspensive condition, the right to enforce it does not accrue until the occurrence or performance of the condition.

When an action is brought on an obligation before the right to enforce it has accrued, the action shall be dismissed as premature, but it may be brought again after this right has accrued.

C.C.P. Art. 641   Joinder of parties needed for just adjudication

A person shall be joined as a party in the action when either:

(1) In his absence complete relief cannot be accorded among those already parties.

(2) He claims an interest relating to the subject matter of the action and is so situated that the adjudication of the action in his absence may either:

(a) As a practical matter, impair or impede his ability to protect that interest.

(b) Leave any of the persons already parties subject to a substantial risk of incurring multiple or inconsistent obligations.

C.C.P. Art. 2504   Specific performance; court directing performance by third party

If a judgment directs a party to perform a specific act, and he fails to comply within the time specified, the court may direct the act to be done by the sheriff or some other person appointed by the court, at the cost of the disobedient party, and with the same effect as if done by the party.

C.C.P. Art. 3501   Petition; affidavit; security

A writ of attachment or of sequestration shall issue only when the nature of the claim and the amount thereof, if any, and the grounds relied upon for the issuance of the writ clearly appear from specific facts shown by the petition verified by, or by the separate affidavit of, the petitioner, his counsel or agent.

The applicant shall furnish security as required by law for the payment of the damages the defendant may sustain when the writ is obtained wrongfully.

C.C.P. Art. 3601 Injunction, grounds for issuance; preliminary injunction; temporary restraining order

A. An injunction shall be issued in cases where irreparable injury, loss, or damage may otherwise result to the applicant, or in other cases specifically provided by law; provided, however, that no court shall have jurisdiction to issue, or cause to be issued, any temporary restraining order, preliminary injunction, or permanent injunction against any state department, board, or agency, or any officer, administrator, or head thereof, or any officer of the state of Louisiana in any suit involving the expenditure of public funds under any statute or law of this state to compel the expenditure of state funds when the director of such department, board, or agency or the governor shall certify that the expenditure of such funds would have the effect of creating a deficit in the funds of said agency or be in violation of the requirements placed upon the expenditure of such funds by the legislature.

B. No court shall issue a temporary restraining order in cases where the issuance shall stay or enjoin the enforcement of a child support order when the Department of Social Services is providing services, except for good cause shown by written reasons made a part of the record.

C. During the pendency of an action for an injunction the court may issue a temporary restraining order, a preliminary injunction, or both, except in cases where prohibited, in accordance with the provisions of this Chapter.

D. Except as otherwise provided by law, an application for injunctive relief shall be by petition.

Appendix III

CASES — ILLUSTRATIONS

CHAPTER 1 — OBLIGATIONS IN GENERAL

Article 1 — Classification of Obligations According to Their Sources

Article 2 — Classification of Obligations According to Their Object

Johnson v. N.O.P.S.I.	293 So. 2d 203 (1974)
Alexander v. Alton Ochsner Medical Foundation	275 So. 2d 794 (1973)

Article 3 — Classification of Obligations According to Their Effects

Thomas v. Bryant	639 So. 2d 378 (1994)
Succession of Irene B.B. Jones	505 So. 2d 841 (1987)
Succession of Harrison	444 So. 2d 1191 (1984)
Succession of Burns, et al	7 So. 2d 359 (1942)
In re Atkins Estate	30 F. 2d 761 (1929)

CHAPTER 2 — KINDS OF OBLIGATIONS

Article 1 — Patrimonial Obligations

St. Jude Medical Office Building Limited Partnership v. City Glass and Mirror, Inc.	619 So. 2d 529 (1993)
Mc Guffy v. Weil	125 So. 2d 154 (1960)
Bogart v. Caldwell	66 So. 2d 629 (1953)
Cambais v. Douglas	120 So. 369 (1929)
Johnson v. Levy	43 So. 46 (1907)

Article 2 — Modalities Affecting the Exigibility or the Existence of an Obligation

Southern States Masonry, Inc. v. J.A. Jones Const. Co.	507 So. 2d 198 (1987)

Article 2   —   Subrogation

Safeway Insurance Company of Louisiana v. State Farm Mutual Automobile Insurance Company	839 So. 2d 1022 (2003)
Bruce Martin v. Louisiana Farm Bureau Casualty Insurance Company	638 So. 2d 1067 (1994)
Cox v. Heroman	298 So. 2d 848 (1974)
Pringle Associated Manufacturing Corporation v. Eanes	226 So. 2d 502 (1969)
St. Paul Fire & Marine Insurance Company v. Gallien	111 So. 2d 571 (1959)
Standard Motor Car Company et al v. State Farm Mutual Automobile Insurance Company	97 So. 2d 435 (1957)

CHAPTER 6   —   PROOF OF OBLIGATIONS

State ex rel. Hebert v. Recorder of Mortgages	143 So. 15 (1932)
Succession of Mrs. A.R. Montgomery	506 So. 2d 1309 (1987)
L. Meltzer v. S. Meltzer	662 So. 2d 58 (1995)
G. W. Jones v. W.S. Mason	99 So. 2d 46 (1958)
L. Jackson, Sr. v. Gulf Insurance Company	199 So. 2d 886 (1967)

CHAPTER 7   —   EXTINCTION OF OBLIGATIONS

Article 1   —   Voluntary Performance

§ 1   —   Performance

Fletcher v. Rachou	323 So. 2d 163 (1975)
J. Weingarten, Inc. v. Northgate Mall Inc	404 So. 2d 896 (1981)

§ 2   —   Imputation of Payment

G.M. Porche v. T.S. Waldrip	597 So. 2d 536 (1992)
A. Payton v. W. Colar	518 So. 2d 1104 (1987)
Chaisson v. Chaisson	690 So. 2d 899 (1997)

Article 2   —   Impossibility of Performance

City of New Orleans v. United Gas Pipe Line Company and Pennzoil Company	517 So. 2d 145 (1987)

Hanover Petroleum Corporation v. Tenneco Inc.	521 So. 2d 1234 (1988)

Article 3 — Novation-Delegation

Polk Chevrolet, Inc. v. Vicaro	162 So. 2d 761 (1964)
Crescent Cigarette Vending Corporation v. Toca	271 So. 2d 53 (1972)
First National Bank of Abbeville v. Greene	612 So. 2d 759 (1992)

Article 4 — Remission of Debt

F. Arender v. J.C. Gilbert	343 So. 2d 1146 (1977)
A. Arledge v. Bell	463 So. 2d 856 (1985)

Article 5 — Compensation

In re Canal Bank & Trust Co.	152 So. 578 (1934)
First National Bank of Commerce v. A. Dufrene	525 So. 2d 298 (1988)
A Confidential Limousine Service, Inc. v. London Livery, Ltd.	612 So. 2d 875 (1993)

Article 6 — Confusion

Deshotel v. Travelers Idemnity Company	243 So. 2d 259 (1971)
Hibernia National Bank v. Continental Marble and Granit Company, Inc.	615 So. 2d 1109 (1993)

INDEX

[References are to sections and appendices.]

[References are to sections and appendices.]

[References are to sections and appendices.]

[References are to sections and appendices.]

[References are to sections and appendices.]